IN THE MIDST OF CHAOS

IN THE MIDST OF CHAOS

Caring for Children as Spiritual Practice

Bonnie J. Miller-McLemore

John Wiley & Sons, Inc.

Published by Jossey-Bass
A Wiley Imprint
989 Market Street, San Francisco, CA 94103-1741   www.josseybass.com

Jossey-Bass books and products are available through most bookstores. To contact Jossey-Bass directly call our Customer Care Department within the U.S. at 800-956-7739, outside the U.S. at 317-572-3986, or fax 317-572-4002.

Jossey-Bass also publishes its books in a variety of electronic formats. Some content that appears in print may not be available in electronic books.

Credits are on page 250.

Library of Congress Cataloging-in-Publication Data

Miller-McLemore, Bonnie J.
In the midst of chaos: caring for children as spiritual practice / Bonnie J. Miller-McLemore.
p. cm.—(The practices of faith series)
Includes bibliographical references and index.
ISBN-13: 978-0-7879-7676-7 (cloth)
ISBN-10: 0-7879-7676-8 (cloth)
1. Parenting—Religious aspects—Christianity. 2. Child rearing—Religious aspects—Christianity. 3. Christian education of children. I. Title.
BV4529.M56 2006
248.8'45—dc22
2006022132

Printed in the United States of America
FIRST EDITION
HB Printing   10 9 8 7 6 5 4 3 2 1

The Practices of Faith Series
Dorothy C. Bass, Series Editor

Contents

With thankfulness to dear friends and colleagues
who shape my work and grace my life
Dorothy Bass
Stephanie Meis
Pamela Couture
Brita Gill-Austern

Editor's Foreword

In Kent Haruf's novel *Plainsong,* a wise high school teacher asks a pair of elderly bachelor brothers to take a pregnant teenager into their home. They are astounded. Why would she choose them for this unlikely task? Her answer is clear: "You're going to die someday without ever having had enough trouble in your life. Not of the right kind anyway. This is your chance."

This is not how most people become parents. But the teacher's notion that receiving a child brings the right kind of trouble into one's life makes a great deal of sense. Caring for kids, whether newborns or adolescents, can be exhausting and confusing in ways that introduce plenty of "trouble" into our homes, our schedules, and our sleep. But oh, how right that trouble can be: right for youngsters who receive a safe place in which to grow, and right for adults who learn in the presence of children to love and to forgive, to play and to listen, to bless and, finally, to let go.

In this book, Bonnie Miller-McLemore delves into the experience of life with children in a way that is devoid of sentimentality but full of joy. At a time when many busy adults wonder whether households like theirs can even aspire to be places where a life-giving way of life is nurtured, her reflections on how God's grace emerges in the shared daily life of adults and children point directly to the heart of Christian faith. God is with us in the flesh, Christians have long proclaimed (though this truth is easily forgotten, and often has been). God has embraced all the messy details of human existence, and it is in the midst of these that God loves and transforms adults and children alike. How could it be otherwise for a God portrayed in Christian scriptures as one who joined the human family as an infant laid in an animal's eating trough, who blessed small children others impatiently tried to push aside, and who suffered rejection, injustice, and death while opening a way to new life?

In the Midst of Chaos offers a lively, winsome invitation into a rich spirituality that not only has room for busy caregivers but that also finds redemption taking place in the midst of their often hectic lives. Through practices that give shape to the life of a household, Miller-McLemore shows, adults and kids can find themselves sharing a way of life that is abundant in love, mercy, and justice—a way of life that can also contribute to the well-being of others beyond the household, where so many of God's children suffer injustice and want. *In the Midst of Chaos* offers no easy remedies or grand solutions, to be sure. Yet its down-to-earth depictions of everyday practices that sometimes become vessels of God's love humbly point toward signs of hope and pathways of faithfulness.

I am delighted to add *In the Midst of Chaos: Caring for Children as Spiritual Practice* to the series on the Practices of Faith, which offers wisdom drawn from the deep wells of Christian belief and experience to those who long to live with integrity in today's rapidly-changing world. The series's initial book, *Practicing Our Faith: A Way of Life for a Searching People,* found such wisdom in twelve practices that shape a way of life attuned to God's presence and the well-being of all: honoring the body, hospitality, household economics, saying yes and saying no, keeping Sabbath, discernment, testimony, shaping communities, forgiveness, healing, dying well, and singing our lives to God. By participating in these practices together over time, Christian people address fundamental human needs in ways that reflect and respond to God's grace to them and to the whole world in Jesus Christ. Each subsequent book in the series has focused on one of the practices that received only a single chapter's exploration in *Practicing Our Faith.*

In the Midst of Chaos brings a new approach to the series. Rather than focusing on one of the practices in *Practicing Our Faith,* this book considers how a constellation of practices creates openings within which the grace of God can be known by those whose daily lives are deeply shaped by the presence of youngsters in need of their care. A practices approach to the life of Christian faith seems especially appropriate to this particular situation. Attention to practices keeps faith from abstraction and fosters reflection on hands-on ways of addressing the fundamental needs of actual human beings. Moreover, this approach acknowledges that practices emerge from a rich and complex history that spans generations—a dynamic encountered here at close range, as one generation and the next struggle to comprehend each other's somewhat different cultural style. Finally, being attuned to the practices that comprise the life of Christian faith shifts our understanding of how faith is passed on from one generation to another. It helps us to see the formative power of faith as it is lived out around the family table, in the play of children, and in daily acts of blessing.

Throughout the twenty years that I have been a mother, Bonnie has been my friend and encourager in the effort to live faithfully "in the midst of chaos." We met soon after each of us gave birth for the first time, and by the time our eldest children were weaned we were both teaching at the same seminary, where we often took time between classes to alternately celebrate and commiserate about the early years of parenting. Both of us had moved by the time our kids became teenagers, but our conversations continued over phone and e-mail and in occasional visits. Gratitude for the privilege of having benefited from Bonnie's reflections across two decades makes the task of commending this book to readers especially sweet.

This same gratitude reminds me to commend you, readers, to one another. Those who seek a life-giving way of life in these uncertain times need one another's insight and support if we are to grow in practicing our faith and in honoring the true sources of well-being for all the world's children, including ourselves. As you explore these pages and ponder how you may grow in your care of children and in your life with God, I hope that you too will find companions with whom to discuss, pray about, and live the practices considered here. To assist you in this endeavor, other resources on Christian practices, including a *Guide for Learning, Conversation, and Growth* based on this book, are available at www.practicingourfaith.org.

September 2006   Dorothy C. Bass
Valparaiso, Indiana   Editor, Practices of Faith series

Preface

If you read the comic strip "Zits," you have a first-rate window into my own home with three teenage boys (of course, my kids don't laugh at "Zits" half as hard as I do). A recent cartoon taped in front of my desk shows a mother hunched over her keyboard. Her son comes up behind her. "I know you're working," he says, "but can I ask for one tiny favor?" "Sure," she says. "Will you sew this button on my shirt, drive Sara and me to the movie, pick us up when it's over, drop us off at Pierce's for band practice, pick us up again, and swing by Sara's Dad's apartment so she can drop off a book on the way home?" "Yeah," answers the mother, "I guess that's not asking too much." "So," her son wonders in the final caption, "do you have that book written yet?"

Bingo.

I am not complaining (although I've been known to). I love my kids, and I love their interruptions. My life is better for it. I'd rather be interrupted than not. Like the mother in "Zits," I would probably say the same thing—"That's not asking too much." I strongly believe I owe my kids bountiful love and attention, not the kind that indulges their every whim or puts their success ahead of other children's, but the kind that cares deeply about their maturation into compassionate, faithful adults.

It is not always easy, however, to tell the difference. Helping children become compassionate, faithful adults who love God and care for themselves, others, and the world around them is an enormous challenge. Life is "always running amuck," I heard a mother exclaim recently. Life with kids is trying; it is confusing, bewildering, and overwhelming. Even those with resources struggle. "Thanks to flexible schedules, short commutes, quality day care, and an egalitarian relationship," one father told me, "my partner and I have worked out a semblance of 'balance.' Yet I often feel torn." We romanticize children if we do not recognize that life is also hard for them. Kids are human, stresses children's author Katherine Paterson, "with all the glory and the anguish the word implies."

The fast pace of society and changes in the family create unique difficulties for faithful living today. It isn't merely a matter of learning how to juggle the demands of kids and life in general. Adults and children together face a more fundamental question: How does one sustain a life of faith in the midst of all this? How does one combine spiritual life with family life?

Within my own religious tradition, Christianity, faith and spirituality have usually been defined by adults who stand at a great distance from children. Spirituality, in this dominant view, is something that requires quiet and solitude and that is best experienced in disciplined settings of prayer, worship, or bible study. Children and families can participate in these practices to some extent, it is generally acknowledged. However, the overall effect of this view is to portray faith in a way that keeps it separate from the daily experience of children and those caught in the mundane toil of their care.

I want to redeem the chaos of care as a site for God's good news. What would happen, this book asks, if we were to search for spiritual wisdom by looking closely at messy, familial ways of living? What would happen if we considered how people discover God not just when alone, in worship, or on the mountaintop, but when with others—specifically when with children and all the turbulence and wonder they bring into our world? Thomas Merton's genius, asserts one scholar, was to "articulate monastic spirituality for people 'in the world.'" What would happen if we claimed that those most proximate to children have something comparable to offer?

This book is an invitation to discover God in the midst of chaos, not just through silence, calm, prayer, or meditation but by practicing faith within the tumultuous activity of daily life. It is about the chaos of family life and how people might find God within it through less commonly recognized practices of faith such as playing, reading aloud, deciding where to live, or figuring out how to divide up household chores. Revising our conventional understandings of faith and the spiritual life in these ways requires us to see children anew as more fully embodied and more fully knowing than some conventional views suggest, lots more trouble but also much more alive and wondrous. It also prompts us adults to look deeply at the dynamics of our own lives of faith.

Understanding care of children as spiritual practice is important to the formation of faith in children and adults alike, and we consider both throughout this book. My emphasis, however, is on the faith of adults. Yes, parents raise children. But raising children also raises adults. Children dramatically transform the lives of adults who care for them. Although these two aspects are integrally related—I can hardly talk about one without the other—this second dimension has received less attention. Yet even before one has children (as a colleague anticipating the birth of a child any day reminds me), one begins to see the world differently.

When I claim that care of children is spiritually transformative for adults, I mean something quite different from recent New Age portraits of parenthood as one more self-gratifying spiritual adventure. Parenting isn't spiritual, I insist, because it might be personally gratifying. Rather, care of children as a practice of faith transforms us adults by summoning us to be committed to the well-being of children—not just our own but all children—as an essential dimension of the common good of the human family. Religious traditions acknowledge that children are bestowed as a divine gift—on parents and on all adults open to receiving them—for the flourishing of the world. Life is not all about our own kids, these traditions forcefully remind us. Instead, care of children as a spiritual practice demands that we ask how parenthood and the shape of family life make us and our children better persons in the world as a whole.

For kids and adults, the family is a kind of workshop or laboratory for honing practices of faith that nurture such generosity and justice. The family is a small community of practice, complicated by its many overlaps with other communities and dependent on the grace that allows us to love one another as gifts and on the trust that God has first loved us, even if we sometimes experience this with uncertainty. Practices of faith can give rise to new wisdom. They can set the conditions for recognizing the "risen Lord" within our midst, even under the oddest circumstances. At the same time, if not attended to with care, practices can also degenerate into rigid, destructive patterns that impede encounter with God.

The most important communities with which families overlap are the religious congregations in which families share the life of faith with adults and kids from other households. Throughout the book, I assume the importance of religious traditions that uphold the practice of just, compassionate love and the essential role of religious communities that sustain these traditions. Amid the chaos of contemporary life, neither adults nor children can do without the support and wisdom these communities and traditions hold. In fact, neither family nor congregation can embrace faith, pursue justice, enact compassion, or love God easily or well without the contribution and grace of the other.

Each chapter of this book explores one practice that allows adults and kids to grow in faith in the midst of chaos. The practices I look into are illustrative examples, not exemplary ideals. The last thing those caught in the demands of family life need is one more exercise to implement, one more ideal to live up to, one more task to execute. If anything, I want to lighten the load by offering a child-friendly, caregiver-supportive, nonelitist understanding of faith and theology. Nor is this a seven-step success story of how I got off the fast track and found God in the family van. Instead, it is my effort to share a sense of the grace that can come when we are honest about the difficulties and attentive to the blessings present in everyday life.

Throughout the book I use the terms *children, parent,* and *family* in intentionally open ways. When we take kids to the movies or theme park, the ticket person says "children are twelve and under." We pay the extra money even though we know "a thirteen-year-old is *not* an adult" (as I once announced). Some chapters of this book, such as the one on pondering, focus more on younger children, whereas teenage boys in front of video games figure prominently in the chapter on play. Throughout the book, I often use the term *kids* because it covers this broad and nebulous age range in which kids still depend on and powerfully influence adults. This term, it seems to me, stretches a bit further than *children* to include teens and young adults.

When most of us hear the word *parent,* we immediately assume biological parenthood. But I have long admired groups and cultures that stretch the word beyond its immediate origin and recognize the importance of "othermothers," as black feminist Patricia Hill Collins designates those who bear responsibility for children not physiologically their own. Because I draw from my own experience, many examples in this book come from a so-called nuclear family. But my remarks are not limited to biological parents and their immediate children. I also write for people who spend extraordinary amounts of time with children: those who teach, those who work in nonprofit organizations for children, and those aunts, uncles, grandparents, and partners who adopt children in their extended family network as their own. These people know that long hours spent with kids radically influences them, and I hope that they too will appreciate the importance of reclaiming this chaos as spiritually transformative. In my view, then, a parent is anyone who cares for kids and is changed by it. For all such adults, not just biological parents, I hope to reclaim the faith-transformative elements already active in their lives. Ultimately, the book is for all those frustrated by narrow definitions of spirituality and eager to rethink faith, spirituality, and families.

I sometimes use *parent* instead of mother or father to flag a commitment to gender inclusivity. I also specifically refer to mothers and fathers and recognize important differences in the contributions they make and the experiences they have. But I advocate here, as I have in other places, shared responsibility among women and men and mothers and fathers for the care of the next generation. Women are not innately gifted at tending to children's needs. All women and men have a capacity, to a greater and lesser extent, to learn how to empathize with a child's anguish. This itself is one of the rich spiritual implications of the practice of close attention to a child. Similarly, both men and women deserve comparable power to make household decisions and owe equal engagement in domestic work. Both also deserve adequate means to pursue other vocations in the public realm outside the family.

I have lived around boys all my life. I grew up between two brothers. Then I had three sons. So I have lots of boy stories. I try to use this particularity as a source for insight while also recognizing how it limits my understanding of care of children as a spiritual practice. I am also shaped and limited by a variety of more complicated characteristics: my middle-class values, European American background, Christian beliefs, academic vocation, and heterosexual motherhood. I see each of these particular locations as both a resource and a place from which to work toward greater understanding of those in quite different locations. The experience of finding faith in chaos arises in families of many shapes and sizes today, and I try to respect and point toward that.

Several wonderful readers help expand my horizons. In particular, I am indebted to Susan Briehl, Kathleen Sprows Cummings, Stephen Ringo, and Dorothy Bass for their meticulous review of the manuscript, copious notes, and lovely stories and insights, many of which now grace the text. A special appreciation goes to Dorothy. This book began in earnest with her encouragement in 2002, when I realized that my book *Let the Children Come* could not contain all I wanted to say about the care of children. But I've been circling around this subject since I began teaching, when my first son was nine months and I had an office next to Dorothy's, twenty years ago. There is really no way I can thank her adequately for the wonderful conversations over the years on dilemmas related to this book, and for her amazing work—most recently as muse and midwife, drawing out ideas, shaping chapters, refining sentences, and laughing, mourning, and celebrating over life with me. Along with Craig Dykstra, she led the way in reconceiving faith as practice, and my understanding of it owes much to her work.

Two other good friends—Stephanie Meis and my husband, Mark Miller-McLemore—helped me sort through the mess of rough drafts and figure out what I wanted to say. I am grateful for how they make my life and practice of faith fuller, richer, better, enhancing but going way beyond this book.

Unlike the teenager in "Zits," my sons, Chris, Matt, and Daniel, actually never asked if I had the book written yet. But my editor, Sheryl Fullerton, did and I thank her. Her confidence, conversation, and work on details helped turn ideas into reality.

My kids simply remarked, "We thought you *said* you *finished* that book," as I kept revising, editing, and copyediting. I am blessed, as I've noted before, that they, along with Mark, just went on living their lives, subjecting my argument to its most rigorous test by demonstrating before my eyes our common foibles and fulfillment. I thank all four for allowing me to use their stories. Throughout the book, I say "one of my sons" rather than identify them by name to leave them a semblance of anonymity.

I also give thanks for wider institutional support provided by the Divinity School of Vanderbilt University; my dean, James Hudnut-Beumler, and colleagues; and the research assistance of Melinda Mc-Garrah Sharp, Elizabeth Zagatta, Kevin Fisher, and Emily Heath; the Lilly Endowment and the Valparaiso Project on the Education and Formation of People in Faith, as well as participants in several Lilly consultations on family, children, and practical theology; and members of the Study Group on Theological Dimensions of Family at the Society for Pastoral Theology and my cochair, Herbert Anderson, in particular. I thank those who shared their thoughts and experiences with families and faith over the past two years at Holden Village, an ecumenical Christian renewal center; Woodmont Christian Church (Disciples of Christ); the American Academy of Religion session on children and spirituality; the Focus on Children Conference of the United Methodist Church; the Boreham Lectures in Pastoral Care in Fort Smith, Arkansas; the Hein-Fry lectures at four Lutheran seminaries; and the Paul S. Allen Lectures at McCormick Theological Seminary (including wonderful colleagues in pastoral care in the Chicago area who dined with me afterwards).

Living in the midst of chaos means living with time and its continuous relinquishment. I end the book with the practice of blessing and letting go. This practice reminds us that we are not finally in control, that we are limited and finite. Ultimately, we are called to release our children in lament and joy. We turn them over to others and the rest of the world in trust, and we give them back to God in love. To bless is perhaps the most ordinary of all the practices in this book, something we do when we say "hello," "good-bye," "good morning," and "good night," greetings that hold forth the hope that God will be with others as they come and go.

Now I release this book, imperfections and all, and bless it on its way to you. Rather than additional burden or guilt, I hope it will free you to practice your faith more abundantly, loving those around you in the midst of life's craziness and letting go of failures, faults, limitations, and sorrows to live more deeply in grace.

Bonnie J. Miller-McLemore

IN THE MIDST OF CHAOS

Chapter 1

CONTEMPLATING IN CHAOS

I have a vivid memory of a scene in *Shadowlands,* a film about the renowned theologian C. S. Lewis. He sits alone in his quiet study, thinking, praying, and perhaps developing the theology that has had such an impact on many Christians. Then his housekeeper arrives with tea and asks him if he needs anything.

This scene is not an especially important or memorable part of the film, which tells the poignant story of the love and bereavement Lewis experienced late in life. But it stayed with me because it planted a question I've lived with ever since: Do we know more about Christian faith as those like Lewis experienced it and wrote about it—in the quiet sanctum of a study, needs secured, free from the immediate demands of others—than about the faith experienced by parents and those who care for children?

Consider this scene next to the opening frames of the film *Parenthood.* Credits roll as a mom and dad inch their way from a baseball game to the family van, juggling, dropping, and picking up kids, souvenirs, bags, and other paraphernalia. The father, played by Steve Martin, is determined to be a better parent than his own father, who, as he has just reminisced, didn't even bother with things like baseball games. His father had simply dropped him off at the ballpark and paid an attendant to watch him.

In spite of this character's resolve to be a good parent, however, the scene also shows how hard it is, as the oldest son starts singing a ditty about diarrhea on the hot, sweaty ride home and the parents exchange a look of hopeful, despairing resignation. *Parenthood* depicts the entanglement of being a parent and being a child, having parents and having children, across several generations. Even the perks of middle-class suburban life cannot allay bedlam, comically yet honestly depicted.

When people think of the spiritual life, they typically picture silence, uninterrupted and serene—a pastor's study, a cloister walk, a monk's cell. Thinking of parenting, by contrast, they imagine noise and complication, dirty diapers, sleepless nights, phone calls from teachers, endless to-do lists, teen rooms strewn with stuff, and backseat pandemonium. By and large, these portraits are accurate. The life of faith requires focused attention that comes most easily when one is least distracted, while caring for children is one of the most intrusive, disorienting occupations around, requiring triage upon triage of decision and response. Can one pursue a "spiritual" life in the midst of such regular, nitty-gritty, on-the-alert demands?

SPIRITUALITY ON THE INSIDE

The Western world has a long history of saying no. One extreme example is Jerome, a fourth-century advocate for monastic life. Like many Latin authors of Roman antiquity, he deemed procreation and the love of children undesirable. He didn't have anything against children per se but rather shunned child rearing for one primary reason: children are a big roadblock on the highway to heaven.

Even those early church leaders who were relatively sympathetic to marriage and family accepted them as a concession to human weakness and sexual desire rather than as a valuable way to live a faithful life. In the Greek context of early Christianity, marriage and children, like other temporal concerns, were thought of as a potential trap for the soul, which ancients understood as yearning for the unchanging immaterial world of beauty and truth. Patristic treatises on the virtues of virginity offer detailed lists of the horrors and tribulations of domesticity—the risks and discomforts of infertility, pregnancy, and childbirth; the drudgery of domestic work; the conflict and violence of the homestead; and anxiety about infidelity, servants, and family members' deaths.

These early church theologians do not have a uniform outlook on marriage and procreation by any means. Although Jerome tended to see them as the baneful result of humankind's fall into sin, Augustine believed instead that the family was part of God's original, good creation and thus a part of God's plan for people from the beginning. Other leading thinkers, such as Gregory of Nyssa and Ambrose, fell somewhere in between. But they all agreed on one thing: family life is inferior to the celibate life of religious heroes and saints. Only lesser mortals (of whom there are many, to be sure) settle for it. If these folks could only learn its hardships prior to the experience, Gregory remarks, "then what a crowd of deserters would run from marriage into the virgin life."

Few people today would flock to celibacy as an alternative to family drudgery. But this legacy of what constitutes the authentic life of faith still seeps into our outlook more than we realize. Several years ago, at a consultation with a group of systematic theologians working on Christian practices and theology, one well-regarded scholar who is particularly interested in the contemplative tradition offhandedly remarked to the rest of us that after the birth of her first child her "discipline of prayer" became impossible. She gave it up.

Like many parents, this scholar gazes with envy over the shoulders of what seem to be our "more spiritual brethren," people refreshed by long retreats uninterrupted by the nagging demands of others. Are these not, many of us ask ourselves, the "true 'spiritual athletes' whose disciplined life of prayer brings them daily closer to God?" Guidance from priests and pastors often affirms this "received" or traditional view. When a young, exhausted Anglican mother found her devotional life in disarray after the birth of her child, Janet Martin Soskice reports, the mother received this advice from three priests: "The first told her that if the baby woke at 6:00 A.M., she should rise at 5:00 A.M. for a quiet hour of prayer. The second asked if her husband could not arrange to come home early from work three times a week so that she could get to a Mass. This advice proved threatening to life and marriage. The third told her,

'Relax and just look after your baby. The rest of the Church is pray-ing for you.' "

Anyone who has had children knows how difficult the first sug-gestion really is (as if babies keep a regular schedule and parents have energy to get up an hour ahead of them). Most contemporary parents also know how much the second idea—negotiating for more child-free time, much less time for prayer—can disrupt and even tear apart relationships of those who jointly care for children. The third sugges-tion was clearly meant to comfort and uphold the importance of the church community's pledge in baptism or baby dedication to pray and care for children and parents. But the remark also implies that the faith life of a busy parent must simply be put on hold. They are "Christians on idle," taking some years off from their faith life while others seek God on their behalf.

Not too long after I joined the ranks of those encumbered with young children, a news article caught my eye. It proclaimed the benefits of a "new" technique called "centering prayer," revived by the Catholic monk Thomas Keating—one more development in a rejuvenated in-terest in spirituality and monastic practice over the last few decades. The article said in part that the "search for God starts by entering a room, the private inner room of the soul. . . . There, a person finds God waiting, beyond the noise, beeps and defeats of life 'outside.' " Beyond the noise, beeps, and defeats of life outside? One finds God on the in-side? So the common tradition of prayer and faith seem to assume.

Thomas Merton, a well-known twentieth-century Catholic monk and mystic, profoundly revitalized this view. His compelling journey from a tumultuous youth to life in one of the more austere monastic orders, the Trappists (a journey recounted in his books, pub-lished in many languages, reprinted frequently, and bought by mil-lions) gave this kind of meditative spirituality new visibility and appeal. Even though Merton himself combined strict ascetic discipline with political action on race, peace, and civil rights, his writings often assumed a conflict between the internal and the external, as if one al-ways needed to dig deeper within to find the real self before God. "Contemplation is not and cannot be a function of this external self," this "superficial 'I' . . . that works in the world," says Merton in one of his most widely read books. It is the "work of the 'deep self,' " an awakening to God's mystery within the "depths."

Psychologists writing during Merton's lifetime, such as Carl Rogers and Carl Jung, proposed the same idea from another angle. One must peel off the outer layers of the "false self" or the "persona," like an onion, to reach the authentic core at the center. Some truth does lie in this advice to question our external attachments and strip the mask that hides our flawed motivations. But this spatial perception of inner over outer, higher over lower, which is woven through so much spiritual and psychological advice, also ends up demeaning the external, the bodily, the earthy, and the material and obscuring their actual connection to our real self and our authentic spirituality. "Certain active types," Merton even argues, "are not disposed to contemplation and never come to it except with great difficulty." Well, this would seem to exclude many parents and children.

Before my husband, Mark, and I became parents, we co-led an adult class on prayer in a small, mostly working-class congregation. We used a classic text by Harry Emerson Fosdick, *The Meaning of Prayer*. The slender volume is designed around daily readings and, like many books, suggests setting aside time to pray at regular intervals. This might require getting up earlier, starting work later, or cutting lunch short.

Such instruction seems simple enough. Yet most of the adults in the class balked. They had kids and jobs. Repeatedly, they had tried and failed. They were too tired in the morning, too tired at night, and too overwhelmed in the hours between. They were already cutting corners. At that time Mark and I were without kids; we pressed these good church folk to persist. Now we look back and laugh at our slightly pretentious naïveté and confidence that *we* at least knew how to make space for prayer in *our* busy lives.

These folks were simply trying to adapt a pattern of faith that is deeply embedded in Western society to the incompatible pattern of their physical, material life with children, partner, and domicile. The embedded pattern simply does not fit the contour of most people's lives today.

"Few of the great remembered pray-ers of our tradition were married. Few had children," notes church historian Wendy Wright.

But this is not all. Many of the esteemed champions of the faith tradition modeled an entire way of life at odds with the life of these church members. They pursued God through the "silence and solitude of a hermit's cell or the mobility of unattached apostolic life." They sought to extend love "to all dispassionately" rather than to particular persons. Indeed, they "radically cut ties with families" and forbade pursuit and satisfaction of sexual desire and bodily need. Ardent devotion to God required transcending the body, voluntary poverty, and pilgrimage far beyond the bond and boundary of home.

Here lies a wholly distinct pattern for the Christian life—whom and how to love, how to work, where to live, how to care for the body, how to spend one's money. Has anyone ever outlined so clearly and carefully an alternative to this traditional view that has comparable weight, integrity, and cohesiveness? A huge gulf lies between this pattern and daily life for most of us—marriage, children, and passionate attachment to specific people; immersion in bodily, sexual activity; commitment to one location; ownership and care of material possessions; and the daily grind of making a living and maintaining a home.

Ambivalence about the family as a place of faith goes as far back as Christian scripture itself. In all three Synoptic Gospels, Jesus himself disclaims his own biological family and proclaims a new family of believers, not related by birth but by commitment to doing God's will (Matthew 13:55; Mark 3:31–35; Luke 8:19–21; all scriptural citations are NRSV unless otherwise specified). Certainly these passages are meant to challenge the extended family clan and the authority it wielded rather than dismiss marriage and procreation themselves. Other passages, such as Elizabeth and Mary greeting motherhood with joy, or Jesus blessing wedding wine, forbidding divorce, and welcoming children, indicate high regard for the bonds of marriage and the love of children.

Nonetheless, Jesus' own model of discipleship and that of his first followers planted seeds of unrest. He was, after all, single and without children, and he asked those who followed him to leave their family. The Apostle Paul never married or had children and thought the imminence of God's kingdom advised accepting whatever situation one found oneself in. Even Paul's identification of the early Christian community as the new "household of God" subtly shifted the locus of faith from the hearth and family as the center of religious practice to new extrafamilial relationships within the church. In many cases, the early church did precisely what Jesus predicted: set brother against brother, father against child, and daughter-in-law against mother-in-law (Matthew 10:21, 35–36; Luke 12:52–53). These characteristics, mixed with the otherworldly leanings of Greek philosophy, made development of a Christian theology of family faith difficult, right up to our time.

Christian perception of faith as something that happens outside ordinary time and within formal religious institutions, or within the private confines of one's individual soul, still pervades Western society. This is true despite recent popular movements and publications affirming everyday spirituality, and despite long-standing movements within Christian history that have encouraged integration of faith into daily life. Some of these movements are receiving renewed attention today, as growing interest in Ignatian and Benedictine spirituality demonstrates. Ignatius of Loyola was the sixteenth-century founder of the Jesuits, a religious society that combines contemplation with action designed to change the world, and Benedict of Nyssa was a fifth-century monastic who created an order that balanced prayer and daily work. Today thousands still belong to these religious orders and many more benefit from retreats, books, and other instruction in these distinctive spiritual paths. Efforts to disseminate these traditions more widely are an important corrective to the understanding of faith that continues to shape many church members, texts on spirituality, and my colleague who thought having kids disrupted her faith.

By and large, however, twentieth-century theologians continue to look past the sheer messiness of daily family life. Similarly, disregard for the material basis of life continues to frustrate contemporary believers' efforts to embrace their faith daily. Bias against "outward" forms of spirituality, as enacted by the body in the midst of family and community, marginalizes many Christians. Limiting spirituality to the "inner" life and restricting theology to the life of the mind ends up excluding a huge portion of life from both faith and theology.

SPIRITUALITY ON THE OUTSIDE

I now recognize a moment of awakening, when I began to have serious doubts about this way of understanding the life of faith. In a quintessential act of multitasking over a decade ago, I sat in the bathroom, watching two of my young sons in the tub *and* reading *The Way of the Heart,* Catholic priest Henri Nouwen's book about spirituality. I was reading his meditation on the *Sayings of the Desert Fathers* because I'd assigned it in a ministry class and wanted to enliven my own practice of faith.

Drawing on one of the Desert Fathers, Abba Arsenius, Nouwen (a twentieth-century priest and spiritual leader) names solitude, silence, and prayer as the three means to love of God. Flee, be silent, and pray. "The words *flee, be silent* and *pray* summarize the spirituality of the desert . . . 'these are the sources of sinlessness,' says Arsenius." Solitude with God frees us from compulsive conformity to the world's standards and propels us toward compassion. Silence reorients the heart. Silence and solitude are paths to God.

No doubt there were many times when I wanted to flee motherhood, or at least some of its daily duties, over the months and years. But I couldn't—at least not to the extent Nouwen implied. There were also times when I yearned for silence, most often when I had other work to do, or as the day waned, infants turned inconsolable, and I tired. When silence came, I appreciated it but was far too spent to use it to fulfill what felt like more obligations of pious devotion. With three children under six and a full-time teaching job, silence and solitude were rare. But without solitude or silence, could I ever experience God?

My youngest son's babbling drew me from my reading to babble back, and another thought crystallized. Why were silence and solitude so absolutely crucial to spiritual growth? Although helpful and important, were they sufficient unto themselves? I looked up from Nouwen's lines about the danger of wordiness to witness one of my sons, not much over a year old, playing with words.

I watched as he grasped the power of language. As with most young children, water fascinated him, and he held a cup, poured water, tried to connect his utterance not only to these objects—"cup," "wa wa"—but also to voice more elusive thoughts and feelings about the joy of pouring ("oooh") or the frustration of having me pull the plug ("aghhh," "no!"). Words opened up worlds for him. They became a source of self-knowledge, meaning, relationship, and, dare I forget, power (here is one reason we fear the day toddlers learn to use the word *no*). They allowed him to begin to conceptualize different orders of reflection and gave him the authority to name and share his experience. Certainly "words lead to sin," as the Desert Fathers say, and silence "keeps us pilgrims" and reminds us of our fleeting nature. But silence can also lead to sin or stagnation and words can build a home.

Words traded back and forth, words mimicked, words slowly stitched into whole sentences. Recently, while cleaning out the attic, I ran across a note on my oldest son's first full sentence: "Mommy come pick me up after work," a life-saving sentence for him that I probably wrote down with mixed feelings about leaving him to go to work. Words in books, rhyming Dr. Seuss words, *Good Night Moon,* and books with only one or two words per page, picture books without words for which we made up stories. Words shared around the dinner table, words sung by heart on Mark's lap with guitar about Casey Jones the railroad engineer, words rejoicing in worship, words debating language for God, words spilled in anger, words recanted. Words with holy potential. The Word as the holy itself. "In the beginning was the Word, and the Word was with God, and the Word was God" (John 1:1).

All these words made up the essential warp and woof of our daily life in those days and now, just as essential to faith as any period of solitude and silence. Such words had the potential to breathe life into our lives. None of the words were God, but all could potentially invoke the Word "with God." Piled one on the next, they worked to weave together convictions and convey tradition, story, song, and prayer. They confirmed the place of conversation alongside silence and connection alongside solitude as vital components of a faithful life.

I did not then and do not now want to rule out silence or solitude as part of the Christian life, or of any life. Indeed, I have a job that requires large amounts of both. I pursued my particular vocation

9

partly because of these built-in qualities and my need for them. To write this book, I even had to ask my husband to take his laptop out of our shared study and find another place to (as I said not too nicely) "tap, tap, tap." Silence and solitude have their place.

I simply want to widen the circle of faith for the sake of children and parents. Millions of other parents must have also asked how to live a life of faith when silence and solitude are rare. I know that I am not the first to raise this. I join a centuries-old search in the Christian tradition for similar streams of thought, bubbling up in Ignatius, Benedict, and beyond. I am, however, among a smaller number who have wondered about the life of faith in direct relationship to children and those who care for them.

WIDENING THE CIRCLE OF FAITH

We give birth and raise the young. We seek God. Why has loyalty to the former, such a potentially rich source of spiritual inspiration, seemed to impede, derail, and compete with the latter? How might we sustain and adjudicate both these fundamental human needs? Perhaps we are now at a juncture where we have means not available before to take up this question once again and find fresh solutions.

More than two decades ago, Ernest Boyer, a lay Catholic minister and father of three sons, had a pivotal experience like my own. He sat in frustration while listening to a lecture at Harvard Divinity School on the Desert Fathers. Although tempted by the image of solitary prayer commended by the speaker, who made points similar to the ones I read in Nouwen's book, Boyer was also troubled. At the conclusion, he approached the speaker and asked (with a smile), "Is there child care in the desert?"

Boyer indicts the Roman Catholic Church for standing so insistently in the "shadow of the monastery." Catholicism certainly places a high value on the family. But this emphasis is often undermined by the Church's tradition of celibacy and male-only priesthood. Not surprisingly, married women, as Catholic theologian Elizabeth Johnson points out, are few in number among canonized saints. The closer one is to the life of the family, it seems, the farther from God and the less accessible one's priestly gift.

Few religious traditions escape the tension between family and religious life, and most have explored ingenious ways to deal with it. Catholics themselves have attempted to mediate the hierarchy of celibate spirituality over spirituality of the home by identifying the family as a "domestic church," a small-scale model of the Church itself, an idea that goes back to the fourth century and that has enjoyed resurgence in the past two decades. Jews in eighteen-century Eastern Europe separated spiritual practice along gender lines, with religious study reserved for men and care of family the obligation of women. Hinduism regulates the problem chronologically, dividing the life cycle into four periods devoted to various concerns and with a special stage of "householding" for rearing children. Seventeenth-century Puritans sanctioned the home as a "little church" but then elevated the father to the role of pastor, nearer to God than others—with all the potentially destructive and even violent consequences of this equation.

As this indicates, these patterns of the past were often based on gender hierarchy and inequity. As a result, they cannot adequately address the question of how to combine faith and family today without considerable modification. Changes in women and men's roles in family and public, as well as the pressure of raising children in contemporary society, mean that we need fresh perspectives.

Now more people share responsibility for family and work in ever new ways—single and divorced mothers and fathers, grandparents caring for grandchildren, blended families, partners and spouses with two careers. More theologians, women and men alike, challenge previous hierarchies of soul over body, culture over nature, reason over emotion, and men over women and children. Perhaps now, with more people seeking God at the busy crossroad of parenthood, we can also challenge the hierarchy of inner over outer and begin to ask how to live faithfully amid noise and distraction.

My own pursuit of a more satisfactory answer has arisen gradually. Several years ago, a ministerial colleague told me that she had used my book *Also a Mother* to facilitate a church retreat on spirituality. I was surprised. The book does make rather dramatic claims—

Contemplating in Chaos

that utterly physical acts of birth and care can be a powerful spiritual catalyst, that walking "according to the pace of children" can deepen faith, and that children have much to teach adults about the life of faith. But spiritual guidance was not in the forefront of my mind. It has only dawned on me slowly that I was then and am still now caught up in a much larger historical and cultural debate about the nature of faith, contemplation, chaos, and children.

LIVING ON A SLACK LINE

Yesterday I took a break to follow my oldest son outside, where he had set up something called a "slack line," a flat, brilliant red webbing tied (low—only a few feet off the ground) like a tightrope between two trees. He wanted me to watch him as he practiced walking on it. It looks easy. It's not. He can take several steps and is working on turning around. I can't even stand up on it. Muscles matter, although it's not all muscle.

Holding the tension between silence and words, solitude and company is something like this: hard to sustain, a resounding pleasure when one succeeds. No wonder many Christians either hop off the slack line toward silence and solitude or give up altogether.

I write on a slack line that runs through the center of our home. My desk sits in a living room converted to a study, smack dab in the middle of family solace and bedlam. Sitting here writing, I can hear the phone, the dryer buzzer, interrupting questions ("Do you know where . . . ?"), and lots else (did I mention my oldest son plays drums?). I've become good at abiding through all this, choosing what to ignore and when to respond. But in neither realm am I at my best.

Drawn into the rhythm of meals, laundry, and kids' schedules, work goes poorly. I sometimes return to home life in a daze, like a sleepwalker, not really hearing my sons or my husband, or, as one of my colleagues did during a major project, making hamburgers to cook for breakfast ("Mom—it's *breakfast*"). At least my sons no longer run through my office chasing each other, although tomorrow could prove me wrong.

At certain overwhelming moments, I consider changing my mind about this strategy. But all in all, I am placing my bets on what I might learn from trying to walk this particular slack line. I do indeed get "more done" when no one is around. But this is only true if measured in the literal (and limited) sense of work produced, and not in the sense of wisdom gained and life deepened.

This particular arrangement is not for everybody. I recently read a lovely poetic book by a friend about the "art of faith and family." In the time-honored pattern of many writers, he retreats from the urban fray to a prairie farm to compose at a geographical distance from his family. He incorporates wonderful journal entries, fresh with insight spawned by the antics and wisdom of his three young children, jotted down right in the middle of it all. Yet I could not help but wonder how the book might have been different had he written at home. Maybe it wouldn't have happened at all. This is the hazard. But as it is, one of his pressing concerns—how to steady oneself in dual careers, multiple children, and escalating expectations—is somewhat defused. When he looks up, he sees birds, lilies, and spiders, not domestic debris, dirty dishes, and runny noses, or a time clock, phone messages, and a stack of deskwork.

My friend in the prairie henhouse suggests how hard it is to attain attention, not to mention artistic production or prayer, without fleeing. It may be that for him leaving home isn't fleeing at all. Rather, he says his time away is less "a retreat from my family than a journey back to them." This solitary reflective time is necessary to his ongoing ability to attend to faith in family.

When I once commented to a senior woman colleague about how hard it was to get my work done, she encouraged me to do what she did: get away for six weeks. Of course, when I told my husband, he just laughed. Exactly how were we going to do that? When would he get his turn? Hadn't I already had an unfair amount of time away on work trips? And so forth. But both of these folks illustrate that a key for faith and chaos lies in finding one's own necessary pattern for balancing, one's own particular slack line between solitude and connection.

Widening the circle of faith for the sake of children and parents means balancing profound silence and fruitful words, potent solitude

Contemplating in Chaos

and invigorating company. A fine balance. A precarious balance. Perhaps this is partly what makes faith, as William James said, "strenuous."

REDEEMING MARTHA

Learning to walk the slack line of faith is a step in the right direction. Each person does have to find a particular way through the chaos of life. But widening the circle of faith for children and those who care for them requires more than individual dexterity. I am actually suggesting a deeper transformation. We must get off the slack line and back on the ground. This means changing our minds about Martha and what she has stood for.

Women as a group have probably worried more over the story of Mary and Martha in Luke 10:38–42 than over any other five verses of the Bible. When Jesus visits the home of Mary and Martha, Mary sits at his feet and listens while Martha is "distracted by her many tasks" (Luke 10:40a). When Martha asks Jesus to tell Mary to help with the work, Jesus says, "Martha, Martha, you are anxious and troubled by many things; one thing is needful" (Luke 10:41 RSV).

Many women identify acutely with Martha and despair over their domestic unfaithfulness. A long history of biblical interpretation has indeed esteemed Mary as the model of faithful attentiveness and peace, able to put aside dinner preparation and cleaning to appreciate Jesus fully. Even bible commentary simply presumes that Jesus' approval of Mary stands in contrast with his disapproval of "Martha's unneeded acts of hospitality (the more usual woman's role)."

Not surprisingly, women long for a "Mary heart in a Martha world," as one recent popular book is entitled. Mary has it all. Martha is equated with everything in the world that distracts us—daily chores, life's demands. Few escape feeling ashamed and guilty right alongside Martha before Jesus, responsible for and worried about so much.

Other New Testament passages seem to reinforce this. "Do not be anxious about your life, what you shall eat, nor about your body, what you shall put on," Jesus tells his disciples (Luke 12:22 RSV). "Do not be anxious about tomorrow" (Matthew 6:34 RSV). Although few in number, these passages are heavy in influence. They do remind us to put aside petty obsessive worry and "seek first God's kingdom," a central imperative of Christian faith. But over the long haul, the tradition has also interpreted them to mean that anxiety about material needs and desires itself is bad. In theological language, this anxiety is proof that we are fallen.

Years ago, as an anxious graduate student, I was considerably relieved to read the words of the twentieth-century theologian Paul Tillich to the contrary. In those days, I saw no constructive place for anxiety. First I felt anxious about my life; then I felt bad that I felt anxious. Tillich helped me understand just how foolish this was.

Following his nineteenth-century inspiration, Søren Kierkegaard, Tillich insists that anxiety precedes the human fall into sin. In other words, it is part of our creation as human, what he calls the "ontological nature of being," not a distortion of our nature. It is not inherently bad or a problem in itself. Feeling bad about feeling anxious simply compounds distress unnecessarily and unfairly.

Certainly anxiety can become what psychologists call "neurotic." Jesus sought to allay anxiety that grows out of unfaith or distrust in God's love. Both Christian conviction and psychology help us notice when distorted, excessive, or faithless worry contribute to our distress. But some anxiety is natural, normal, and a needed part of life.

Anxiety moved me forward to undertake the creative work needed to finish a graduate paper and get through exams. It accompanied me as I ventured out with my yet-to-be husband for dinner. It foreshadowed the birth of each child. It is part of what is helping me finish this book. In instances such as these at least, I am not anxious because I am bad or flawed, but sometimes because I have love, hope, and desire for my work or for another person. For such possible goods, it is indeed proper to be anxious. In such instances, anxiety is a sign of faith, not faithlessness.

Likewise, Martha is not the epitome of unfaithfulness. In her concern about her work, she solicits and prepares for God's grace. It is not, in fact, entirely self-evident that Jesus rebukes her. Or so argues the thirteenth-century Dominican theologian and mystic Meister Eckhart.

Contemplating in Chaos

Those who want to redeem Martha today have an unusual ally in Eckhart. In his sermon on the Lukan passage, he praises her. She is worried about Mary, he says, because Martha has "lived long and well" and "living gives the most valuable kind of knowledge" about God. Mary, she fears, has mistaken enjoyment for genuine faith at work. One can imagine another scene untold where Jesus says as much to Mary.

So Jesus is not chastising Martha at all, according to Eckhart. That he calls her name twice is itself an indication of his blessing and her "perfection" or completeness. Our "work in time," just as Martha's activity and service, can indeed bring us as close to God as the "most sublime thing that can happen to us, except for seeing God" in God's "pure nature." When Jesus says Martha has many cares, he means she is "so grounded in being that her activity did not hinder her. Work and activity led her to eternal happiness." She only wants the same for Mary.

REDEEMING CHAOS

This summer, I worshiped in a sanctuary that had a sign on the wall in big bold print, "May the Spirit of God Disturb You." These words were posted to honor Gertrude Lundholm, a Lutheran woman who deeply shaped and inspired all generations in the community and who had died only the week before. During Eucharist, she would pass the peace in just this way. "May the Spirit of God disturb you," she'd say as she embraced her neighbor.

What did Lundholm mean? "Many Christians," she told a friend, "seem to think that the peace of God is just about their own internal peace of mind, as if being a Christian is kind of like being on a kind of tranquilizer. But God intends to stir us up . . . to make us notice new things, to keep us from being complacent." She came by this conviction rightfully. Martin Luther himself said faith is a "lively, reckless confidence" in God's grace. But "we Christians like the part about confidence so much," she observes, "that we often overlook the part about being lively and reckless." Sometimes God's peace brings rest.

But sometimes it turns our world upside down, makes chaos of all our plans, and challenges the limited horizons of our self-built lives.

"As hectic as life and work may be," argues Gabriel Fackre (a Protestant theologian and industrial mission pastor who served churches in a steel mill town and a growing suburb for eight years), one finds a peace with God different from that of cloister and cell. Rather than "contemplative union," the "missioner looks for God . . . in the swirling currents of time" and all its material demands. He proposes the churning "River of God" as a better image of faith and ministry than the still, silent "waters of Siloe," the ideal of spirituality defined by Merton.

"Merton's vocation and counsel stand in radical contrast," Fackre believes, "to what the Protestant missioner is and does." In place of vows of obedience, chastity, and poverty, one bears responsibility for endless decisions, negotiates complex long-term intimate relationships, and balances material need, money, and its just use. Yet this "foaming stream of livingness" with "people moving, people building, people tearing down, people drifting, people fighting, people forgotten" is "God's river." In essence, life's busyness is not an utterly secular wasteland. Faith and meaning can emerge *in* the mess.

We do not like the feeling of chaos. We like to think we're in control, contained, ordered. We fear disorder within and dirt, dust, and debris without, perhaps because they subtly remind us of the very fragile, transitory, dependent reality of our own created lives. We often associate chaos with violence and evil.

These associations are well warranted, of course. Seeing faith as something that arises in the midst of chaos is risky. Chaos is not always so promising. There are aspects of chaos that are evil and destructive. The chaos of war, violence, holocaust, and natural disaster comes immediately to mind. Children raised in complete chaos suffer and fail. Complete chaos is not good for anyone.

Not surprisingly, therefore, distrust of chaos runs deep. It even colors how creation itself has been understood and misunderstood. When we read the creation story in the Book of Genesis, we often focus on the first verse, where "God created the heavens and the

Contemplating in Chaos

earth," and skip right past the mysterious second verse: The earth "was a formless void" covered by darkness over which God's spirit or "wind" sweeps. The long history of biblical interpretation has also largely ignored this verse, insisting instead that God creates the world out of nothing—*creatio ex nihilo.* But chaos was there from the beginning, before the beginning, as part of the beginning.

We need to recover the "lost chaos of creation," *creatio ex profundis,* creation out of "the deep," argues Catherine Keller, a theologian who has been trying for a long time to promote a more sympathetic reading of chaos. Doctrines of creation that claim God created out of absolute nothingness (creatio ex nihilo) distort the original narrative. In Genesis 1:2, God moves over the "face of the deep" and actually creates amid chaos. In place of the usual opposition between chaos and cosmos, she argues for a more wondrous oscillation—what she calls a "chaosmos." Her ultimate goal is to foster a fragile peace among us all that is predicated on warmer acceptance of chaos. Perhaps if we can recover the lost chaos of creation, she says, we can live "more creatively with the inner and outer chaos—the uncertainty, unpredictability, turbulence, and complexity of our lives."

Recent explorations in physics support this rehabilitation. The universe is not governed by inexorable laws that order things from the smallest particle to the most distant planet, as we once thought. Instead, chaos theory suggests a universe teetering on the edge of chaos and order. Order emerges only spontaneously as a result of infinitesimally small uncertainties in a complex interrelationship between motions. Disorder is the baseline and the rule, order the exception. It is the "precondition," remarks a scholar of science and religion, Ian Barbour, for order.

Ultimately, redeeming Martha and rethinking anxiety, peace, and chaos changes our understanding of God. God is no longer an all-powerful, unchanging Lord in the sky. Instead we glimpse a more puzzling, raging, weeping, shouting, pleading, disruptive, disturbing, and even evolving God, moving within the deep, appearing in unexpected and unplanned places, and sometimes even coming to us as the "Discomforter" as well as the Comforter. God bestows peace not as a promise of perfect serenity or an end to chaos, anxiety, and strife but as a source of strength in turmoil. This is good news for those caught up in the many divergent tugs of family, children, and work.

REDEEMING THE WAKING, WALKING ROUTINE

Some Christians have endorsed exemplary models of prayer as a way to counteract the dissipation common to domestic life. One model is "breath prayer," an ancient discipline that involves multiple repetitions of a phrase short enough to be spoken in one breath ("Jesus is Lord") from the earliest creed of the church, for example, or a phrase from the Psalms. Others turn to a discipline suggested by Brother Lawrence three centuries ago, in which the person "practices the presence of God" throughout the day regardless of external circumstances. Despite his menial household work as a lay brother in the Carmelite order—cooking, washing dishes, cleaning hallways—Brother Lawrence managed to reach a point where work was no different from prayer. "In the noise and clatter of my kitchen," he says, "I possess God as tranquilly as if I were upon my knees before the Blessed Sacrament." Nouwen also recommended a kind of unceasing prayer for those who "are not monks and do not live in the desert." Some African Americans carry over into daily life the "tarrying" of worship, a similar practice of lingering in conversation with God, saying over and over words of praise, thanksgiving, or confession. Howard Thurman believes such prayer anchors social engagement and creates an "island of peace" within oneself, and within the island a "temple" where God dwells.

As helpful as all these aids to prayer are, however, they still require an interior focus of mind, will, and heart that one can rarely find in family life. They call for a kind of stepping outside of one's routine, or for bringing something that is outside one's routine—God, spirituality, tranquility—into it. One participates in these disciplines "despite" or "regardless" of the chaos. They still assume one meets God in a quiet inner space.

What I am trying to describe, instead, is a wisdom that somehow emerges in the chaos itself, stops us dead in our tracks, and

Contemplating in Chaos

heightens our awareness. I am talking about a way of life that embraces the whole of family living in all its beauty and misery rather than about individual acts of devotion, as important as they are to sustaining the whole. In other words, I am not trying to recommend a better way to pray. I am suggesting that faith takes shape in the concrete activities of day-to-day.

I want to redeem the waking, walking, buzzing routine itself. In saying this, I do not mean that our everyday busyness will make us righteous or earn us salvation; not even our "good works" can do this. Nor am I implying that we can get this routine into perfect working order. Rather, I want to insist that grace is active not only when we're passive and quiescent or tranquil and mindful but also when we are deeply involved in the activities of childhood and parenthood themselves. People respond powerfully to Brother Lawrence precisely because he seems to suggest that our actions themselves might become prayer.

Practicing the presence of God. I like that. It is close to what this entire book is about, but in a particular way. This book is about practicing the presence of God not through a prayer discipline that sustains a peaceful inner life but rather through practices that invoke, evoke, and form faith in our outward lives. We already participate in such practices in the varied contexts where children and adults live together: playing, working, eating, talking, learning, fighting, making up, arriving, departing, and otherwise making a home. Out of this great hubbub, I select a few that come a bit more easily for me than others: sanctifying the ordinary, pondering, taking children seriously, giving to others and oneself, doing justice, playing, reading, and blessing and letting go. These are the practices I invite you to consider with me in the chapters ahead.

Chapter 2

SANCTIFYING THE ORDINARY

One day several years ago, when my kids were little, I stood next to my husband, Mark, in what we called the "train park" because it was next to commuter and freight trains rumbling in and out of Chicago. My boys were thrilled to get as close to the roar and speed of engine and caboose as parental nerve could tolerate. That day they weren't doing anything particularly different from any other day at the park. Yet something about their sheer joy and abandon in running from slide to swing sparked a sudden, unanticipated rush of matching joy. I looked at my husband. He knew it too. We lifted it up, and the moment passed.

Standing over the stench of a dirty diaper, wiping the bottom of a child, occasionally had the same effect. I would stand there caught in the intimacy of eye-to-eye, face-to-face, body-to-body contact with this small being, overwhelmed by a flow of love toward my sons that somehow did not feel restricted to them. We laundered those diapers ourselves. Although one of my good friends thought our effort Herculean, especially by child number three, we took it on as a small token connecting our care for our kids to care of environment, but also because cloth seemed soft, warm, more human than disposable plastic (not to mention cheaper). How could I explain this unlikely sense of God's presence and blessing?

This sense of faith in, with, and under the mundane routine of rinsing, washing, drying, folding, and piling up a fresh stack of clean diapers—a stack marking stability in a cycle of messiness—gained a foothold. Although Mark and I share laundry, I have yet to get help or to ask my kids to do their own, apart from sorting socks and underwear and putting everything away. On occasion, there's something for me of God in the sheets, towels, and material surrounding of my family.

Apparently I am not alone. When Kathleen Norris published an essay about laundry in the *New York Times Magazine*—specifically, about the "joys of hanging clothes on the line to dry"—she received at least a hundred letters in response. Except for one tired mother with small children and a long commute who exclaimed that Norris "must have way too much time" on her hands, her recognition of the holy in the mundane struck a chord.

We should certainly heed the justified suspicion of the overworked, and the feminist warning about women's domestic exploitation. These dangers should be taken seriously, better understood now thanks to the women's movement. But there is truth in Norris's claim that "women's work" can ground us rather than "grind us down." She subtitles a later book on the mystery of the "quotidian"—the daily, the ordinary, the commonplace—*Laundry, Liturgy, and "Women's Work."*

Of course, laundry is sometimes just one big brain-numbing chore. The last time I made my way through multiple baskets of whites, darks, and assorted colors after returning from a vacation, there was absolutely nothing enlightening or inspiring about it. Little in life is pure—pure faith, pure joy, pure love. Yet doing laundry, as other quotidian aspects of life, can hold the symbolic and the material in incredibly close proximity. One of my friends, a mother of twins, told me she once found herself crying over a huge pile of unfolded clothes. She cried as she folded, both out of frustration that her husband refused to help *and* out of recognition that her days of being this close to her children's underwear were so very short-lived, so fleeting.

We need to honor and savor these moments. They befriend and uphold us through less savory times. Yet apart from Norris, I have not heard many acclamations of diapers, laundry, or playgrounds in sermons or Christian theology. I remember the train park incident not because I earmarked the moment when inspired by church worship or reading theology later that week. I remember it because I lifted it up first with Mark and later in supervision and therapy during my pastoral counseling training.

Psychology, for all the popular ridicule of its navel gazing, has often sparked valuable soul searching of the most concrete kind. If most sermons, liturgies, and theologies do not in turn create space to mark the sacred in the daily and celebrate the intricacies of parenthood as a faith-filled vocation, how will we stop to notice and know? My clinical training fostered good parenting and deepened my faith. It did so precisely because it honed my capacity for attention and empathy for the earthy intricacies of life. Can Christianity claim as much?

PROTESTANT HISTORICAL AMNESIA

A wise friend and Presbyterian minister with grown children, grandchildren, and a great love for the church once said something to me that allays any fear of faith being impractical after childbirth because one "can no longer pray" as one did before. The ordinary, he asserted, is often the most significant for faith. Most of the time we miss it. It takes discipline to notice the distinctiveness of the ordinary. Moreover, to notice the theological nature of the ordinary, to connect the ordinary to the conviction of religious tradition, is even harder. It requires a particular kind of theological vision and valuing of the ordinary.

Protestants have long upheld the practice of sanctifying the ordinary. But our awareness and disciplined enactment of this practice has waned. Norris herself is a good example. Of all her spiritual memoirs recounting her journey from secular disbelief back to her Presbyterian roots, her book honoring the quotidian is by far her most Protestant. But even she doesn't explicitly recognize its Protestant roots. She is more inclined to commend the monastic Benedictine community.

Neither Catholics nor Jews have hesitated as much as most Protestants in claiming a distinctive approach to spirituality in family life. Mainstream (or "old-stream") Protestantism has a long history of significant denominational support of family and children's ministries and programs of advocacy for children in need. Indeed, it has created so many educational resources, church directives, family surveys, child-rearing pamphlets, and so forth that when historian Margaret Bendroth traces what it means to "grow up Protestant" she has to draw lines around what she can and cannot cover. If gauged by all the "forest slain in behalf of the written word," she observes, the mainstream has a long history of extensive attention to parenting and children. So why doesn't this translate into a confident, recognized pattern of family spirituality?

Many factors engender Protestant amnesia about our tradition of sanctifying ordinary family drudgery. Protestants often privatize faith as primarily a personal conversion and see faith "practice" as limited to private devotions, such as prayer or Bible reading. In my own church, we have actually changed the confession of Jesus the Christ as "Lord and Savior of the world" that appears in our denomination's affirmation of faith to a confession of Jesus as our "personal Lord and Savior." Many churches perpetuate an equally unhelpful view of faith as a cognitive, intellectual, disembodied endeavor taught in the Sunday School wing. Protestants also believe that Christians are justified by faith, not works. So anything that smacks of "works righteousness" or the attempt to earn our way to spiritual perfection, including the very phrase *spiritual discipline,* is suspect.

Human experience itself is sometimes distrusted. A friend recently compared the model of prayer in Protestant theologian Karl Barth and Catholic theologian Karl Rahner. One of the most striking differences is Rahner's complete sacramental trust that God is found in all things and by contrast Barth's lower estimation of human nature and his conviction that God's Word enters the world only from outside it. Barth is considerably less sure than Rahner that human action mediates divine presence. The chance that our family lives will distort God's Word rather than force an encounter with it is far greater. Our distant Puritan history just accentuates these deep misgivings about ordinary embodied experience.

Then, of course, there's modernity. Baby boomers inherited from their own parents a cautiousness about making religious claims that no longer measure up to modern scientific standards. In a major study of Presbyterian baby boomers, Dean Hoge, Benton Johnson, and Donald Luidens reveal that the parents of baby boomers were "considerably less likely than previous generations to impose their particular religious beliefs on their children." Even though these families went to church each Sunday, faith was "rarely a topic of discussion" in the home. So also did its practice decline. Active church participation "apparently did not result in familial Bible study, devotions, or prayer sessions— other than grace at meals." Gone was the earlier tradition of family worship promoted by Presbyterians until the early twentieth century.

So when Presbyterian theologians gathered in the late 1950s and 1960s to debate the role of the family, many argued that there was little theological warrant to sanction the family as a redemptive mediator of grace or as a place of faith formation. People looked instead to the trained professional in church and the academy to mediate grace. Meanwhile, these same professionals were slowly shifting their own gaze from children to individual adult development. The family, with its growing array of problems, did not appear to be a promising agent of salvation.

This pattern is not unique to Presbyterians or Protestants, of course. The Methodist class meeting, in which congregational members gathered in small circles for Bible reading and prayer, shaped the moral ecology of families throughout the nineteenth century, but it largely disappeared in the twentieth. Emotionally vibrant Catholic spiritualities, as with use of votive candles and the rosary, flourished in pre–Vatican II homes, sometimes in genial contrast to the cognitive slant of formal doctrine, but decreased in the 1960s.

Modernity also brought technology, and technology has had a real impact on patterns of daily life. Listen to one historian's depiction of the centrality of Martin Luther's family fireside: "After the day's labors were over, Luther would often gather his family around him to tell stories, play melodies on his lute, and teach them little songs, games, and prayers. It was also around the family hearth that Luther patiently taught his children the fundamentals of the Christian faith out of the *Small Catechism* which he prepared specifically for the religious nurture of the common folk."

I am struck here by the pivotal place of the hearth and the question this raises about the impact of central heating on domestic routine and family faith in our own time. For Luther and many premodern people, the hearth was a source not only of heat but also of food, light, company, amusement, story, song, conversation, and faith. People assumed a certain amount of family time spent in "table talk" and around the fire. It may not always have been pleasant, but if people wanted to stay warm, if they wanted light, that was the place to go. Where the warmth of the hearth virtually compelled people to gather, central heating sends us to all corners of the house.

My concern here is not the decline of devotional practice. Rather, all these factors—modern technology, decline of family worship, faith as private and limited to acts of personal devotion, wariness about ordinary experience, fear of spiritual discipline as works righteousness—contribute to an amnesia about our particular spiritual history of embracing ordinary family life as a place for faith.

It dawned on me only slowly when I first had children that I held major responsibility for forming them in faith. Nor did I anticipate just how much they would form my own faith. This oversight is pretty astounding. It seems like a no-brainer, but sometimes it was all I could do to brush my teeth and feed and clothe my kids. I didn't really see faith formation as comparable to these necessities. I knew faith had touched my life richly in my own family of origin through how we lived and what we did daily. I had a graduate education in religion that included study of faith development. But I still saw the institutions of religion—church, synagogue, mosque—as where faith happens. I, a good Protestant, had forgotten my history.

RECOVERING MY MEMORY, RECOVERING COMMUNITY MEMORY

A distinctly Protestant conviction about the sanctification of the ordinary fuels my own desire to rehabilitate the practice of parenting as faith-filled. Early in my years of graduate study, Clark Williamson, a theologian in my own tradition, came to speak at the house where I lived with several other students. His topic, "Theology and Forms of Confession in the Disciples of Christ," was "notoriously difficult" for Disciples, he said, because as a rule we react negatively to the mere hearing of the word *theology.* Alexander Campbell, a founder of this early nineteenth-century American-born frontier tradition, actually forbade the teaching of theology at one of the movement's colleges. Like creeds, systems of theology often encumber, truncate, or distort the truth of Jesus as the Christ as much as they confirm or embellish it. Despite all the problems, divisions, and conflicts, this reformation movement sought to restore two pivotal principles of the Protestant Reformation: *sola scriptura* and *sola fide,* scripture and faith alone as the foundation on which to stand.

I still have my tattered yellow copy of the prepublished version of the manuscript Williamson presented with my initial reactions— "good" and "yes . . . my own experience"—scrawled in the margins. What most interested me then and now is Williamson's articulation of theology as practice. Disciples want to avoid abstracting faith "from the whole of life," he noted, "rendering it into a property to be owned, dividing believers from one another, and substituting propositions about God for communion with God." Faith is a "way of life," oriented to practice and confessed primarily through deeds as much as creeds.

"There was no clear line," begins the popular novella *A River Runs Through It,* "between religion and fly fishing" in the family of Norman Maclean, son of a Scottish Presbyterian minister and practiced fly fisherman. "In a typical week of our childhood," Maclean reports, "Paul and I probably received as many hours of instruction in fly fishing as we did in all other spiritual matters." There is much to be learned about faith through fly fishing and ordinary life.

Also descendants of the Scottish Presbyterians, early Disciples followed the Puritans in observing the Sabbath, a practice that church theologians such as Augustine had rejected out of hostility to Judaism. Disciples chose to honor the Sabbath precisely because the practice is an effort to usher in God's purpose in the world. As in Judaism, what one does and how one does are primary ways to declare one's faith. Williamson also calls this "ethics as a form of piety" or a theology of sanctification.

As a questioning preteen, I once asked my mom why we went to church every Sunday. She thought for a second and then, perhaps receiving no further inspiration, said, "Out of habit, I suppose." At the time I thought this a rather lame answer, and I think she did also. But now I see it as part of a richer understanding that faith does partly rest on good habits, not on ideology or confession but on material embodiment and patterns. The word *habit* is also the root of "inhabit," "habitation," "habitat." We make a home not only out of words woven together in conversation but also out of habits of faith.

In fact, the spirituality of "Golden Rule Christians," as sociologist Nancy Ammerman calls mainstream Protestants, "is not just a paler" version of contemporary evangelicalism. It is different in kind and deserves to be understood on its own terms. Golden Rule Christians value "right living more than right believing." Compassion and doing good for others are more important than prayer, witnessing, and Bible study on the one hand, and radical efforts to change the world on the other hand. These Christians are not exactly out to convert others to their beliefs (not even their own children) or overhaul the world. They would just "like the world to be a bit better for their having inhabited it."

In a wonderful little book, *Protestant Spiritual Exercises,* Joseph Driskill insists that "Protestant spirituality" is not an oxymoron. But he defines this spirituality in a particular way. Luther, Calvin, and the Wesleys all suggest exercises of examination, prayer, and so forth. However, these exercises are oriented toward a distinct kind of embodied spirituality. They demand ethical action on behalf of others. They require critical reflection on faith claims. Ultimately, they suggest healthy suspicion of superficial assertions about immediate access to God's will. So, rather than declaring that one has prayed about a problem and heard God, one hopes to manifest faith through living authentically day-by-day.

WHAT A FRIEND IN LUTHER

I do not remember the day I discovered what a friend I had in Luther. But I am glad for it. I know it came after I was well warned about the patriarchal legacy of our Christian forefathers. As it turns out, the Reformation theologian Martin Luther still knew a great deal about family living and prayer, even if his wisdom came with the inevitable baggage that the father is the ordained head of the household. He might even be called the father of the effort to reunite the holy—previously reserved for cloistered priests, nuns, brothers, and sisters—with mundane, dirty, daily life. To put his own sixteenth-century principles of religious reformation into action, he renounced his vow of celibacy and wed Katherine von Bora, a former nun. Together—and she was a wonderful, straightforward, hard-working partner who knew how to hold her own—they raised a large and boisterous family that included six of their own children and four orphans. They couldn't begin to imagine the abundant wellspring of knowledge and deep faith that marriage and children would bring.

When I first read Luther's remarks, I was disarmed. Here was a male theologian saying he also found God in stinky diapers, adorned as if with jewels! He declares such domestic work "holy, godly, precious":

> When . . . our natural reason . . . takes a look at married life, she turns up her nose and says, 'Alas, must I rock the baby, wash its diapers, make its bed, smell its stench, stay up nights with it, take care of it when it cries, heal its rashes and sores, and on top of that care for my wife, provide for her, labor at my trade, take care of this and take care of that, do this and do that, endure this and endure that, and whatever else of bitterness and drudgery married life involves? What, should I make such a prisoner of myself [one hears echoes here of the Greek view of the body as a prison of the rational mind and soul]?
>
> What then does Christian faith say to this? It opens its eyes, looks upon all these insignificant, distasteful, and despised duties in the Spirit, and is aware that they are all adorned with divine approval as with the costliest gold and jewels. . . . I confess to thee that I am not worthy to rock the little babe or wash its diapers, or to be entrusted with the care of the child and its mother. . . . O how gladly will I do so, though the duties should be even more insignificant

Sanctifying the Ordinary

and despised. Neither frost nor heat, neither drudgery nor labor, will distress or dissuade me, for I am certain that it is thus pleasing in [God's] sight.

God "smiles" on all this. In fact, Luther says that "those who sneer . . . are ridiculing God." They are themselves the "devil's fools." Luther speaks here to those religious heirs of the early church fathers who demoted marriage and children. When done in faith, raising children pleases God.

Parenting, says medievalist scholar Elizabeth Dreyer, is the "ascetic opportunity *par excellence*." Traditionally asceticism referred to the use of disciplines of self-denial and world renunciation, such as celibacy and fasting, to draw closer to God. Dreyer turns this usage on its head. If regarded from the right angle, a parent's daily life has an oddly haunting resemblance. Unbidden and unexpected, opportunity arises for a similar kind of disciplined religiosity: "A full night's sleep, time to oneself, the freedom to come and go as one pleases—all this must be given up. . . . Huge chunks of life are laid down at the behest of infants. And then, later, parents must let go." Here, in a nutshell, is the life span and extremes of child rearing: loving, losing, and letting go.

I cannot say how relieved I felt when I first came across these words several years ago. They allowed me to see my early parenting life as somehow connected to my faith. The first question commonly traded among new parents runs something like, "How many hours does she sleep?" or "Is he sleeping through the night?" or "Are you getting any sleep?" Now I see: on one level this is a deeply spiritual question about faith, care, and the practice of love, even if this dimension goes largely unmentioned and unnoticed.

One of my sons didn't sleep much. Even in the hours after birth, when pregnancy books and midwives assure parents that their newborn will sleep, he didn't. For the next few years, we ran through the entire book of sleep-inducing tricks. None worked. Mostly, we got up. We stayed up. We walked, talked, comforted, nursed, changed diapers, walked, talked, comforted more, and put him back down crying. Sometimes we gave up and left him crying. We tried to sleep, to no avail. We spent our days a bit delirious. We teetered on the edge of exhaustion and poor judgment. We learned, as most parents do, just how hard it is to be a good parent and just how much support one needs to avoid abuse. I cringe to remember now the time I told him that if he didn't lie down and quit crying the boogieman would get him (a terrible remark on my part that only quieted him temporarily in any case). To see this daily regimen of care, restraint, self-extension, and craziness as part of a larger practice of faith, a means of learning patience, charity, endurance in fidelity, receptivity to the other, long suffering, and humility, sanctioned the work that filled my life and placed it in a new light.

Parenting as a Religious Practice

One Sunday morning several years ago, I lugged one infant in my arms, shouldered a diaper bag, nagged two small kids out the door to the garage, heaved the garage door up, cajoled all three into the van, and then, as I backed out to drive to church, hit the van's spoiler on the partially opened door. I jumped out of the van, tossed the spoiler aside, and went to church anyway. But I wonder then (and many other times) whether getting to worship was worth the cost, not of van repair but of repairing all the other damage done to all of us in transit from home to sanctuary. How is this—this tending to family— a religious practice? Acts such as communion, baptism, fasting, and centering prayer at least try to invoke God's presence explicitly, whether they succeed or not.

When we hear the phrase *religious practice,* we usually think of ecclesial acts, such as baptism and communion, or devotional acts done on our own or in a small group, such as scripture reading and personal prayer. Religious practice, we assume, refers to a specific ritual action with a structured format. Parenting bears only a faint resemblance to this. It is not religious in this sense. In fact, many parents feel guilty because they struggle to sustain just such practices amid the intensity of family life. But parenting is a rich spiritual practice in another sense.

One way to understand parenting as a religious practice is to picture a series of three concentric circles of sanctification. The inner ring is made up of those acts and rituals that immediately come to mind on the individual and community levels. This does not, however, exhaust the meaning of religious practice. A second circle of ordinary time and space circumscribes this inner circle. Daily life is, as Dorothy Bass and Craig Dykstra argue, *"all tangled up with the things God is doing in the world"* in very down-to-earth bodily gestures, embraces, and actions and in the elements that address basic human need, such as food, water, words, and song. In *Practicing Our Faith,* they and their collaborating authors join together to identify several activities that each contributes to a Christian "way of life": honoring the body, household economics, saying yes and saying no, keeping Sabbath, testimony, discernment, shaping communities, forgiveness, healing, dying well, and singing. Each practice is a cooperative pattern of activity that people do together and that rests on a complex tradition of interactions over a long period of time. These practices sustain faith in daily life, embody deep religious values, and preserve and convey faith across generations.

An empirical study of "growing up religious," based on interviews with two hundred diverse people conducted by sociologist Robert Wuthnow, confirms that embedded practices matter. Religious practices, "firmly intertwined with the daily habits of family routines, of eating and sleeping, of having conversations, of adorning the spaces in which people live, of celebrating the holidays, and of being part of a community," are pivotal to faith. The "act of praying was more important" than the specific content of people's petitions. "Being in Sunday School was more memorable than anything they may have been taught. Fried chicken or seders or statues of Mary provided the texture of their spiritual understanding."

This does not mean that formal teaching, specific kinds of prayer, and worship are unimportant. A wise pastor suggested a wonderful analogy to Bass and Dykstra. She said that acts of worship, such as communion and baptism, are to daily life like "consommé to broth." Consommé is "thick and tasty, darker and richer" than the broth of everyday life. The sacraments of worship contain a concentrated dose of faith, a distillation of all its many meanings. The communion table, for example, richly weaves together common practices of hospitality, shared meals, forgiveness, stewardship, and so forth.

PARENTING AS A VOCATION

Parenting is not exactly a self-contained practice in this second sense either, however. It is actually a cluster or group of many practices, a third concentric circle around ritual practice and daily practices of faith. If ritual is to daily practice as consommé is to broth, then raising children is more like a big pot of stew than either consommé or broth. It takes consommé, adds water for broth, and then tosses in lots of other stuff. In essence, parenting might be best understood as a religious practice whose many parts make up a more encompassing religious vocation.

This word *vocation* has had hardships of its own. We often ask others, "So where do you work?" or "So what kind of work do you do?" We hardly ever say, "So what is your vocation?" In a distant way, we recognize that vocation carries a residual elevated religious connotation. We're not sure we want to get into this. Some Catholics today still equate vocation with vowed religious orders.

On the other hand, when the term is used to talk about "vocational counseling" or "vocational schools," it is often simply reduced to something one is paid to do—a job or a career. Some people restrict it to particular service jobs, such as ministry and teaching. In this usage, a pastor might have a vocation but the rest of us do not.

Vocation actually has a more radical meaning than any of these uses. One's vocation is that to which one is especially called by God. It is the good use of one's gifts and desires to glorify God and contribute to the good of the neighbor. In the often quoted words of novelist and theologian Frederick Buechner, vocation is "the place where your deep gladness and the world's deep hunger meet."

When Luther insisted that life outside the cloister was as spiritual as inside, he rested this claim on a fundamental redefinition of vocation. In the Middle Ages, vocation meant a call away from the family, work, and other temporal concerns into a separate community of celibacy, poverty, and obedience. If one had a vocation, one was a priest, a nun, a monk. Luther and other reformers declared that God calls people into every walk of life. This included not just bakers and craftsmen, farmers and peasants, but also mothers and fathers. Indeed, Luther christens marriage an "estate of faith" alongside the two other more widely recognized estates of church and society. He did so to underscore the extent to which parenthood as a religious vocation is not simply an occupation but a life of faith that extends to all one's relationships and involvements.

Sanctifying the ordinary, including ordinary domestic work, is not unique to Protestants. Luther's spirituality was deeply informed by his own Catholicism. Even before the Reformation, as theologian William Placher observes, "groups like the Brethren of the Common Life in the Netherlands were pursuing 'callings' to more deeply religious lives that kept them in their secular occupations." In the last century, the Second Vatican Council affirmed household and general labor as a way to serve God.

PARENTING AS FORMATIVE

One primary reason I call care of children a spiritual practice is precisely because of its formative impact, for children and for parents. When Justus Justin, Luther's friend and colleague, told Luther that he'd placed a cherry bough in his dining room to remind him of God, Luther replied, "Why don't you think of your children? They are in front of you all the time, and you will learn from them more than from a cherry bough." Marriage and children are every bit as much a "school for character" or training ground for virtue as the monastery. "Babies give birth to their parents" as much as the reverse, "also launching them into a brand new life," one of my friends and father of three ruminated.

Parenting is about more than raising children in faith. It has the potential to foster religious transformation in the one who attempts such care. Engaging in the practice of parenting gives rise to new knowledge and a new way of being, not in sacred time and space but in the very concrete minutiae of life in all its messiness. With young children, I had to practice an altered mode of being: walking and playing *with,* not *ahead of* them, walking according to their pace. "Nothing has ever subverted my peace of mind," I claimed several years ago, "as has living according to the pace of my small sons, and yet nothing has ever taught me as much about myself and my location in the world."

I hear this echoed again and again whenever new parents talk honestly about parenting. Wendy Wright says it is motherhood that "has most profoundly formed me," even though she spends considerable time on spiritual retreat, reads and writes extensively on spiritual disciplines, and serves as a religion professor and spiritual director. She is not using the term *formation* lightly here either. She is talking about formation as it has been "classically understood in the world's spiritual traditions." Her definition is helpful: it is "conscious engagement in a series of spiritual practices that enable one to emerge as a transformed person," which for Christians means "putting off the 'old person'" alienated from God and "becoming new in Christ."

A recent "Zits" cartoon captures the humorous irony of children forming parents rather than the other way around, as we usually assume. "Dear Mom," the mother reads on a card in her hands, "All the trouble I've given you over the years has only made you a stronger person. You're welcome. Love, Jeremy." The father, next to her, puzzles over the message and says, "Well, *technically* I guess it qualifies as a birthday card." Yes, children do give gifts in a way a cherry bough cannot.

CULTIVATING PRACTICES

When Bass and Dykstra categorize distinct practices, their intention is to help people reclaim the many ways in which such practices form people. But these practices actually intersect with and enrich one another. Keeping the Sabbath, for example, includes the practice of saying yes and saying no to particular demands. The practices can also be broken down into smaller components, as in a companion book for youth, *Way to Live,* written by young people and adults together. It looks at bodies, food, work, play, "stuff," time, justice, music, choices, justice, forgiveness, grieving, friends, and so on. Although rooted and nurtured in religious congregations, such practices occur in a variety of communities to which people belong, including the family.

No one can excel in all the component practices. Instead one cultivates favorites, those toward which one naturally gravitates, by which to live and raise one's kids. As Dykstra and Bass suggest, "Get started on one and you find yourself in the middle of another." To "focus on even a single practice," they observe, "can lead you into a new way of life."

Practices have a way of spreading. A few summers ago, I spent a week in an ecologically minded family retreat village. I did my duty in "garbology," their euphemism for the smelly, dirty job of sorting village trash into piles of recycling and nonrecycling and then taking the leftover food to the compost heap. I'd threatened to start a compost pile of my own at home—a practice of honoring the goodness of God's creation and giving back what you use—but found lots of excuses why it wouldn't work. My current one (that we didn't have a good place to put one in a yard that bumped up to three finely manicured homes) no longer held; I've discovered that they make plastic compost containers.

I bought one. I haven't yet turned out incredible fertile soil because I don't do all the proper steps (monitoring moisture, layering with particular materials, etc.). But last summer, growing right out of the bottom on the left side, despite the unpleasant circumstances, was a beautiful butternut squash vine. We ate lots of squash last fall, even though one kid declared, "I'm not eating this if it came from the garbage."

A few days ago, at the beginning of one more summer, I spotted another vine. I think it's a melon plant. Gardening is one of those practices of care for creation that we haven't yet figured out how to transplant to our midsouth climate of intensely hot summers, red clay soil, and weekends dominated by kid sports. But plants have sprouted nonetheless through a different practice.

Several practices that form faith through family living have germinated in our lives. The next several chapters explore some of them. They are not meant as some new parent ideal. They are illustrative, not exhaustive.

Each family faces its own circumstances and has unique talents. I simply pick my favorite practices, those with which I am most familiar and those we sometimes do well. Parenting is guilt-inducing enough, especially if one has teenagers happy to tell you that you mispronounced a word, made a revolting meal, or do not know as much as they do. My intent is not to offer a list of the things you should do but rather to empower you to notice what you are already doing to embody faith in the daily life of your family, so that you may practice it more consciously.

Chapter 3

PONDERING ALL THESE THINGS

Last summer, during a bible study led by a rabbi on the story of Moses and the burning bush, I saw that "sanctifying the ordinary" is not just a Protestant idea. In the story (Exodus 3), Moses is out in the wilderness tending sheep when he notices a bush that is blazing with fire and hears God's voice speaking to him from within the bush. During the ensuing conversation, Moses receives his vocation as leader of the people of Israel. But before this happens, God instructs Moses to approach the bush with reverence.

"Take off your shoes," God says. When I heard this, I instantly thought of my mom shouting at me from somewhere inside our new home on a freshly seeded lot when I was in third grade. "Get rid of those muddy shoes," she would call through the house as my brothers and I entered. So we did, and at least part of the dirt stayed outside. I have yet to shake the habit of kicking off shoes when I enter my home.

The author of this ancient text, I'd like to think, lived in a household where his mother also ordered him to take off his shoes. If so, he knew this practice held associations with home and feet and maternal care. He connected attention to God with a lowly, common act of entry into the familiar sanctum of family. The author also knew that taking off shoes does not just keep the floors clean and make us more comfortable. It makes us more vulnerable.

When we were invited to remove our shoes a few times during worship connected with the bible study, I noticed a lot of us didn't. It wasn't just that our feet were ugly beneath our sandals and tennis shoes. We felt exposed without these coverings. We didn't venture to bare ourselves before others, much less before God. In inviting Moses to take off his shoes, the author suggests, God was inviting Moses, and us, into a place where we can risk such exposure, into a "home" that is deep and profound.

One particular Midrash read by the rabbi caught my attention. (*Midrash* is a Jewish term for interpretative commentary on scripture, recorded as early as the second century and still being discussed and written today. It isn't Bible commentary as Christians often understand it; it has considerable authority, there are many readings of each passage, and debate is welcomed—even expected.) Why, the author wondered, did God appear to Moses from a thorn bush, especially when genuine leaders sought God on mountaintops? Why from a lowly bush, the least of trees, rather than from a mighty tree? "To teach you that there is no place without the Divine Presence," answers the Midrash, "not even a thorn bush." The ground on which Moses stood is the same ground as before: the common ground, the desert floor, the patch on which his sheep grazed and made themselves at home only moments earlier. God is present and available to us on the most mundane spot and in the most "godforsaken" situations.

Care of children as a religious practice has deep roots in the Jewish tradition and its claims about the goodness of all creation. The sense of God's lively participation in human life runs through Hebrew scripture. In the Hebrew worldview, humans are a wonderful unity of body, spirit, and soul, with the soul and spirit no closer to God than the flesh. The very incarnational dimension of the Christian faith—that the "Word became flesh and dwelt among us" (John 1:14a), carnal and holy—builds on this Jewish tradition of valuing life.

ATTENDING ALL ALONG

My friend and colleague Herbert Anderson sometimes speaks of "ordinary awe." As a Lutheran who sees all walks of life as potentially luminous, he comes by this idea of wonder pervasively lurking in daily routine rightfully. For him, ordinary awe provides a rich connection between formal theological doctrine and the experience of living as a Christian. For me, the phrase captures in a nutshell what happens when faith is active in life.

Awe can so easily become tamed and lost in the ordinary rather than noted and celebrated, however. This is partly because we fear what awe ultimately means. Awe tips us toward the unknowable nature of life, the very mystery of our own beginning and ending.

So we truncate and dilute our responses. We say "wow" all the time, but as Anderson points out, we don't really mean it. Curious about this, he took an informal survey: What do people mean when they say "wow"? An exclamation that was once an expression of awe, he concluded, has become just another casual colloquial way of saying "you don't say" or "no kidding," a "socially acceptable alternative to 'holy shit.' " We say "wow" when we don't know what else to say.

What if we stood up and took notice when we say "wow"? Awe is an integral Christian "disposition of the soul," Anderson contends. It leads us into and disposes us toward faith. Luther himself said, "Wonder brings faith." Such a disposition is what actually connects belief and practice. Without an outlook tilted toward awe, belief becomes a hollow platitude and practice turns into empty habit. Building on Luther, Anderson emphasizes, "We will be more disposed toward moments of extraordinary awe if we have been attending all along to wonder and awe in the ordinary."

"Attending all along." Here, I think, is an active way of being that supports all the practices of faith and that is integral to good parenting. Yet so often we parents neglect this. On our way to prayer, on our way to church, on our way to all the other places where we think God abides, we pass by ordinary awe much too quickly. But greater openness and attentiveness, often sparked by caring for children, can come through the practice I call "pondering."

Small children in particular are no strangers to awe, of course, but kids of all ages invite us into this experience. Attending all along to children means we adults are also permitted to see the truly awesome—not only to wonder at them, as fond parents readily do, but also to see and share their own wonder at the world. Children both catch our attention and reorient it. Being present to all the ways in which *they* are growing—to their focus and pursuits, their curiosity and capacities—also leads *us* to deeper faith. If attended to, if noticed, if pondered, the routine of caring for kids in ordinary time offers up ample opportunity for wonder, for entering as adults more deeply and alertly into the presence of God.

In the story of Moses and the burning bush, a common, ordinary bush becomes a place of God's presence, not simply because God says so or because God is there to set it afire. Moses also has to turn to look. He says to himself, "I will turn aside and see. . . ." He has to stop and notice. So also do we. Only when God recognizes that Moses has "turned aside to see" does God call out to him.

THE CATCH OF TIME

One real catch is the press and stress of time itself. When I talked with parents a few years ago about the challenge of parenting and the role of faith, I received one consistent response: "We just can't seem to find the time." The heightened pressure of time crosses over many differences of class, ethnicity, and tradition, standing out as a common denominator that makes the practice of faith difficult for many people.

One parent described his biggest problem as one of "managing our children's lives." In an immediate sense, *managing* meant coordinating the endless details of pick-up and drop-off schedules, as well as needing to plan the whole summer by March—camps, vacation, time with grandparents—because "we have to sign up for day care." These difficulties were compounded for another parent in a blended family. She and her partner faced the complications of figuring out, with a nonresidential parent of another faith, weekend and vacation visits as well as questions of religious upbringing and extracurricular commitments.

"I can barely remember our life without children," says a father after ten years of parenthood, "a life where I wasn't so lifted up *and* so weighted down, so blessed *and* so utterly confused, so stunned by wonder *and* stung by worry." The *and,* repeated in each phrase, stands out as the hitch. It rises up and underscores the ambiguity of parenting as at once awe-inspiring and debilitating. For this father, English professor Tom Montgomery-Fate, the birth of each child stopped measured time, or *chronos,* and ushered in "an immeasurable, uncontrollable" *kairos,* or fullness of time, bursting with unparalleled meaning and beauty. Lots of parents identify childbirth as a (or even the most) spiritually significant moment of their lives. There is hardly anything more momentous.

As kids grow (and even sometimes from the very start), it is hard to sustain this sense of kairos while responding to chronic demands. "In the past few years," the father observes, "as the girls have started school, and fallen into their own schedules, I have lost much of the kairos sense of time that birth teaches." It is often true that the older one's children, the harder it gets. Although moments of inspiration do not disappear and even continue to happen in unusual ways, they are fewer and farther between with adults and teenagers than with infants, toddlers, and young children. Kairos is by its very nature fleeting, fragile, and (perhaps because of this) precious. But age and growth take their toll.

Sometimes managing the details of work and family feels like putting together a thousand-piece interlocking jigsaw puzzle. Each spring I live in a kind of dread as I fill in a five-column grid, one column for each family member, of week-by-week summer plans. When one piece won't fit, I have to reconfigure the whole puzzle. Only a domestic administrative secretary could straighten it out. Sometimes I really do wish I had one.

Most parents today—single, married, divorced, women and men—work *and* care for kids. In the theological language of the last chapter, they do not live out their faith through one primary vocation, whether at home or through their employment, as might have been the case for their own parents. They pursue dual, triple, even multiple vocations, in venues more sharply divided from one another—the workplace and the home front—than during any other era in human history.

Our efforts to handle multiple vocations of work and family often force us to confront the terrible tyranny of time. The ambiguous, loaded accusation that some of us "want to have it all" finally crashes against the reality of time, finitude, and limits. Time is where we face conflict among the competing fidelities of our multiple vocational commitments.

National trends toward longer work hours for everyone, documented by Juliet Schor and others, are intensified for those with primary responsibility for their families. People attempt to cope, of course; time-use studies suggest that they often do so by sleeping less (and, some argue, by having less sex and fewer kids). They seek elusive "quality time" with their children. They cut out nonessentials— vacuuming, home-cooked meals, or friends. They work a "second shift," in Arlie Russell Hochschild's notorious term for the "extra month of twenty-four-hour days a year" women work in the home above and beyond their husbands. Contrary to the impression of this finding that men do not face a similar quandary, some men have also added a second shift of their own. In other words, people just do what I try to do: squeeze more in.

A chaotic family life can be a faithful life. But unrelenting, brain-numbing activity is not good for anyone. We have to be extremely careful about calling this spiritual.

This is a terribly important caveat. Although I want to reclaim faith in the midst of chaos, not all chaos is redemptive. An overflowing calendar does not contribute to faith in daily life if it leads to depletion. Some of our busyness is just that: a deadening busyness that distracts and destroys the capacity for joy and awe. We are too worn down. Or we stay busy so we won't have to think about finitude, limits, death, and our utter dependence on life, others, and divine hope.

Rather than glorify all this running around as somehow spiritual and sanctified, it makes sense to question the pace at which we live and to consider how to slow down. We can and should change a way of life that is debilitating, scheduling less, facing our unhealthy addiction to an inhumane routine, and sustaining practices that help us discern how to say no to experiences and stuff that our culture says are essential for children.

I want to suggest, however, that a fully adequate response involves more than this. The whole idea of time management rests on a rather questionable modern assumption that time is a controllable quantity, something we own and possess rather than something given to us, a divine gift to be received in all its complex and sometimes confusing and messy quality. Sometimes suggestions in popular books on "simplifying your life"—such as working fewer hours, living on half your income, or getting rid of the car or phone—are unreasonable or impossible. Other tips—such as "speed cleaning," cutting grocery shopping time in half, dropping Christmas cards, or completely skipping the holiday—can quickly degenerate into yet another entrapping regimen and source of guilt. Such tricks even deprive us of the good of giving gifts, for example, or of strolling through the grocery store or farmer's market, marveling at the colorful bounty of the fruits and vegetables.

Adhering strictly to strategies of simplification can impede the tumultuous richness of life by trying to clean it all up. Sometimes, realistically, it is impossible to simplify life with children. Instead we must find ways not to flee or control time but to live graciously within its entanglement.

PONDERING

One Advent season several years ago, I sat in worship, eight months pregnant, as people in the church reenacted the Christmas story. Even though a birth is the main event, I was suddenly aware of how little attention we Protestants give to the mother in the story, even at Christmas. In the pageant I was watching, Mary literally faded into the shadows—hidden, to those of us in the pews, behind numerous male figures, including God incarnate. Have male clergy and god imagery so completely suppressed Mary, I wondered, that we no longer even see her, much less consider her role as mother and mediator of God? If we have ignored Mary, have we also repressed or lost her wisdom?

For most Protestants, Mary makes a brief appearance in an annual pageant and then disappears from the liturgy, imagery, prayers, hymns, devotions, and theology of the church. Indeed, her disappearance began centuries ago, when she all but vanished from Protestant theology and religious practice. Saints, including Mary, do not mediate grace, Reformation theologians insisted. So, as a well-socialized Protestant, I never really looked to Mary in my search for a way to bring together faith and motherhood. She simply isn't a figure we talk about, much less someone to whom we might pray.

Feminist theologians have retrieved lots of female figures in the Bible during recent years. But few warm up to Mary. Given her ambiguous track record among Catholics, this isn't surprising. As Catholic theologian Elizabeth Johnson points out, the understanding and veneration of Mary have been limited by male theological interpretation that emphasizes two of Mary's characteristics to the exclusion of others: virginity and obedience. The idealized combination of sexual virginity, spiritual purity, and motherhood that she embodies has been unhelpful and utterly unattainable. Beatific portraits of Madonna and child are far removed from the real grit and grind of motherhood. One mother of four small children declares, "How could I identify with a perfect mother who has a perfect child?"

So I never paid much attention to the stories of Mary as a woman who was "pondering all these things"—until I became a mother myself. Mary's "pondering" appears in two places in the Gospel according to Luke. In the narrative of Jesus' birth (Luke 2:1–20), shepherds tell Mary that angelic hosts have announced that her child is the Savior, the Christ, and amid the wonder of those around her she "treasured all these words, pondering them in her heart." Later the twelve-year-old Jesus gets lost in Jerusalem; he is found three days later in the temple. On returning to Nazareth to watch an "obedient" son grow in "wisdom and in stature," Mary is described again as one who "treasured all these things in her heart" (Luke 2:51b).

I have heard these stories all my life. But when I returned to them with children in tow, the words literally jumped off the page. I underlined them. I wondered about them. I found myself drifting toward amazing sculptures of Mary in cathedrals when I traveled. I saved art postcards with images of Mary and tucked them onto the windowsill at my office. Only after several years did I realize, flipping through my book *Also a Mother,* that I too have been one who "ponders." There on the first page, staring me in the face, was the same word. I ponder the dilemmas of mothering as one of many callings rather than my sole calling. I ponder the virtues of the "good mother" as culture and religious tradition define them.

I have sneaked admiring glances at Mary's pondering from a distance for a long time. Initially, I wondered if her experience as mother, captured in brief scriptural passages, even remotely resembled my own. Now, I see that Mary's pondering shows faith as it is practiced in family. Maybe one way to live more faithfully within the ordinary time of family life is to deepen our appreciation for the practice of pondering. Reviving Mary's practice of pondering undermines sanitized, desexualized portraits of her, but it also affirms the activity of pondering, with all its physical, emotional, and spiritual turmoil and possibilities, as a "saintly," faithful dimension of the Christian life. After all, in good Protestant tradition, even if I can't entertain a feast day for Mary and Mary cannot serve as an intercessor between the divine and me, she can still serve as a model of faith, as early Reformation theologians themselves said. I can even keep pictures of her.

The two passages in Luke that tell of Mary's pondering are more suggestive than complete, and the rest of the scriptural canon tells us little more. Yet I find her pondering provocative. It reveals Mary face-to-face with the challenge of caring faithfully, first for a tiny newborn and then for an independent-minded preteen. Here in the small word *ponder* is an image of a mother in turbulent spiritual waters, wading through the emotional swings of care, who like the father we met earlier, caught between chronos and kairos, also feels "stunned by wonder *and* stung by worry."

Although some have interpreted the sparseness of these Lukan passages as just one more instance where male authors and male tradition have silenced women's voices—and there is truth in this accusation—I would like to think there is more going on. The author of Luke deserves credit for his brevity. In these two instances, he does not put words into Mary's mouth. He restrains himself, perhaps recognizing the limitation of words, the magnitude of the situation, and the integrity of his subject.

When we view this with fresh eyes, we can understand Mary's pondering in quite new terms. Far removed from the idealized Renaissance portrait of a blonde woman robed in blue, gazing adoringly at an infant, Mary lived on the margins of a war-torn society. She actually shares much more in common with women in Iraq today or Vietnam a few decades ago than with middle-class women in the United States, as Johnson suggests. Even more important, although she undoubtedly deserves ample credit for raising a son as generous and good as Jesus was, mothering was one of many, many tasks she took on to ensure her family's survival. She had other children. Besides her role in the family, she also served as witness and disciple. In a word, she had many vocations, of which parenting was only one.

What was Mary thinking and doing in the Lukan passages, then? It was simply too much to put into words. But this pondering is not the same as silence and passivity. The miracle and messiness of birth—the miracle and messiness of Christ's birth—had to be "carefully weighed," as in one dictionary definition of *ponder*. Mary didn't (and couldn't) go off to a special place to do this. She was busy with an infant who, we can be sure, was not well described by the line "no crying he makes" in the famous Christmas carol "Away in the Manger."

Webster's Collegiate Dictionary offers other definitions of *ponder* as well: to deliberate about or think about earnestly. It suggests synonyms: meditate, ruminate, and muse. To differing degrees, all three terms imply a focusing of one's attention for the sake of deeper understanding. Pondering is prolonged consideration. Equally important, pondering is often inconclusive. As one author notes, the very tone of the word *ponder*—its "heavy, slow sound"—suggests a lack of resolution different from the sense evoked by sharp-sounding words such as "assess" or "analyze." The sonorous effect is magnified by its location: in "her heart" rather than in her mind.

Pondering in one's heart does not negate thinking, as the conventional opposition between the thinking mind and feeling heart might imply, but rather emphasizes the wisdom found within and through one's passions and actions. Keeping thoughts in one's heart means keeping them at the core of one's being. Wisdom is located at the juncture of physical desire and mental aspiration—not when one transcends the body and world, as modern scientific rationalism and some Christians assume. Pondering connects thought and action.

Nothing makes the connection between mind and body, thought and action, clearer than the acute physical demands of pregnancy, childbirth, and infant care. In lactation, for example, when the mother recognizes the baby's hunger and her milk "lets down," she *knows,* through a muscular ache that defies artificial boundaries between body and mind, self and other, theory and practice. Much knowledge in early parenting is body-mediated. This practical, tactile form of knowledge is not, as some philosophers and Christian theologians have thought, the least and lowest or the simplest and most intuitive of human senses. Potentially it is the richest and most powerful, the hardest and most challenging. How does one discern when bodily knowing has hit the mark and when it has missed? Only with practice. The pondering needed to tend children interweaves physical sensation, momentary cognition, responsive behavior, and an intellectual reading of the results of each act. Then one starts the process all over again. With young children especially, one repeats this trial-and-error pattern endlessly, sometimes to the point where one borders on fear for one's sanity and needs other adults nearby ready to take over.

As this implies, pondering ultimately involves accepting limits and realities that go beyond our understanding. Pondering includes attention, appreciation, and amazement to be sure; it embraces potential anguish too, an aspect of parenting hidden in Mary's pondering to which we turn in the last chapter. For now, it is enough to recognize human limits in the care for others and the reality of failure and loss.

Through her pondering, Mary becomes one of the first theologians of the Christian tradition, turning over and over in her mind just who this child is and what God has to do with it. She does so in the very midst of her mothering—not when she moves away from it all.

ATTENTIVE LOVE

I picture Mary's pondering as an early Christian version of what several women, inspired by feminism, have celebrated as "maternal thinking." Philosopher Sara Ruddick stunned the staid world of philosophy by boldly claiming that mothers think. This seems so obvious. Of course they do.

The Western world, however, has denigrated this—along with women themselves—and defined genuine knowledge as something far removed from the care of children. Knowledge has been defined as the pursuit of objective truth by the detached, disembodied rational self (the "I think, therefore I am" of Descartes). This view dismisses the routine labor, talk, and knowledge of parenting, often carried out by women, as trivial, mindless, and instinctive. Women's talk is just "chatter," and household labor is nothing but "drudgery."

To the contrary, not only do mothers think but their thinking is deeply embedded in and arises out of a rich social practice of care for children. An entire array of intellectual capacities, judgments, attitudes, and values are evoked, developed, and affirmed through the particularities of parenting. In response to the "historical reality of a biological child in a particular social world," Ruddick argues, the mother "asks certain questions rather than others; she establishes criteria for the truth, adequacy, and relevance of proposed answers; and she cares about the findings she makes and can act on." In essence, she develops a "conceptual scheme" or "vocabulary and logic of connections" that orders and expresses the practice.

Central to this practice is the activity of attentive love. To describe the capacity of attention and the coinciding virtue of love, Ruddick turns to the philosophy of Simone Weil and the writings of Iris Murdoch. Attention entails a kind of patient hovering, an anticipatory openness, a "waiting upon truth," as Weil says.

Weil isn't actually thinking of parenting here at all. Instead, she turns to a more intellectual enterprise, "school studies." But she shows nonetheless how even such a mind-centered act, like poring over a geometry problem or translating a Latin text, constitutes a richer embodied practice because it potentially hones attention. Ultimately, Weil argues, attention is a way of looking that asks genuinely of the other, "What are you going through?" Any parent knows that this question is a refrain, a litany, an utterly essential and sometimes tiresome part of the cycle and pattern of parenting. What are you going through? What is wrong? What do you need? What is your world like?

The ordinary parent, then, who learns to ask again and again in so many ways "What are you going through?" without rushing to give the answer or act on it embodies parental attention. This requires seeing children as fully real, without seizing or using them. Indeed, it takes incredible forbearance not to use a child to meet one's own desires for solace, affirmation, and success. This is especially difficult in a society where parents spend so much time marking the child's first step, word, and achievement and then watching endless performances, whether in sports, music, spelling bees, or school plays. To ward off this temptation demands cultivating an attitude and posture of "holding" governed by the "priority of keeping over acquiring," in Ruddick's words. This keeping over acquiring means sustaining, shaping, and supporting without possessing or controlling, "conserving the fragile" vulnerable growing edges of children and "maintaining whatever is at hand and necessary to the child's life."

Attending, as we have seen, also involves activity, physical contact, direct touch, material response. It happens in the most rudimentary moments and movements, in the "innumerable small acts of watchfulness, many almost as involuntary as lactation," says theologian Janet Martin Soskice. Parents of toddlers scan "any new surrounding for steep steps; sharp, breakable, or swallowable objects" and move to avoid them and protect their kids. They may not think much about this, but they do it all the time. At "apparently empty and everyday moments," says Murdoch, "we are 'looking,' making those little peering efforts of the imagination which have such important cumulative results."

"Attending all along" to minutiae also changes the adults who attempt it. One might even say, in contrast to Descartes, "we care for children, therefore we are who we are." It is interesting to note that, as a secular philosopher, Ruddick does not attempt to argue that this kind of practice hones faith. But attending is precisely what Weil compares to prayer. Prayer, she says, "consists of attention" when the whole of one's being is turned toward God. Attention forms faith. Not surprisingly, when Ruddick spells out the capacities and virtues that mothers develop, among them humility, holding, trust, compassion, and renunciation, we hear echoes of the attributes of Mary herself,

Pondering All These Things

something theologian Sara Coakley notices, even though Ruddick claims no allegiance to traditions about Mary.

Although we often call this practice of attending "empathy," there are important differences. Empathy involves identifying with the other. In attending, we may not be able to use our experience to connect. A parent often has to attempt to attend even when she is unable to make any "sense of what she hears," observes Ruddick, or when he "can barely tolerate the child" he is trying to understand, a point all parents reach eventually.

When one of our sons was small, he hated bumps in his socks. Right before heading out the door, he'd put on one sock, then the shoe. He'd say he felt "bumps." So we'd take off the shoe, adjust the sock, put on the shoe again. Again he'd announce, "bumps." We'd repeat the attempt endlessly, or so it seemed. And we still had the second shoe to go. Was this a bid to stay home longer for more time with us (my guilty conscience asked)? Was it pure impetuousness (said my angry temper)? Did the bumps hurt (thought my more attentive side)? Our capacity to attend and comprehend took different spins each time.

Just the other day at the dinner table, we all laughed together as we recalled this amazingly tedious scenario. Over a decade later, he tells me the bumps were not around his toe at all as I'd always assumed but underneath the arch of his foot. "I don't know how both of you could stand that," another son never bothered by bumps chimed in, "I would have lost it." Well, sometimes we did, and we'd just carry an unhappy, crying kid to the car without his shoes.

None of this is easy; none of it comes immediately or naturally. All of it involves practice and living with an endless variety of demands and mistakes. Paying attention is a practice for the long haul. It requires patience and steadfastness that do not arrive instantly with birth and that we do not always have in the many moments that follow. Sometimes all it takes to make attentive love impossible is feeling overwhelmed or exhausted. Ultimately our ability to sustain attentive love of another rests on our own shaky trust that we too are loved, on our own experience of having been loved ourselves, fragmented or limited though it may have been.

There is much about parenting itself that makes this practice challenging. Ruddick presents a long litany of difficulties: the "intensity of identification, . . . the daily wear of maternal work, . . . indignities of an indifferent social order, and the clamor of children themselves." Rather than provide attentive love, we are often tempted instead to proffer "indifference, passivity . . . anxious or inquisitorial scrutiny, domination, intrusiveness, caprice, and self-protective cheerfulness."

Nor is the birth experience or any other such moment always a spiritual highpoint. "I entered the hospital one person," explains a mother of a ten-year-old, who did not find birth so miraculous, "I left as two. The full magnitude of this hit me hard. Giving birth did not seem like a high spiritual moment for me. I looked the same but now I had another person, another body who needed me, depended upon me, and to whom my own life would be forever tied. It was several weeks before this helpless, sucking, pooping creature made eye contact or smiled."

This mother's warning is well taken in a culture still obsessed with biological motherhood and unsympathetic to deviation from it, despite feminist efforts to offer women other scripts in life. Some feminists derided motherhood as oppressive when seen as the sole role for women. They felt justifiably hesitant to reclaim its virtues. Society has romanticized and idealized the attentive love of mothers for their children as innate and unconditional. This has kept women in their place, and it has kept men from believing they had any significant role in— or anything to learn from—attending to children. But other feminists, such as Ruddick, insist that in this rejection we have cast aside a basic biological, emotional, and social practice of care that stands at the center of human community and should concern women and men alike. I am arguing that it is also a practice of faith central to life and demonstrative of God's love.

Soskice depicts attention as native, almost involuntary; Ruddick says it requires effort and self-discipline; Weil sees it as a gift, a "miracle" rather than a "discipline." Though these thinkers seem to disagree, I think all three are right. Attentive love is part instinct, part effort, and part gift. It builds on early, almost involuntary responses, as when a mother's milk comes in on hearing a baby's cry. But it also involves hard work and constant discernment of what to look for, what to ward off, and how to scan the horizon for dangers. Yet, for all this, understanding the other is never predictable or controllable. One cannot command attention by sheer will power or muscular concentration. Attention evolves out of joy, as Weil says, and its fruits come as a grace.

AN ART ALL ITS OWN

Last summer I spent a week at a family retreat center on the grounds of an old copper mine in the mountains. The mine is now closed, but its refuse is still there, visible in the tumbling iron structure of its original building and a huge pile of discarded nuts, bolts, wires, and machine parts. I hiked past this pile many times with nary a notice. Then I joined a class on making art from found objects.

The teacher began the class with an Emily Dickinson poem:

> Perception of an object costs
> Precise the Object's loss—
> Perception in itself a Gain
> Replying to its Price—
> The Object Absolute—is nought—
> Perception sets it fair
> And then upbraids a Perfectness
> That situates so far.

Then he said something even more interesting before we hiked up to the old mine: "Just let yourselves become attached or caught up by an object."

I was dubious, but I started looking. My first find, of all things, was a rusty flattened oil can that captivated me (even though someone next to me said, "*What* do you see in *that*?"). I also became "attached" to a piece of rusted wire, so much so that when someone eyed it on my collected pile I was quick to say, "Hey, that's mine."

54

Found-object art challenges traditional definitions of art and the very nature of art itself. It can potentially turn almost any ordinary piece of junk into art. It is, as my teacher remarked at one point, about the "salvation of material things." I like that: the salvation of material things.

So also the found-object art of parenting and pondering can free us to scavenge for salvation within almost any piece of the ordinary. We may then discover that parenting as a faith practice is an art form all its own. We can sometimes practice "found awe and amazement" with our kids, and when we do it's not only about perception but also about being moved by, connecting with, getting attached to, holding, picking up, putting down, protecting, admiring.

The teacher said he owes his love for found art partly to a mother who knew something about attending to the sacred in daily life. One summer decades ago, when his family of origin spent a few weeks at this same retreat center, he hiked up to the mine and found an old, rusty, breadbox-sized slot machine whose colors and levers fascinated him. Later that day he told his mother about his wonderful find. "Go get it," she said, to his surprise, and he did. When they packed up to return home later that week, he assumed he would have to leave his cumbersome treasure behind. But again his mother said, "Go get it. Bring it along." On many occasions, other distractions, worries, and needs probably prevented this mother from attending to her son. But not on this one.

PONDERING = FAITH IN TIME

The practice of pondering resists the modern fantasy that we can master time. Instead it seeks renewal of faith within the ordinary boundaries of a day that is received as God's gift. This practice resists the spiritual and theological disdain for the impermanence of time that was common among ancient Christians influenced by Greek philosophers. These "Church fathers" solved what they saw as the problem of time by picturing God as changeless and the spiritual life as a pursuit of the eternal and unchangeable. Living with children, by contrast, thrusts one into change.

Pondering All These Things

Like bookends, right before and right after Luke's story of the twelve-year-old Jesus who stays behind in the temple, lost from his parents for three days, provoking Mary to ponder (Luke 2:41–51), is testimony that Jesus "grew" in wisdom and in favor of God (Luke 2:40 and 2:52). Growth and change are the bookends of parental pondering. That Mary "kept" all this in her heart (2:51 RSV) points to the attention, wonder, and anguish that pervade oversight of a child's growth.

Just when my six-month-old fell into a predictable sleep pattern and I thought we had it all together, he grew and changed and we had to adjust. The need to adjust persists now that he is a teenager, even if the rate of change has slowed. After I thought I'd grieved over my oldest son's departure to college, he moved back for the summer (not that I was unhappy about this; it is just that I have to mourn again). Now I hear he wants to travel to New Zealand.

The profoundly interminable and shifting nature of the work of parenting is both its challenge and reward. More than this: many parents would agree that in this practice of attending, they must learn, change, and develop or the child will not thrive. For decades, modern psychology presumed that parenthood required little or no change in the already existing mind-set of the parent. Most developmental theory completely ignored the complicated interaction between the growth of the child and the formation of the adult, particularly the moral and spiritual development required of an adult who cares for a child. Only recently has it begun to dawn on us that birth and rearing children are powerfully transformative for parents and children alike.

If I attend well to my sons over time, there is opportunity, however irregular, for astonishment—by spontaneous humorous comments, by their sheer persistence in the face of daunting challenges, by shoes larger or shoulders taller than mine, or by small acts of gratitude and love returned to me unasked for and unexpected. Children's author Judith Viorst has learned, from watching her three sons, that "it is possible to find delight in just hanging around the kitchen while one kid is making a chicken salad sandwich and the other is tossing a napkin into the trash and missing." It is just this potential for joy in the most mundane moment, pondered and attended to with care, that

In the Midst of Chaos

leads her to conclude, "Family life is better than most any other thing going on in the universe."

Recently, a pastor who is also a father admitted to me apologetically that family devotions fall by the wayside in his household. "I come home midafternoon," he said, "to be around when our two kids come home from school. My wife works until later in the day. We barely squeeze in dinner between her return, my evening meetings, and our kids' activities." Our conversation got cut off abruptly when one of his children ran up to pull him in another direction.

Here's what I wish I could have said. Although family prayer has its important place (I am not dismissing concern about its decline), prayer and scripture reading do not alone determine faith. Faith is not one more thing to check off the list. Family prayer; check. Bedtime prayer; check. Ritual for dead hamster; check. It is not something set aside outside regular time. It is what we do in time and space, with our bodies and through our movements. The practices of this man's family—playing with the children after school, interacting around dinner, greeting and parting, attending and pondering—these practices are formative of faith. They train our eyes to see God amid change and time.

There is no ultimate solution to the dilemma of enacting faith in families in time. One cannot control kairos or schedule an epiphany, although worship and prayer are partly structured toward this end. This is precisely the gift and bane of kairos and epiphany: such moments come unbidden and unexpected. Or they don't. But reclaiming pondering as a faith-filled practice packed full of both kairos and chronos moments offers one way forward.

Chapter 4

TAKING KIDS SERIOUSLY

One night, as I tucked one of my sons into bed, he asked, "What was here before God?" Theologians have contemplated this question about God's relation to creation for centuries. I don't think my elementary-age son wanted to hear about the historical debate over whether God created out of nothing or out of chaos that I began to relay, however (the downside of a theologian parent). He wanted to have a conversation about God's presence and power in the world around him.

I remember trying to ask my dad and then a church camp counselor a similar question when I was close to the same age. "What," I said to each one, "if there wasn't anything at all?" In an inchoate way, I was trying to fathom the possibility of nothingness—something I don't like to think about now but didn't find so scary then. This was not an entirely weird question, I was relieved to learn years later while studying modern philosophy. But at the time I baffled my dad; I don't think he even tried to answer. The camp counselor, a grandfatherly man, did try. He started talking about having kids and "living on through progeny," a response that I thought completely off the subject then but can better understand now.

So when I came across philosopher Gareth Matthews's "discovery" that children "do philosophy on their own initiative," I was not the least bit surprised. Something still troubled me, however. I appreciate Matthews's attempt to establish this fact in a field that hasn't paid much heed to children. But of greater interest and concern to me is why we adults have so sorely undersold kids to begin with. Why has the philosophical along with the spiritual capacity of children been consistently left out of accounts of childhood? How can we begin to see the daily care of children as a spiritual practice if we do not take kids seriously as thinkers, and as our companions in faith?

REDEFINING CHILDREN'S PLACE

When we think of a child's faith, many of us picture something like the image I came across a few years ago in a church flyer. Prominently featured next to the worship schedule was a picture of a young girl kneeling in prayer by the edge of the bed. The girl's pageboy haircut, plaid pajamas, bare feet, and doll make her seem more precious and innocent than earnest and inquiring. The picture leaves the odd impression that authentic faith resides in the naïveté of childhood. Faith, the image assumes, entails a slightly juvenile, female posture; it is something we know when we are little and lovable but that disappears as we lose our prepubescent charm and innocence. (In fact, Freud and other modern thinkers have suggested that outgrowing faith in adulthood is right and good.) This picture tempts us to see both children and faith as cute and sweet rather than thoughtful and challenging.

This view discounts children and distorts faith. It is important to recognize, however, that this view of both children and faith is of fairly recent historical origin. The temptation to romanticize children and exclude children from genuine faith, evident in the worship flyer and elsewhere, is a natural outcome of dramatic changes in Western culture that are only two centuries old.

On a school field trip to a 4-H agricultural center with one of my sons several years ago, I listened as a volunteer explained dairy production on a farm in years past to two classrooms of third grade children. She had an antique butter churn and several other tools used to process the milk. Who, she asked, did they think churned the butter? Everyone just stared at her. So she hinted, "Do you have chores?" There was a resounding chorus of "no" from about fifty eight- and nine-year-olds. No, they didn't have chores. Well, she had news for them. In the distribution of farm labor—not all that long ago, she noted—children close to their age churned the butter.

That these children said no—that they no longer saw themselves as directly responsible for the welfare of their families—may seem like a small matter. But in actuality it exemplifies a sea change of major proportions. In premodern and early modern times, children were subordinates in a highly structured, patriarchal family. However, they did have essential roles. As soon as they were old enough, they participated as best they could in the household economy, whether it meant tending the garden or making clothes or watching younger brothers and sisters. With industrialization, children gradually lost their place as contributing members of the household economy. If they did household work at all, it was more arbitrary and random than a matter of necessity. Their position in the family shifted dramatically from asset to burden. Today children no longer increase a family's chances of survival but instead drain its resources.

Protecting children from much adult work is a positive development, to be sure. Horrendous reports of children's exploitation in societies throughout the world reinforce the value of advances in child labor laws and work patterns. I am troubled, however, that children no longer see themselves as active contributors to family welfare. A capsule definition of adulthood and childhood offered by one of my sons sums this up: "You work; I don't." One day, after I asked him to do something, he said, "You're the adult. You're supposed to do that; I'm not."

The problem is this: If children are not participants and contributors to household economics, how can we avoid seeing them as an economic burden? The idea of calculating the cost of raising a child was unheard of less than a century ago, but today that price is a well-publicized and steadily-rising amount. I remember a cartoon showing two parents staring at the headline: "Cost of Children $233,530." They turn toward their slouching, headphoned, baseball-cap-on-backwards teenager and remark, "Seems our investment's taken a downturn."

The change in children's economic worth does not necessarily mean that children are less cherished in other ways. To the contrary. The less productive and useful children of modernity have become emotionally priceless. In a sense, adults have overcompensated for children's declining material value by elevating their value psychologically. This shift, which took place during the 1800s for the American middle class, was encouraged by Christian theologians such as the New England minister Horace Bushnell, and by social scientists. They advanced an array of arguments claiming that children require the hovering attention of a primary parent (almost always the mother) in the private sphere of the home. At the home's emotional center stood the unselfish, sacrificial love of mother for child.

Increased love and respect for children was a great gain, of course. However, this new ideal also created new problems, especially by giving mothers a mandate to love without limit on parental excess or expectation of return on the child's part. The idea that improper maternal love could permanently harm children's development and determine how they turn out as adults was unheard of in the Middle Ages. But by early modernity, children—at least in the middle and upper classes—were idealized as precious, delicate, and needing vigilant care. Expectations have continued to rise, with little regard for limits imposed by economic class. Parents today experience an incredible escalation in role expectations beyond anything imagined by our own parents. To the job of meeting a child's material needs has been added an elusive, ever expanding list that includes emotional, social, and most recently spiritual development.

Among the many pressures and problems engendered by these expectations, two stand out as especially unjust to children themselves. Most troubling is the fact that people's sentimentalization of their own children is inversely related to their willingness to care about the well-being of other people's children. Children from less privileged classes and nationalities, especially those in underdeveloped countries, are excluded from the privileges that accompany this model of what children need. It might even be argued that the protected, unproductive play of U.S. middle-class children is largely subsidized by the labor and deprivation of less-privileged children in the U.S. and around the world—children who themselves work, or whose parents work, at low wages to manufacture the expensive shoes and electronics more pampered children enjoy.

Another negative outcome of this view is this: the fact that some children are highly prized does not mean that children at large receive the social recognition and support they need. In many ways, children are much less visible in society. With industrialization, children moved farther and farther from the arena of adult activity and more and more into the separate realms of home and school. Children lost steady contact with parents; they also lost contact with the wider world of nonfamily adults.

At the elementary and middle schools across the street from my house, there are multiple car and bus drop-off lanes, but no bike racks. Thanks to traffic restrictions, kids cannot even approach the school on foot or bike. Only adult drivers can get there, and even they only in motor vehicles. This odd example of exclusion brings to mind other supposedly public places—resorts, restaurants, planes, and even parks—where children seem to be less and less welcome. At times it seems that some adults are tempted to designate no-kid areas as if kids are bad for health, like smoking. Society may no longer insist explicitly that children "be seen and not heard," a saying first applied to servants, then women, and finally children a few centuries ago. But we still expect them to fit in with adult choices.

In spite of intense lip service to their importance, children occupy an ever-shrinking place in our society. This is true even demographically. In the nineteenth century, only about 20 percent of families did not include children younger than eighteen. By 1991, at least 42 percent of all families in the United States did not include children. In the twenty-first century, a majority of households will not include children. This is not just a matter of numbers. It is also a matter of money and its distribution. Among households without children, the median income per person is 67 percent higher than among those with two children. Children not only have a smaller number of adults who deal with them in the most immediate sense; the adults who do care about them have less money.

The view of the child as productively useless, emotionally priceless, and yet increasingly invisible also has one more feature: the child as morally and spiritually innocent. Before the eighteenth century, children were thought to enter the world bearing the marks of "original sin." A primary parental task was to suppress and control what was seen as a child's natural depravity through catechism, prayer, scripture, discipline, and reprimand. By the end of the eighteenth century, fewer people accepted this. The child's mind is a blank slate, philosopher John Locke argued, on which anything may be imprinted. The child is by nature social and affectionate, not sinful, Jean-Jacques Rousseau said. By the midnineteenth century the emphasis had shifted almost entirely, although certainly not within all religious circles. Children were now defined as morally neutral, even "innocent" or "sacred."

Questioning children's dire depravity brought immense benefits, notably awareness that harsh punishment of children to "break their will" is inappropriate and wrong. But once children came to be seen as innocent, many people no longer thought of them as moral and spiritual beings at all. Adults saw children as cute but less often as capable, intelligent, desiring individuals in their own right. Portraits of children as innocent allowed adults to treat children as passive, trivial, and available to adult objectification, exploitation, and abuse.

Although, as we shall see, this endearing, soft image of the naturally innocent child is passing from the scene, it is hard to dispel. During my second pregnancy, I sat on my obstetrician's examination table and stared straight ahead at a framed poster of a beatific mother and child, creamy skinned and all clothed in white. Both were endowed with an almost celestial goodness, pure and unsullied by worldly corruption. Maybe the obstetrician was trying to give future mothers hope for a blissful experience of birthing and raising children. With one birth behind me and a toddler at home, I knew better by then.

KNOWING CHILDREN

We now stand astride a major rethinking of who children are. The romantic view of the child has run its course, and today Americans tend to see children as neither wholly depraved nor wholly innocent. Our image is more complex. The art historian Anne Higonnet calls this new image "the knowing child."

Provocative portraits of children from contemporary photography, art, and advertising—think of the infamous Calvin Klein underwear ads—prove Higgonet's point. The children seen here are not adultlike figures in grown-up fashions and regal poses, as they were in colonial portraits. Nor are they the soft Impressionist cherubs of the Victorian era. Instead they look rough and tumble, sometimes alluring, often disturbing.

Pictures of "knowing children" challenge the notion of children's innocence by portraying children with consciously active minds and bodies. The "romantic child" defined children in terms of what adults were not: "not sexual, not vicious, not ugly, not conscious, not damaged." Such absolute distinctions between adult and child stranded adolescents, of course, as if they ought to metamorphose overnight from one to the other. The knowing child presents a more complex alternative. As Higonnet remarks, today children are as much about "difficulty, trouble, and tension" as they are about "celebration, admiration, and passionate attachment." This confronts adults with "many more challenges as well as many more pleasures than any idea of childhood has done before." Those who thought of children as innocent didn't have to take them seriously as thinkers, doers, and companions. Now we must.

What is required now is not just a shift in our understanding of children. Rather, we must consider how our new regard for their complexity is expressed as we practice our faith within the daily rounds of family life. Taking children seriously entails not just what we believe or how we think about children; it also involves new ways of including them in the shared life of faith. Children are active agents and participants in the practices of faith, even if they bring their own perspectives, capacities, and insights. Now we must figure out what this means for our lives together.

LET THOSE WHO HAVE EARS HEAR

At the age of three, the godchild of author and pastor Marjorie Thompson stopped what she was doing midstream to listen to a recording of Mozart that was playing in the background. Her parents noticed and asked if she knew who had written the music. "In a hushed and solemn tone," Thompson reports, "the child responded, 'God.'"

A Methodist pastor once told Thompson that his child came home from Sunday School to tell him, "God is bigger than our whole house and bigger than our whole yard." The father responded, "Yes, that's true." Unable to resist a little adult theological correction, he added, "You know, God also lives in our hearts." The child thought a moment, and then asked, "If that's true, then why aren't our hearts bursting?"

Given our history, we are tempted to see these children and their stories as sweet or cute. But this assessment distorts their power. These children see something that adults have ceased to consider. They see through and behind our given reality to the heart of matters that adults have defined, categorized, mastered, and forgotten—the beauty of God's music, the magnitude of God's love. For "those who have ears to hear," children often correct and edify us. They know more than we give them credit for knowing. Sometimes just attending to them can challenge and change us.

Illustrations of children's profundity abound. If you are reading this book, you probably have stories of your own. You already know about "taking kids seriously." Still, like me you may have trouble remembering some of the simple but profound observations you have heard children make. Fortunately all sorts of people have captured the wisdom of children. Philosophers such as Matthews, social scientists such as Robert Coles, and journalists such as Jonathan Kozol have made it part of their life's work to record their conversations with children for posterity. It is not just what kids say. Our focus on the verbal and the conceptual should not prevent us from noticing the extent to which children's spirituality is tactile, shaped in part by what they sense and know physically, by what they do and how they respond.

One young North Carolina girl told Coles how she managed to sustain herself during the battle over segregation in 1962. "I was all alone, and those [segregationist] people were screaming, and suddenly I saw God smiling, and I smiled," Coles reports. The girl continued, "A woman was standing there [near the school door], and she shouted at me, 'Hey, you little nigger, what you smiling at?' I looked right at her face, and I said, 'At God.' " This child, as Coles observes, "knew exactly how and when to invoke God" and how to stop a white heckler dead in her tracks.

Children's wisdom entails "an *activity* of knowing," suggests Tobin Hart, a psychologist who has spent several years doing empirical research with children. It is not just what they know but how it gets "walked out into" their lives and translated into "character and compassion." Hart describes a kindergartner who sensed his teacher was having a bad day and offered her his pencil after noticing that she had broken her own, despite her order that everyone stay in their seats with their heads down. He also tells about a preschooler who stood her ground for several days with a biting, pestering, difficult classmate by initially reprimanding him ("No!" she said, like a parent) and then finally hugging and including him. As these children demonstrate, children's wisdom—their proclivity for attention, sensitivity, pondering, and wonder—is not just what they know and say but how they live and embody their knowledge in daily life.

WHAT ABOUT THOSE TEENS?

Of course, anyone who lives or works with teenagers knows this wisdom takes a fresh turn in adolescence. In a "Zits" cartoon from last summer, the son is looking down, we're not sure from where, as he says to his friend, "Scientific studies show that the decision-making areas of the human brain aren't fully developed until the age of 25." The next frame shows the two standing on a rooftop with a long, unwieldy slide they've just constructed to carry them from the second story to the ground. "So we have an excuse for this then," says one of the boys. "Factory installed," replies the other.

When I showed the cartoon to one of my sons, he actually said, "Cooooool" (translation: "I'd like to try that"). Fortunately he is the only one of my three who is regularly up to something like this. The other day I caught him with a giant rubber band contraption—the kind they use in football arenas to shoot shirts into the stands—launching rotten grapefruit, left over from the band sale, down our steep driveway into the street below. A small crowd of admiring teens—his two brothers and a couple of friends—had gathered to watch. The splat *was* kind of fantastic, and, I have to admit, I didn't stop him until I'd watched a few sail.

Here we have an easy, ready definition of *childhood*: childhood continues until the brain reaches its adult capacity or age twenty-five, whichever comes first. The United Nation's 1989 Convention on the Rights of the Child defines a child as any one below the age of eighteen. I sometimes prefer the term *kids,* which for me seems to stretch a bit further than *children* to cover teens and young adults. Basically, children are those literally and immediately dependent on us (in a dependency that outlasts the length of any other mammal's). Partly because human childhood lasts so long, it requires an immense amount of care, protection, and guidance from adults over the long haul. No wonder we can learn so much and go crazy at the same time.

Of course, we also have to take into account what my car mechanic said the other day: "Your kids are always your kids, no matter what age they are." Moreover, for adults a lively faith involves keeping in touch with the child within ourselves, whether by watching kids shoot grapefruit or by being attentive to our own all-too-occasional childlike experiences of wonder.

Faith defies conventional chronological definition. It does not develop in the same way as other parts of our bodies and minds, growing from small to large and from immature to mature. Developmental theorists in biology, psychology, and moral education have traced growth through stages. Baby teeth fall out and adult teeth appear. Baby thoughts, talk, and activity move toward the thoughts, talk, and behavior of young children, adolescents, and adults. Abstract universal reasoning replaces concrete value judgments.

Theologians have tried to follow suit, drawing on these theories to formulate stages of faith development. Faith, however, evolves more curiously, less obviously and quantifiably. Its progression through childhood and adolescence into adulthood resists easy assessment and handy measurement. There is no assurance that simply by growing up we grow in faith. Indeed, the power of faith, like that of philosophical exploration, rests on a freshness or vitality that is as likely to be lost in adolescence and adulthood as to grow. Even if faith involves much more than wonder and awe, such qualities are, to borrow Matthews's words about philosophical inventiveness and zest, "much to be prized."

"All too often," Matthews continues, "maturity brings with it staleness and uninventiveness." Faith, like philosophy, requires the ability to set aside assumptions and trust our naïve observations, an outlook that is hard for teens who are searching for a code to live by and for adults who have made their bed and must lie in it. Such freshness and daring come more readily to children. Children have an eye for incongruity and perplexity, and they are less inhibited about communicating what they see with candor. A stage model of faith, in other words, may help us understand some aspects of human development, but it gets things wrong when it comes to religious and philosophical wonderment. It is hard to have a stage theory that does not overvalue the final frame as an improvement over the first and that does not, indirectly at least, devalue children and even teens.

The important twentieth-century Catholic theologian Karl Rahner made a similar point in a short but powerful essay on a theology of childhood. Childhood has "unsurpassable" value, Rahner insists. That is, childhood has value that adult faith cannot surpass. It is important to note that this value is not the result of innocence, in Rahner's view, for he saw that childhood faith is "already and inevitably" conditioned by the "guilt, death, suffering, and bitterness" of human life. Like the rest of us, children suffer and fail and try to make sense, theologically, of these experiences.

Children certainly must grow up in faith, seeking greater understanding and discovering how to turn self-centeredness into care for others. But Rahner questions our ordinary subordination of childhood to adulthood. For him, the adventure of faith includes "remaining a child forever." He is not talking here about a Peter Pan flight to Never-Never Land but about retaining certain aspects of childhood: an "infinite openness" (or openness to the infinite) that persists in adulthood in spite of experiences that invite us to shut down. Children touch on the "absolute divinity of God" in a special way. Hence for adults Christian faith does not mean moving "away from childhood in any definitive sense," but toward it and its eternal value in God's sight.

Unfortunately, in old-school style Rahner says at the very start of his essay that his exploration is not intended to aid those looking after children. That, he asserts, "cannot be the aim of the theologian." Why not, I ask? Indeed, how we understand children and childhood faith has everything to do with how we live with them and how we practice faith as adults, whether we embrace childhood and children or try to get away from it and them.

Kudos to Rahner nonetheless. That he actually wrote an essay on children when his colleagues at the time had little, if anything, to say about them is wonderful. As one commentator notes, Rahner's careful attention to childhood is a natural consequence of his Jesuit and Ignatian convictions about the "mysticism of everyday life" that finds God in all things, including children.

Making Space for Kids and Faith

Overt expressions of awe tend to taper off as kids approach adolescence. Now it's more likely that my sons will roll their eyes or look away than join in when we gush over a sunset or muse about life's deeper meaning. "Mom's in another one of her 'poetic moods,' " says one of Wendy Wright's daughters when Wright waxes religious.

The change, of course, could have as much to do with socialization as with sinful human nature, which Augustine thought progressed across a lifetime from the sinfulness-in-waiting of infancy to the outright disobedience and malice of age. Schools and society often discourage faith-filled wonderment as well. Children learn to ask the " 'useful' questions expected of them," as Matthews suggests. After age eight or nine, spontaneous excursion into philosophy "goes underground, to be pursued privately, perhaps, and not shared with others, or else becomes totally dormant."

Yet if we gave kids more space, would this always be so? Curious to know, Matthews developed a "technique of writing story-beginnings in which the characters, mostly children, stumble, unaided by adults, on some philosophical issue or problem." When he visits classrooms, tells the story-beginning, and asks how it should go from there, kids of all ages launch into surprisingly spirited discussions. Matthews discovers, on these occasions, that kids who are given a chance to be philosophers are eager to embrace the opportunity. This makes me wonder what we do as adults and as a society to push kids underground as they grow, why we do it, and how we might act differently.

With some encouragement from us and a few fortuitous friendships, my children have managed to stay active in local and regional church retreats. They may drag their feet to church or protest going to youth choir. But when the flyer for fall or winter retreat and the form for summer camp arrive, they do not hesitate. They have chosen summer camp over competing opportunities, including long-favored family trips to the beloved lake where grandparents and cousins gather. I imagine that part of the reason, beyond having a good time, is that this mid-Tennessee campground, with its rustic cabins, tiny lake, old swimming pool, and notoriously bad food, is still one of the all-time best space makers for wonder, for pondering big questions, for faith.

Mark and I occasionally hear stories from camp about our own kids that surprise us. One friend told us about an evening during his first time as a counselor at this camp. He was sitting a bit awkwardly apart from others during a special communion service where kids joined in informal small groups to pray with and for each other. One of my sons, a rather quiet "guy of few words," as I sometimes call him, came up to this friend and asked if he would like to pray with him. Well, "wow" was about all I could say. Sometimes—not always, or inherently—church youth programs offer a space that fosters behavior like this, encouraging the exercise of forms of active wisdom that the philosopher Alfred North Whitehead calls "activity in the presence of knowledge." Especially when parents are no longer quite the right or most desirable persons to provide this space, we can be grateful for settings that do so.

Years ago, while my oldest was still in elementary school, I volunteered to be his classroom's "art lady." (Later, in an effort to be more gender-inclusive, the title would be changed to "art volunteer.") Trained by docents at the Art Institute of Chicago, we art ladies took a piece of art into the classroom each month. Our goal was not to instruct, although I often furnished information about the artist and the work. Rather, the aim was to look at art together. Together we tried to learn to look, and learn to look more carefully.

So into the classroom I went each month with a print I had picked out from the large collection shared by the school district. I avoided questions for which I already had the answer (for example, "Who do you think painted this?") and instead asked questions whose response might be found by looking at the work itself. I took Grant Wood's "American Gothic" or Paul Gauguin's "Tahitian Landscape" or a Magbo head piece from Nigeria and spent a fascinating hour that began with something like, "What do you think is happening in this picture?" "Why are these two people standing together with a pitch fork?" "Are they mad at each other?" "Would you like to go to this island?" "Why did the artist use these bright colors?" "Why would someone wear this mask?" "How would you feel if you put it on?"

There was never a wrong answer or a dull moment. I never saw the particular artwork in the same way again. I'd like to think the kids wouldn't either. They might not remember every piece I took or particular facts about the artists. Still, I hope that they will remember a way of seeing and will occasionally recognize a piece they once regarded with great openness.

Being the art lady was similar in some ways to what I learned during the same years, while training to be a pastoral counselor. Practicing therapy also involves opening up space, inviting shared participation, awaiting surprise, following fresh leads, reconsidering alternative avenues, trying on theories to see what fits, offering my own honest thoughts. Both had immediate relevance for my own practice of faith within my family. One of the better pieces of art-lady advice I wished I'd followed more often at home is, "Don't be afraid to say 'I don't know, what do you think?'" I wish I had thought of that when my son asked me what was here before God.

One of the most remarkable aspects of psychiatrist Robert Coles's work with children, about which he has written in his widely recognized trilogy on their moral, political, and spiritual lives, is not the particular content he gleans from children but rather the method by which he discovers it. He attends to children in a truly remarkable way, partly because of his psychoanalytic training. When he becomes a "field worker" instead of an analyst, he carries into his conversation with children a style and demeanor honed through years of patient listening. His method is essentially to offer "acceptance of the immediate, the everyday, the objectively visible and audible—all worthy of respectful attention for their own sake."

Before Coles could hear faith concerns, he had to reconsider the presumptions about religion and children he held early in his career. He missed a great deal, he confesses, before he became aware of this. "Years later, as I look back and go over old transcripts," he writes in a footnote, "I realize that the children I met were eager indeed to speak of their religious and spiritual interests, concerns, worries, beliefs—but the doctor listening to them had his own agenda, some of it a consequence of a professional ideology all too well learned." For example, at first he could only hear eight-year-old Connie's desire to talk about a religious movie she saw as a defense against raw sexual feelings. One day she finally confronted him in "blunt, earthy, child's language," saying something like, "You're not interested in my religion, only my 'problems.' But without my religion, I'd be much worse off, don't you see? How about *encouraging* me to talk about that movie, about what I experience when I go to church, instead of sitting there, bored, waiting for God to pass from this conversation?"

So Coles changes his approach. When he adopts the "truly humble" pose of his own supervisor, trying to "learn from this girl," new doors open not only with her but also with other children. Kids, he realizes, are as anxious to make sense of life as the rest of us. He learns to listen carefully to the "blooming buzzing confusion," as William James describes it, of daily religious experience.

Making space for children is never easy, never entirely successful, and always prone to distortion. It happens only in mundane time and over the long run. The remarkable comments Coles catches and the insights he uncovers are hard-earned. "Prolonged encounter" is the essence of the psychoanalytic method he learned and of the work he currently does. It is also the essence of practicing faith within the family. For Coles, each child "becomes an authority." His job and ours "is to put in enough time to enable a child . . . to have her say."

Knowing Children of Faith

Recognizing children as knowing spiritual and moral beings has consequence for how we treat and interact with children economically, psychologically, and socially. Children need greater participation in the family economy and welfare, but we have only begun to scratch the surface of what engaging children more actively in this realm might entail. Does faith and the Christian life have anything to say about this? Kids are, as Christian feminist theology suggests, *agents,* people with the capacity to participate, even if only gradually and rudimentarily, in the decisions that affect their bodies, minds, and general welfare, as well as in the labor that a household and society require. Only recently, for the first time, did I hear a colleague even raise the idea that children themselves might have a vocation. Whether this vocation includes assuming a share of household and community labor awaits further discussion. But no matter how we answer, there is clearly something wrong with the picture in my own household, where my husband and I run ragged from washing piles of laundry to cleaning the toilet while our kids play video games.

Knowing children also have a new role in household psychology and the emotional sphere of love. Kids need close attention and care. But do they need the obsessive hovering of a singular mother isolated in the private household? Not to the extent we have presumed. Neither kids nor adults benefit from the kind of unconditional self-sacrificial love that some Christian theologians and modern psychologists have foisted on mothers in particular. But we really do not know what mutuality looks like between children and adults. Lots of theologians who have talked about mutuality simply assume the subjects are adults, not adults *and* kids. These folks might benefit from a few long road trips with kids, where they have to reach a "mutual" decision about where to stop to eat. Adults and parents bear the difficult task not only of modeling a new kind of mutuality between themselves but also of helping children find their own place in the complicated give-and-take of family love.

Knowing children also deserve greater social visibility in decisions as far-ranging as how to make schools accessible to them by bike and whether to spend immense social resources on a war in Iraq. Society and church have made small gestures in this direction, orchestrating "take a child to work" days or making space in adult worship for children's sermons. But as both of these examples reveal, such efforts can easily become token rather than truly representative and inclusive.

A few years ago, I attended the ordination of a woman who had worked closely with children in the congregation. She decided to include them in the service. However, my heart sank as I entered and received from one of the children an otherwise inviting colorful stole to wear. I appreciated the cheerful gesture, but I immediately worried that it might be the first of many ways the children would be superficially "used" during the service because they're "cute," as often happens in the children's sermon.

I could not have been more wrong. These children had learned from this new minister an entire way of worshiping that engaged them holistically in prayer, singing, and leadership. They were used to leading worship in their own context, and they took charge of the service in a way I had never before experienced in a "youth Sunday" service or otherwise. They guided us through each element of the service, including communion, turning our usual patronizing admiration for their charm into respect for their leadership and insight.

In the popular novel *Gilead,* the narrator, under the duress of poor health and aware of his own impending death, says to his son what all of us should say to our children: "I'm writing this in part to tell you that if you ever wonder what you've done in your life and everyone does wonder sooner or later, you have been God's grace to me, a miracle, something more than a miracle." Few of us try daily to put this into words, partly because even as we speak, as the narrator later acknowledges, words fall short of the hopes we have for them. Our intent gets truncated or trivialized. Besides our own ineptness, let's face it: children are not always so mystical or amazing.

Embedded within the minister's words of "miracle" and "grace" are other words from the Jewish and Christian traditions that might support us. Like all adults, children are created in God's image. They have value as ends in themselves, not as objects of study or means to adult ends. They are, in essence, "gifts," a phrase too easily reduced and cheapened in a market economy that has lost sight of the genuine nature of a gift.

75

In each sphere—in our work, our love, and our social inclusion of children—Christian conviction that children are *essentially gifts* becomes primary. This conviction could hardly be more important or more difficult to sustain in an economy that judges everything and everyone (even children) by monetary expense, worth, and productivity. For the Jewish tradition, the gift of children assures the continuation of a nation and the blessing of the covenant of faith between God and the people. For the Christian tradition, children herald God's reign, not because they were humble, pure, or innocent, as romantic interpretations of Jesus' welcome of the little children have argued, but because their vulnerable status and marginal social and political position show them to be among the "little ones" dear to God. In both renderings, children are not a burden but a blessing.

Children are not only gifts, however. They are entrusted to us, and this very knowledge provokes and mandates adults to ensure their welfare. They are a gift but they are also a *task,* a task that inevitably requires lots of hard work, time, energy, and common participation by adults and society at large.

The narrator of *Gilead* stumbles upon the mystery of our obligation toward children most powerfully through the "face of an infant," his own daughter whom he held only briefly before she died soon after her birth. She opened her eyes and looked right into his own, he believes, even though experts says a newborn can't see. "You feel your obligation" when you see and hold a child. There is "nothing more astonishing than a human face," he realizes, and this "has something to do with incarnation." Any face has a claim on us because of its singularity, loneliness, and courage, but this is particularly, even mystically, true with an infant.

If adults diminish children as active participants in religious practice, we both reduce the vitality of our own life of faith and overlook the human complexity children already possess. If we want to experience the daily care of children as a spiritual practice, then we must take kids and their faith seriously. Taking children seriously—as created in God's image, as sinful, as agent, as gift, and as task—has the potential to enrich the lives we share, in faith, with children.

Chapter 5

GIVING UNTO OTHERS . . . BUT WHAT ABOUT MYSELF?

Our first home was a white frame three-bedroom colonial with a green tile roof and a big back porch. Mark and I were childless when we moved in, possessing only two old lawn chairs for the porch. When we moved out thirteen years later, we had three young children, more furniture, one very whiny cat named Mistletoe, and a ten-gallon tank with several cold water fish that survived the eight-hour trip south with the aid of a battery-run pump. How the many pieces of raising kids can clutter life.

That ten-gallon fish tank is a story in itself. First, my oldest son came home proudly clutching a plastic baggie with a languishing goldfish he'd won at the school fundraising fair. (He landed a Ping-Pong ball in its bowl, but they don't give you the bowl.) So off we went to the store to buy a small container—and then home we came with pebbles, fake plants, a ceramic mermaid, and a second goldfish to keep the first company. Or was it to replace the now-dead fish? Before we knew it, we'd given in to a five-gallon and then a ten-gallon and then a twenty-gallon tank because, the salesperson said, the "larger the tank the less often you need to clean it." No other sales pitch could have persuaded me so easily.

There was hardly a better adventure in those days than entering the local pet shop's backroom, lit only by the blue hue of the many bubbling aquariums, and picking a fish. (I was happy to escape the store without snake, rodent, or rabbit.) When we moved, the half-filled tank was the last thing left in the otherwise empty house before I unplugged it and wedged it into the back of our jam-packed van. A neighbor snapped a picture on the outside chance that we might forget the moment.

Last week, I placed an ad on our neighborhood list serve, "Does anyone want our twenty-gallon tank, fish included?" I'm truly tired of cleaning it and I don't want anything bigger. I'm not sure when the kids quit identifying the fish as "theirs," but they have. So why am I still cleaning that tank?

Kids have a way of moving into your life and moving you right out. Originally the desk where I worked stood in one of the three upstairs bedrooms, which we transformed into a study. When our first son arrived, we returned the room to its original purpose and my study became the baby room, despite its dark-red, too-busy, paisley wallpaper. I moved to a small room at the back of the house off the kitchen. Just as I finally felt settled, along came sons two and three. Too much in the center of all the action, I moved out again, this time back upstairs to the one space left, a desk right next to our bed. Talk about conflict of interest.

Parents make space for kids over and over, in small and big ways, and for an extended period of time. Just tonight, I had planned to go with my husband and youngest son to the Friday night high school football game. (Where else would I want to be on a Friday night in the fall?) We own a fifteen-year-old van we've sworn to drive to its death or until the last kid leaves home, whichever comes first; and, in some bizarre quirk of car buying, two small non-gas-guzzling Mini Coopers. Earlier today my oldest borrowed the van for a camping trip with friends. My middle son took off to school in one of the Mini Coopers and then rode the team bus to the game. My youngest son invited two friends. This left us with a two-door, four-passenger vehicle and five riders: my husband, myself, my son, and his two friends. I volunteered not to go; it seemed like the best solution. Squeezed out again.

In the Midst of Chaos

Now, I don't intend this in a mean or accusatory way. Most of the time I'm happy to make space. Take tonight, for example. I didn't mind staying home. I'm just as well off here. I have a moment's peace, an idea or two, and time to write. I don't get football anyway, despite fifteen-plus years of growing up in a family where we went to Big Ten games as regularly as church. Life with three boys hasn't corrected my handicap.

So I don't mind giving up a seat in the four-passenger car to the guys and the game. But thanks to the women's movement, I am also aware that when women grow accustomed to making space over and over and over, pretty soon we become so good at this practice that there's not much space left for ourselves. If you get squeezed too much, you might disappear.

I wanted to see the game. Well, let's be honest: I wanted to watch kids I know, especially my own, run around, even if they all look alike and I don't know what they're doing. Women are more socialized than men to give up the best seat, the last bite, the winning hand, and lots of other things, sometimes including personal sanity, for the sake of children's happiness or to please others. Sometimes it really does make us happy. But not always, and not without mixed consequences.

At long last, a few men—maybe more than we realize—face this also. New pressures to participate more actively in parenting catch fathers in a squeeze play too, raising similar questions of space, time, and sacrifice of desire. How does one work and have a family life also? This is certainly a real question for my own husband, who has shared housework and children with me as justly as possible.

One of my older woman friends says the involvement of her adult sons in caring for their children—her grandchildren—is *"the biggest difference"* between generations. Some people wouldn't agree; hearsay and statistics both suggest that most men are still not carrying their weight in the household. Mark sometimes feels incredibly alone; few men he knows at work or at home shop for groceries, make meals, keep track of doctor visits, fill out school forms, oversee laundry, *and* carry on a day job. But my friend's observation about the difference between today's generation and previous generations still

Giving unto Others . . . But What About Myself?

holds. Many men and women who do not otherwise identify with feminism (including some in conservative religious groups) now reject the idea that the husband should "wear the pants" in the family and instead affirm egalitarian marriage, dual careers, and shared housekeeping, even if they struggle to put all this into action.

Care of others takes priority over and interrupts particular religious disciplines, even in monastic life. "Charity, not silence," Henri Nouwen ultimately admits, "is the purpose of the spiritual life and of ministry. About this all the Desert Fathers are unanimous." But what happens when such a huge proportion of one's adult life is directed toward care and charity? What happens in families where all of life seems like one big interruption?

Not surprisingly, many parents, men and women alike, feel pushed out of their own lives. It's not just about space either. Adults who care for children have a need for care themselves. They also have desires, loves, and interests beyond their children. They must learn to live with relentless interruption (call teacher, buy soccer shoes, defrost meat, take kids to dentist). Figuring out just how to care for others yet still sustain oneself—in all the detail and the broader ethical and spiritual consequences—has important faith-forming implications for adults and for the children for whom we care.

The Giving Tree

Years ago, we made lots of trips to the library and came home to curl up with books, reading aloud to our kids. Mark found a book of poetry by Shel Silverstein, *Where the Sidewalk Ends,* that made us all laugh and learn. I wasn't sure how Silverstein kept humor alive and *still* managed to sneak in a gentle moral message. "Sarah Cynthia Sylvia Stout Would Not Take the Garbage Out." She ends up buried by it all. Or "Smart": "My dad gave me one dollar bill 'cause I'm his smartest son, and I swapped it for two shiny quarters 'cause two is more than one!" "Smart" keeps trading—two quarters for three dimes, three dimes for four nickels—until he proudly has "more" than he had when he began: five pennies.

Poetry with a kick, one might say. So I was caught off guard when I borrowed Silverstein's extremely popular (millions of copies sold and translated into many languages) chartreuse book *The Giving Tree* from our church library and read it for the first time with my oldest son. It begins innocently enough. "Once there was a tree . . . and she loved a little boy." But near the end, the tree has given everything—limbs to climb, leaves to toss, fruit, shade, and wood—at every stage of the boy's life from childhood to adolescence to adulthood. Nothing much is left.

Is this a message I want to convey to my son? Is this my own destiny, I thought as I looked at him looking at me—his tree? Is this the epitome of faithful love? Or if the tree stands in for Mother Nature herself, is this how we are to use the earth's bounty?

Silverstein does plant a note of ambiguity in the final pages. Abandoned by the boy who took and took and took, there sits the lonely stump. She is no longer sure if this is indeed the road to happiness. But her moment of sadness is easy to miss because it is quickly resolved. The boy, now an old man, returns, sits on the stump, and the tree is "happy" again to offer the boy all she has left.

Some mothers today wonder about this kind of endless giving. As one mother put it, "As I strive to 'hold' my daughter, to be more open and responsive to her need to be heard, accompanied, and understood, I come up against my own needs. Who's holding me? And, while we're at it, whose turn is it to make dinner?" Her answer: God, the "real parent" in charge of it all, or better yet, the "ceaselessly generous life-giving, life-sustaining force" picks up where our limitations and failures leave off. We must, as the saying goes, let go and let God.

This is a good answer. But it isn't sufficient. I am not saying God's love isn't enough. I am urging us not to turn to religious platitudes too quickly and thereby avoid facing the hard question of how to enact the love of God in daily life. Who is, after all, going to make dinner?

Assurance of God's care does not answer the concrete question of how God's sustenance shapes day-to-day life with children. While God is holding us, how do we work out the nitty-gritty details of care? Who, along with God or on God's behalf or in the midst of God's care, cares for the caregiver? While adults are busy attending

Giving unto Others . . . But What About Myself?

to the needs of others, pondering, and taking kids seriously, who cares for their very real material and spiritual needs?

As it turns out, "Who cares for the caregiver?" is a relatively new question. Even fathers who assume a primary role in parenting fall into a well-established rut of seeing love of others and love of self as mutually exclusive. One actively engaged father says that he sometimes sees his kids paradoxically as "anchors." They give stability, direction, and commitment *and* they also drag him down. "During my selfish moments," he says, they feel like a "heavy weight that prevents me from moving toward the fulfillment of personal goals." His use of the word *selfish* here is noteworthy. The Christian tradition has had a long history of calling pursuit of one's own desire selfish, an idea that, once again, women have imbibed as much as men or more so.

Once when I was little, my mom admitted that she really didn't care if she won or lost the game we were playing. I couldn't believe it. She didn't care? She didn't want to win? She wanted me to win? What had happened, I thought, to make her this way? I must have also wondered in some dim way whether I could ever be like that. She didn't seem to like candy anymore either. Would I turn out this way?

Not quite. This is not just a difference in temperament, although there is that. I do have a keen competitive streak and always have (long before I could tie my shoe, she says I insisted, "I DO it"). I'm definitely what pop psychology calls a type A high-achieving spirit. But my unwillingness to give up wanting to win also reflects a different moral and spiritual orientation. I'm no longer sure losing for the sake of the other is always a goal toward which women should aspire. But this ideal dies hard.

The quintessential Mother, a product of the Victorian era, forever seeks the needs of others, her children and her husband in particular. Congregational pastor and theologian Horace Bushnell's 1886 *Christian Nurture* represents a key moment in the definition of this ideal, according to historian Margaret Bendroth. Bushnell "codified a powerful new understanding of the family's religious role," with the home as a private refuge and the sacrificial love of mother for child at its "emotional center." This motif "has shaped American Protestant thinking ever since."

Other historians, such as Ann Taves and Elizabeth Pleck, reveal how Victorian ministers such as Bushnell and Henry Ward Beecher, a Presbyterian, "virtually created" a sentimentalized approach to family life in which women "endlessly sacrificed themselves" because they saw this as their primary role. Bushnell, for example, compares God's love to a mother's exhaustive love for her child. A mother, he says, "takes every chance for sacrifice for it as her own opportunity. She creates, in fact, imaginary ills for it, because she has not opportunities enough of sacrifice." A mother is endowed with "semi-divine proportions" of love "measurable by no scale of mere earthly and temporal love." Similarly, Beecher says that "the love most like God's is an 'unselfish' love 'that makes suffering itself most sweet, and sorrow pleasure,' " a love best exemplified by mothers, who are by nature "unselfish and long-suffering."

Wow. *Inherently* unselfish and long-suffering. No wonder the attempt of twentieth-century women to challenge this approach to motherhood is so upsetting. It undercuts a major religious motif portraying God's own love. Rejecting sacrificial motherhood may seem like a direct assault on God Himself (male pronoun used deliberately). Doesn't God love us unconditionally and exhaustively? If not, just how do we understand God's love? Does God need something from us in return?

These ideals of an impassible God and a devoted mother, neither of whom needs anything in return, go hand in hand with the ideal of the ruling father. In fact, models of faith in family life, such as the "domestic church" in Catholicism or the "little church" in Protestantism, were originally predicated on male authority. From early Christian history to seventeenth-century Puritanism, attempts to portray the family as a faith community have presumed male headship, women and children's subordination, and a clear division of gender roles. These images, often seen as biblically based and built into the very order of God's creation, have "lain like a pall" over people's lives across the centuries, as a historian of the New England Puritans remarks. The rules ran something like this: man will make money and major decisions; woman will put family before public responsibility. She will meet the needs of others; he will get his needs met. His

Giving unto Others . . . But What About Myself?

job will take precedence; she will support him. She who works outside the home neglects her children. Those who break these rules will be punished.

Once, after a school open house, a friend who forgot I took my own kids to a sitter while working lamented how sad and unfortunate it is that parents harm their kids by doing so. Granted, long hours in poor day care isn't good for any child. But neither is the idea that a solitary individual, usually the mother, has sole responsibility for and should devote her waking hours only to the nurture of her own children. I doubt, however, I could convince my friend about this.

Reclaiming parenting as a spiritual practice requires us to deal with this ambiguous legacy. This task is made more difficult by the prominence of polarized political arguments about family life. At one end of the spectrum, some say we have to abandon the family altogether; at the other end, some trumpet a new kind of Christian "familism." The former argue that the idea of the Christian family as a little church is hopelessly coupled with patriarchy. "Only the church is essential to the Christian life," religious educator Janet Fishburn insists. Celebration of the family as a place of Christian formation is a form of idolatry, she argues; the church community itself is the locus of Christian formation.

At the other end of the spectrum is the "religious familism" of the conservative right. James Dobson counsels a return to the so-called "traditional" two-parent heterosexual family of the 1950s, a legacy of the Victorian era, as *the* biblical Christian family. He gives only a passing nod to concern about male authoritarianism. The father is still the captain of the Christian ship, the "ultimate decision maker," even if now the "benevolent captain." "If the family never reads the Bible or seldom goes to church," Dobson asserts, "God holds the man to blame."

Most people, however, live somewhere between these polarities of flight from family or fight for one idealized form of it. At a recent meeting, one of my colleagues, a Mennonite, arrived with his eight-year-old son. Both this colleague and I spoke on a panel discussing Christian faith and children, a session where it actually made sense to have children around. Halfway through, his son, who had sat quietly in the front row coloring, came right up to the podium and asked loudly enough for at least the rest of us speakers to hear, "When will this be over, dad?" (Actually, this was exactly the same thing I was thinking at the time.)

During informal conversation before the panel, my colleague had described his wife as a full-time homemaker and then immediately qualified this. She manages to work as an artist, fitting this in around mothering, while he spends a considerable amount of time caring for his four children, especially in comparison with his own father and grandfathers. That he had brought his son with him to the meeting certainly illustrated the point.

He and many others like him still see the family as a site of faith. But they are trying out new models for love and, along with love, new models for power, authority, vocation, and God. They are exploring answers to a relatively new question: "Who cares for the caregiver?" Perhaps most important, they are suggesting through their words and actions that the desire to pursue one's goals, and the frustration that comes when kids prevent it, are not inherently selfish.

Maybe the airlines have caught the flavor of the Jewish and Christian mandate to love the other as oneself better than religious traditions have. Every time we fly we're told, "In case of emergency, put on your oxygen mask *and then* help your child or the person next to you." Learning from this, we might rephrase our question about contemporary families: How are we to create and sustain a balanced Christian life that is neither entirely selfish nor entirely self-sacrificial *and* that doesn't leave anyone gasping for air? Striving to sustain this balance is at the heart of faith when it is active in family living.

THE DANCE OF MUTUALITY

I believe that the ideal of self-sacrifice, as interpreted by church tradition and promoted in society at large, fails many people today and misrepresents both the intent of God's creation and the promise of the gospel message itself. As a theologian interested in mothering, family, and children, I have been pondering the meaning of sacrifice

Giving unto Others . . . But What About Myself?

for many years, and as a result I find myself challenging virtues, values, ideals, and rules that, as I note in *Also a Mother,* "a good person just does not go around defying lightly." I question the virtue of undying sacrificial love that defines the "good woman" and the "good mother." But I also criticize the virtue of self-fulfillment that defines the "good feminist," the virtue of achievement that defines the "good man" and the "good worker," and the virtue of detached objectivity that defines the "good scholar."

So, what Christian values do I endorse if I uphold neither sacrifice nor its ready alternatives? A generic list includes self-respect, mutuality, shared responsibility, interdependence, and justice. However, the ideal I most earnestly seek is not easily summarized but needs to be explained through thick description. Generally, I try to talk about the complicated daily dance of care, work, procreativity, and creativity, as other scholars have understood it and with reference to my own early parenting—nursing children, skipping meetings for the sake of children, forgetting children for the sake of work, reconceiving work, rethinking children, refashioning parenthood and adulthood.

An abridged term for this ideal might be the simple word *mutuality*. Many twentieth-century male theologians, including Reinhold Niebuhr and Anders Nygren, tended to dismiss and degrade this, calling it "*mere* mutuality," not to be confused with the supposedly more authentic Christian love of sacrifice or *agape*. But others, such as the theological ethicist Beverly Wildung Harrison, have protested this dismissal. Mutual love "is love in its deepest radicality," she argues. "It is so radical that many of us have not yet learned to bear it." It requires vulnerability and entails the "experience of truly being cared for" and "actively caring for another" in a complex rhythm of "take and give, give and take."

But what does mutuality actually look like in family life? Frankly, I think people are hungry for detail. If I could name an overriding response to *Also a Mother,* it was something like, "Tell more stories." When I give talks about the book, I almost inevitably end up being asked about how Mark and I "practice" mutuality—how we share cooking, cleaning, and laundry. In the earliest weeks of marriage, long before we had children (I find myself saying to those who ask), we had to figure out how to shop, cook, and clean—the three most obvious and urgent of housekeeping tasks. Sometimes I even went into further detail. I'd say that we alternate cooking and laundry—chores of approximately similar time commitment—and split cleaning down the middle. Whoever cooks shops, and the other person cleans up the dishes.

Working this out took much time and many adjustments, however. Early in our marriage, we realized that cooking every other night didn't work. It didn't even work to alternate every other week. The longer one does something the better one gets. In fact, one of the benefits of traditional gender roles comes from specialization. The more trips one makes down the grocery aisle, the more one knows what's there and the more effectively one shops. We reached a plateau at about a month of cooking, and then we switched. Now we go two months before trading off. We're usually sick of our particular chores, but we have a hard time changing over and relearning "new" skills.

I have also come to realize that it is a good thing we worked at this early in our relationship, because these arrangements aren't things one can change arbitrarily later on, when consciousness gets raised and one realizes the injustice that has by now become habitual. Such patterns do not change easily, especially when they enjoy so little social and cultural support. In spite of Mark's involvement, for example, sitters, schools, doctor offices, and other mothers almost always ask for me when they call. Nor do we have it down. There are inequities inherent in any short-term distribution of the common workload that we hope balance out in the long run. When one of us feels overwhelmed or taken advantage of, we have to declare the felt injustice, fight, and work it out.

Many roads lead to mutuality and shared responsibility. We must, as a friend comments, lead at the point of our gifts. It has taken this friend and her husband almost twenty-six years of marriage to agree that she is better suited for traditional male tasks of home repair and yard care. He has yet to realize, she notes, that he doesn't really have the gift for creative stewardship of family finances that she does. Laundry lovers and gourmet cooks out there need to find their own preferred ways to share the load.

When I talk with people about sharing housework, my main intent is to prime the pump, to get people talking theologically about faith active in life's details. Although most people and a majority of theologians wouldn't see any of this as a theological discussion, I do. In its very concreteness, it's a close look—an "experience-near" look—at God's love active among us through our mutual love for one another. Maybe those who talk theoretically about mutuality should try living in it for a while, and then see what they think.

LOPSIDED MUTUALITY

Mutuality is not just a matter of sharing household chores. Just when Mark and I got that part up and running, along came children to make everything a whole lot more complicated. When this happens, the question is not just how to share the tasks of caring for them, though that is indeed a big and important question. Now the question must expand to include concern about how children themselves will be involved in the mutuality of family life.

Unfortunately, those who espouse radical mutuality have often done so in an adult-centered, chronologically segregated context. Assuming that all the agents involved are equal adults, they ignore children, even though the presence of children is often precisely what makes mutual love between spouses and partners especially difficult. This failure to include children in our definition of mutuality leads to some troubling oversights. First, the failure leads us to disregard the necessity of "transitional hierarchy," the temporary inequity of power and privilege in families. Second, it leads us to ignore the realities of "transitional sacrifice," the temporary restriction and offering up of one's own desires for the sake of one's children.

The dance of mutuality between adults is bound to have an impact on how these same adults relate to children. As many parents strive toward greater mutuality in their own relationship, they also hope for a fairer, less domineering, more mutual relationship with their children. The problem is this: children by definition are not ready for full-fledge mutuality. They lack the physical and cognitive capacity for full reciprocity. They deserve greater latitude and leniency in having their own needs met. They should not feel compelled to meet parental needs and desires (we parents must have other avenues of care, support, and fulfillment to avoid using a child to meet our own ends). Children also need clear limits and guidelines. But finding the shifting middle ground of mutuality between authoritarianism and permissiveness and between parent as authority figure and parent as best friend is hard. In fact, author Barbara Kingsolver calls divining the "difference between boundaries and bondage" the most "assiduous task of parenting."

In a word, mutual love needs to be understood differently in a situation of temporary or "transitional hierarchy," especially when it involves children and those who care for them. Hierarchy has become a bad word; it is often narrowly equated with authoritarianism and sometimes with patriarchy. But hierarchy in and of itself is not inevitably authoritarian or patriarchal. Mutuality cannot rule fully at all times and in all areas of our lives. Transitional hierarchies honor this fact by allowing temporary inequity between people, whether of power, authority, expertise, responsibility, or maturity, undertaken in the hope of moving toward (though it has not yet arrived at) genuine mutuality.

Shortly after we moved and sized up our growing boys, we purchased a new round table large enough to accommodate the five of us. Two of the chairs have arms. The others do not.

One night during dinner, after the kids traded places so the same odd-kid-out didn't always have to straddle a table leg, one of my sons noticed, "Hey, why do you two [meaning us adults] get the chairs with the arms?" Mark and I not only occupied these chairs; we had leg room.

I can't capture the gist of our response, but it went well beyond chairs to a larger portrait of roles and relationships. "We're the adults," we said, though this sounded a bit too much like the "because I said so" response. So we went on. "We are more responsible for your well-being now than you are for ours. We hope this changes eventually, gradually. We generally (although not always) have more experience, knowledge, and expertise."

Giving unto Others . . . But What About Myself?

The chairs with arms are a small sign of transitional privilege. Yet the table itself is round. The heads of the table at which we parents sit are only marginally at the table's "head," since at a round table there is officially no such thing. "We are already trying to empower you in appropriate ways. We try to regard you with respect. We want your participation, as far as you're capable, in decisions that affect your bodies and minds." That our son could protest our table arrangement and ask this question itself marked openness to his seeing himself on close to equal footing with us. But not quite completely equal, not yet.

Salvaging Sacrifice

Difficulties do not end with orchestrating a kind of lopsided mutuality and authority. We also have to figure out just what to do with the rightfully beleaguered ideal of self-sacrifice. If the giving tree seems like a poor model of love, if self-sacrifice is not the ideal we should hang over the heads of women already overprogrammed to give, or over the heads of men who are becoming more willing to parent, is there no room for it at all? Now that we are more aware of its dangers and drawbacks than ever before, can we find anything to salvage about sacrifice?

Salvaging sacrifice. *Webster's Dictionary* defines *salvage* as the "act of saving or rescuing property" in danger of destruction by a calamity, such as a wreck or fire. I happened upon the word partly because of alliteration. But it fits. In a way, we are talking about the church's "property." Sacrifice is a piece of intellectual and ritual capital that has long defined the church. Salvage implies a moderate path forward. The ideal of sacrifice has some value, despite all the damage it has done in women's lives in particular, but the entire doctrine, as religious tradition has upheld it, is not worth saving. Moreover, reentering the site of calamity involves some risk. I tread on, aware of the hazards.

Sustaining family life requires daily self-restriction, whether we call it sacrifice or not. Sometimes the sheer routine of home and work and human finitude itself requires one to postpone (if not forfeit and, yes, sacrifice) one's own desires for the good of the other. One may get a great deal back, but the return is seldom instantaneous or in kind. Sacrifice is not just something that happens between parent and child. It's also something that must be figured into the relationship between parents. Salvaging sacrifice makes particular sense for men who hope to share responsibility for children and home but who have seldom been socialized to put this ahead of their own work and interests.

Sharing the sacrifices required of raising children is the key. A woman cannot, writer Jane Lazarre says, "manage being a mother" not only to her children but also to her husband (or, I would add, her partner). The "husband as grownup" must "care for his own clothes, plan family meals and activities as often as I do, remember his own phone numbers and dates, and spend several nights a week . . . without me while I meet with writers or others who feed my work," Lazarre writes. He must also "learn, as I had to, to respond to the emotional needs of children and to sacrifice the needs of work to the needs of children when this is necessary."

Without some room for sacrifice, the pursuit of radical mutuality between two parents responsible for child care and housekeeping easily degenerates into a parsimonious tit-for-tat computation. In fact, some of the housework negotiations Mark and I conduct almost degenerate into a contest ("Let's just make a list of chores and then we'll just see who's doing more") that each of us threatens when certain we'll come out ahead. We don't follow through because at some level we recognize that this is a no-win situation. In reality, we are both probably doing too much. Recognizing self-sacrifice as a sometimes necessary and transitional part of the larger commitment to genuine mutuality might allow us to suspend such calculation and go about our work without begrudging or calculating the cost so jealously.

There are, nonetheless, some absolutely essential parameters around this activity of salvage. Any act of rescue must recognize that the property will never be quite the same again. Moreover, the entire property itself—all that we have assumed about sacrifice, particularly maternal sacrifice—is not worth salvaging. We need to listen to those who have been harmed by expectations that they make too many sacrifices and to acknowledge that the Christian doctrine of sacrifice has led some into situations of danger and abuse. We also need to avoid oversimplifying our salvage project through taking too strong a stand on either side, completely endorsing or totally opposing its importance. Reclamation comes only after we have recognized the distorted emotional and spiritual reasons that lead women to sacrifice themselves inordinately and destructively and the economic and political inequities that result.

Sacrifice does not rule out self-love. In fact, parents should not be ashamed of the self-interest that accompanies their love. They do better to admit and even affirm the needs they harbor for pleasure and gratification. To acknowledge that we need to give love to our children and to receive their love as well is healthier for all concerned than disguising an offer of love as a "sacrifice" for which they should be grateful. Ultimately, any moment of self-disregard must rest on a bedrock of self-regard, respect, and mutual reliance. Daniel Bell makes this point well: "The recovery of sacrifice hinges on revisioning it not in terms of scarcity, where giving necessarily entails losing, but in terms of abundance, wherein giving is a matter of sharing an inexhaustible surplus. In other words, the recovery of sacrifice entails seeing it as a central practice in a cycle of gift-exchange, in which giving does not result in loss but rather nurtures communion, mutuality, and interdependence." Sacrifice is not the height and epitome of love. Sacrifice stands in service of mutuality.

But how are we to distinguish life-giving from harmful, life-denying forms of sacrifice? Theological ethicist Barbara Andolsen specifies three occasions in which sacrifice is justifiable. First, she says, life-giving sacrifice takes place when those who are privileged make sacrifices for the sake of those who are oppressed. Second, it happens when a party in greater need has a *prima facie* claim on others. Finally, it occurs when those within an enduring relationship make a sacrifice that can be balanced out over the long run.

All three occasions arise when one loves and lives with children. Even if not always oppressed, all children spend long hours around adults who have many privileges, including the ability to tell children what to do and where to go. Moreover, the claims that arise from children's basic needs place a *prima facie* obligation on parents.

In the Midst of Chaos

Giving to children has a good (though not guaranteed) chance of balancing out over a lifetime, as children grow into adults able to care for others.

To discern the difference between exploitative and salvageable sacrifice, one must ask a series of complex questions. Is the sacrifice and surrender chosen and invited, rather than forced or demanded? Is it motivated by fear, or genuine love and faithfulness? Does the person remain a subject, or is she turned into an object and a means to someone else's end? Does the sacrificial loss actually count as a gain in some deeper way and enrich life rather than destroy it? Does sacrifice, in essence, remain in service of a greater mutuality and abundant life? Does it lead to more just and loving relationships?

DUAL (AT LEAST) VOCATIONS

"Mommy," asks one woman's small son one night after she sings his bedtime lullabies, "who do you love better, me or your writing?" The mother, who has been working hard for weeks on a chapter for a book, is startled by the question.

Picturing this scene fills me with dread. None of my sons has asked this. But they very well could. Maybe they have just never said it out loud. Maybe I foreclosed opportunity. On purpose.

I do lots of my work at home, partly so I'm here on teacher in-service days, summer days, snow days (when the mere threat cancels school in the south), and when kids roll in after school. My desk faces the wall opposite the entry to our home. Even as I have worked on this book, I have wondered, "What do my kids think when they see my back day and night as they come in the front door and pass by in the hall?" Does my absorption convey neglect or something worse? Lately I have sat here particularly doggedly trying to finish this book. Should I not be helping them use their nonschool time more constructively than video games—a topic for another day and a later chapter? Should I be taking them out to lunch and to the gym or mall or bowling alley, as the mother down the street does? Am I going to live to regret writing this damn book?

Recently my youngest son called for a ride home from school. He'd missed the bus. I said I'd come pick him up after the buses cleared out. I put down the phone, turned back to the computer, and thirty minutes later suddenly realized he was waiting at school. Did buying him a large sweet tea on the way home make up for forgetting him? I doubt it.

Some say, and I mostly agree, that seeing a mother with other goals and objectives is not all bad. It keeps mothers from excessive hovering and dependence on children to meet their own needs. It models a richer adult life. It encourages greater assertiveness and independence in children themselves. It frees children for aspirations of their own.

These arguments do not completely dispel my panic, however. As many, many women before me and many women around me have asked, Can women have children and books? The question stretches beyond writers and artists. Not surprisingly, it has plagued women in all lines of work more than it has bothered men, who have not usually been expected to rank children ahead of work. But now it is becoming a concern of parents at large. Ultimately, are love of children and love of one's own work mutually exclusive? That is, does one preclude the other?

History has mostly said yes. Men work; women love (religious translation: God calls men to work and women to families). This bifurcation of vocation certainly simplifies things. But does it do justice to a life of faith? Many of us have proven or argued no for years. But whether theological education and society at large can achieve the reconceptualization of work and love required to make it genuinely possible for women and men to honor the various vocations to which many of us seem to be called is another question.

The supposed "choice" between work of one's own and love of family is, in fact, a falsehood. There is no real choice for women, in particular, when distorted ideals and structures go unchanged, whether the assumption about unlimited maternal self-sacrifice or an inflexible eighty-hour work week and denial of benefits and job security for part-time employment. There is also no such choice as Yeats's "perfection of the life, or of the work" in general. As poet and author Wendell Berry argues, "The division implied by this proposed choice is not only destructive; it is based on a shallow understanding of the relation between work and life."

Questioning ideals and structures of work and family is the responsibility of good theology. With all the changes in women's and men's lives and roles, it is time for theologians to rethink what we mean by vocation in particular. The efforts to rethink vocation for women and men that are under way today are every bit as disruptive and revolutionary as Luther's departure from the cloister and proclamation of every walk of life as an avenue for faith.

Many adults now ask, in Presbyterian theologian Cynthia Rigby's words, just how they can be "called *both* to the vocation of raising children and to other vocations"? How are we to handle the multiplicity of vocations to which we are now called? How can we pursue our own talents and gifts and not compromise what we owe our children? How can we care for all the details of the household without compromising ourselves? What about those of us with jobs that are simply jobs, secured to support our families financially with little other gratification? Does any of this nonstop work glorify God? These are tough questions.

Sometimes we know more about what vocation is *not* than what it is. In theologian Nancy Duff's attempt to redefine the meaning of a faithful vocation today, she concludes there are *no* precise definitions of *masculine* and *feminine,* no set rules for gender roles, and no set pattern for the relationship between men and women. All this no-saying, however, leaves us with a slightly empty ethic. What then does positive enactment of faith look like?

I think we can say more: a vocation is not a singular duty to which God calls each person. God's call is multivocal. Good Christians (and the faithful of other traditions) can receive more than one call. Women, as both Duff and Rigby insist, should no longer be forced to choose one vocation to the exclusion of others. Nor, I would add, should men. Mothering is not women's supreme or only vocation, and bringing home the bacon is not the sole vocation to which men are called. Each of us has more than one divinely appointed purpose. Each person glorifies God in a variety of ways. This is, in fact, consistent with Luther's own basic insight: each of us lives out a primary vocation to love God and neighbor within a variety of "offices": as parent, worker, citizen, friend, student, spouse, and so on. Today, however, we can retrieve this idea only as we reconceive the assumptions about gender that once accompanied it.

So perhaps I wasn't so far off base when, in the first few years of teaching, I bucked the system and submitted an annual report to my seminary that stated "parenting my kids" right next to my list of lectures and publications. Let the president, board, and faculty chew on that one for a while. Even though no one else named "family" in their faculty report, I've found seminaries quite receptive to recognizing the importance of multiple vocations. Perhaps they can become "seedbeds" (as their name suggests) for necessary changes in the wider world.

Professing multiple vocations goes against the social grain of seeing vocation as a singular pursuit: one person, one gender, one vocation. "A business card that lists more than one profession," Kingsolver says with a smile, "does not go down well in the grown-up set. We're supposed to have one main thing we do well, and it's OK to have hobbies if they are victimless and don't get out of hand, but to confess to disparate passion is generally taken in our society as a sign of attention deficit disorder."

Multiple vocations do indeed contribute to disorder. At a meeting a year ago, I got so animated by conversation that I forgot my purse on the seat behind my back. Well along my way to becoming the absent-minded professor/mother—or so my mom thinks—I drove half way to Indiana this past summer to meet up with her, and my niece and sister-in-law, before I realized I was a day early. The day before, I had returned from an out-of-town meeting, cleaned my share of the house, went to a minor league game with my family, and glanced cursorily at the load of deskwork awaiting me. Obviously I didn't know where I was or what day it was.

Such is the fallout of pursuing multiple vocations. Kingsolver again: "I'd like to think it's OK to do a lot of different kinds of things, even if we're not operating at genius level in every case." Sometimes I'd be happy to reach average.

This doesn't mean I'm botching everything up, however. The great command to love the neighbor actually summons us to take up vocations that extend beyond the family into the public world. This means that loving one's family alone is great but not sufficient. All parents—mothers and fathers alike—need a public vocation (remember, this does not necessarily mean "job") that carries their gifts to the wider community. To put it bluntly, as Catholic moral theologian Julie Rubio does, "One cannot fully realize the demands of discipleship to Jesus of Nazareth unless one also has a public vocation."

Holding on to multiple vocations is difficult. Sustaining a composite vocation "hour after hour day after day for maybe twenty *years*" involves an "endless expense of energy and an impossible weighing of competing priorities," says author Ursula Le Guin. Author and mother of six Margaret Oliphant hardly had more than "two hours undisturbed (except at night when everybody is in bed)" for her own writing life, reports Le Guin. Harriet Beecher Stowe, also the mother of six, wrote most of *Uncle Tom's Cabin* at the kitchen table. Elizabeth Barrett Browning expressed frustration to her husband about writing in the dining room with "everything else going on."

Le Guin's list of women working and loving goes on. Although she is talking about the literary parenting life and the book-or-baby dilemma, what she says pertains to almost all parents. The angst of multiple vocations is hard to put into words but well known by all who care for children, including many men. Admitting this is itself an important step. Learning to live well within this anxiety may even be the primary spiritual challenge of family life.

A "life lived primarily for others" brings a particular kind of frustration, anger, despair, and emptiness, says minister, writer, and father Ernst Boyer:

> It is frustration at the interruptions that inevitably break into every task, the ringing phone, the need to drive across town to pick up a child, the dishes . . . no sooner washed than . . . dirtied again, the night's sleep shattered by a crying baby. It is anger at a lack of choices, at feeling that

Giving unto Others . . . But What About Myself?

there is nothing else to do but answer others' needs. . . . It is a despair arising from a . . . loss of creativity, a loss of a sense of achievement. . . . It is emptiness that comes of setting aside the urge to become all that it is possible to become to attend to the many details essential to the working of a family.

Of course, others may have an acute reversal of Boyer's portrait. They may feel frustrated about a confining work schedule that takes them far from home and kids; anger at work obligations that arise in late afternoon or evening, when kids often need parents the most; and emptiness from unfulfilling work that seems meaningless in comparison with the needs of kids. For mothers in particular, it seems, a kind of guilt and despair arises around missed opportunities to care for a child that result from devotion to one's work. These are the casualties that accompany a life shaped by multiple vocations. They are also the occasion for pondering and spiritual discernment.

WORK AND FAMILY INTERRUPTUS

I was recently talking with a colleague at a fall barbecue when he dashed off midsentence. His two-year-old daughter had tugged on his leg. Where was the closest potty? Meanwhile my fourteen-year-old, who had accompanied me reluctantly though kindly, was hovering in the shadowy corner of the room, sending a glare that said, "I told you this would be boring" and "You promised you'd leave as soon as possible."

All this was so familiar. I'd been here before. Years ago we had friends over. They had two little kids, and so did we. We started a thousand conversations but finished none. A few years before that, when we went on our first "vacation" with our new nine-month-old, the obvious dawned on me: I might never have another real vacation. I might never complete a full adult sentence again, at least not with anyone under five around. I hadn't yet considered what teenagers could do.

Interruptions are endemic to family life, and their value is "extraordinarily difficult to discern," observes Jewish ethicist Laurie Zoloth-Dorfman. This is especially true when the grass of someone else's relatively uninterrupted pasture looks so much greener. We watch, like Janet Soskice, as our single or childless colleagues spend restful vacations returning refreshed and renewed, while we spend the holiday "explaining why you can't swim in the river with an infected ear, why two ice creams before lunch is a bad idea, with trips to disgusting public conveniences with children who are 'desperate,' with washing grubby clothes, pouring cooling drinks, and cooking large meals in inconvenient kitchens for children made cranky by too much sun and water." This holiday, she notes, is simply a memorable instance of a much "wider whole." The interruptions that constitute family life are not just a matter of daily occurrence but also a pattern that has cumulative effects over decades of steady interruption.

Interruption, however, just might be where faith occurs, as some ministers have argued about the pastoral life. "To live an interrupted life means a recognition of the theological importance of the element of surprise," argues Zoloth-Dorfman. She actually sees the pattern of Jewish Talmud—the dialogical interpretation of a text where interruption, debate, and exchange is essential to knowing God's word—as analogous. A theology of interruption offers what she calls a "foundational pattern" for "radical recognition that the needs of the other compel immediate moral attention." To bear children and take an oath to hear the voice of the other as one's own is the "moment in the faith journey that is the most profoundly ethical."

Adults who live with steady interruption in their care for children experience what anthropologists call "liminality." Anthropologists use this term to describe a phase in religious ritual in which one is dislodged from ordinary patterns and allowed to live "betwixt and between," temporarily free from common expectations and norms. One's social status and role, accepted codes of conduct, and assumptions about the world are suspended and open to redefinition. You can recognize parents at meetings, Zoloth-Dorfman observes, because they are the ones who sit by the doorway, ready to dart out if household need calls. They come late and leave early. They are not fully in

Giving unto Others ... But What About Myself?

the meeting, but they are not fully outside it either. They are caught betwixt and between. Such a place is disruptive and yet potentially transformative.

Interruption can bring focus, teach patience, and foster reconciliation with failure. Daily I face the fact that I am not at my best in any sphere and that each sphere may impede, rather than enhance, my doing well in the other. At the very same time, some dare to hope that the vocation of parenting will enrich their other vocations and vice versa. Some of us not only write in the kitchen but profit from it, observes Le Guin. My entire corpus of work—the classes I teach, the articles and books I read and write, the advising I do—has mostly flourished as a result of having children. Children put us into "immediate and inescapable contact with the sources of life, death, beauty, growth, corruption," says one writer-mother. Looking back on her parenting years, another mother says, "I was more productive, because I was more sensual" or more passionately invested in life and in living "as a human being must live."

My writing "muse," says author and mother Kingsolver, "wears a baseball cap, backward. The minute my daughter is on the bus, he saunters up behind me with a bat slung over his shoulder and says oh so directly, 'OK, author lady, you've got six hours till that bus rolls back up the drive. You can sit down and write, *now,* or you can think about looking for a day job."

Sometimes, however, there is nothing to be learned from, and no redeeming side to, interruption. Interruption is simply frustrating. It stops, it hinders, it breaks in. Sometimes my muse arrives just before my kids do, or not at all. This chapter was written after the summer ended and the semester resumed. I did not get as far as I wanted during the summer. Guess why? I'm still banging away under less optimal circumstances, squeezing in a half day here, circling around and backtracking for hours there.

"You just have to think how good you'll feel," says my good friend, "when you're done." That's nice. That's hopeful. But it won't get it done. That's the vocation of love and faith in family life—often, if not always, half-baked, partly unresolved, constantly interrupted, ever developing, changing, falling apart and coming back together again.

Chapter 6

DOING JUSTICE
AND WALKING
HUMBLY
WITH KIDS

"It's not fair." These may not have been his exact words. My oldest son has not been one to complain much. But when he made this remark several years ago, I readily caught the drift. His younger brothers, he was pointing out yet again, had gotten something earlier and better than he had. I can't quite remember what this something was, but that doesn't really matter now. His point could have applied to any of several grievances: the puppy asked for but delayed, a weekly allowance, late-night privileges, all granted to his brothers when they were younger and perhaps also less deserving than he had been on receiving them. In the years between his requests and those of his brothers we must have given up trying to keep the carpet clean, control our money, or be the last to bed. Mark and I weren't keeping track. But he evidently was, and what he saw was a pattern of injustice.

My son was far from the first sibling to complain about fairness. This is a quintessential human story that appears again and again in myth and folklore, as well as in the memories of countless individuals. It echoes biblically in the squabble between Esau and Jacob, the twin sons of Isaac and Rebekah, as to who would receive their father's blessing and the material and spiritual rewards that accompanied it

(Genesis 27). It also appears in the Parable of the Grumbling Older Brother (Luke 15:11–32, better known as the Parable of the Prodigal Son), in which a brother who has behaved well protests the warm welcome with which the father greets the return of one who has not. It is not only older brothers who grumble, however. I recently received a similar complaint from my youngest son. One of his older brothers got to stay up later and longer; the other one got to drive alone before logging the three thousand adult-supervised miles we require (this charge coming hot off the press: I took him to get his own learner's permit this morning). My middle son registers a reverse complaint: he has done more than his fair share of family chores, so he's not, he says, going to do whatever nasty task I've just come up with.

These are claims we've all made in our own good time to our own parents—claims, indeed, that we continue to make as adults to those parental substitutes for whom we work. I often stumble, as I suspect my own parents did, in trying to offer a reassuring response. The injustice is temporary, I say ("Your time will come"), or justifiable on other grounds ("You got something else"). At other times, there seems to be nothing to say but "Life just isn't fair sometimes."

When that final assertion first fell out of my mouth, I looked over my shoulder to see if one of my parents had come for a quick visit. Then I heard what I had said—really heard it—and thought, *What an understatement.* I had to resist launching into a longer lecture about injustice in the world at large.

Fairness is not just a matter of pets, allowances, late-night fun, driving privileges, and a few household chores. These things, as well as worry about how to divide them among siblings, are luxuries enjoyed by the few. In a world torn by strife, poverty, and prejudice, a bigger and more troubling kind of unfairness affects most children beyond anything my own children have directly known or experienced.

Telling a kid that life just isn't fair, it turns out, is just the tip of the iceberg. Fairness—which is in some ways the kid term for justice—takes shape in negotiations over privileges within the family. But even more difficult questions arise around how a family might address social inequity and foster peace and justice in the wider society. Within Christian and Jewish tradition, a yearning for fairness to all is woven

In the Midst of Chaos

deeply into our sense of God and ourselves. In family life, questions of both kinds arise constantly. One rarely has a better opportunity to learn ethics and practice justice, says mother and ethicist Laurie Zoloth-Dorfman, drawing on philosophical ethicist Selya Benahib, than when one has to "explain to a six-year-old why it is that she cannot make an exception of herself."

Yet so often talk about spirituality in family life today ignores justice. We fail to recognize the family as the heart and soul of doing justice. It is the place where justice is first learned and practiced, and the place where we might begin to turn the world upside down. This is one of the most spiritually challenging and formative arenas for those who care for children.

NEGOTIATING JUSTICE

When our family moved ten years ago, we had to decide where to live. Our children were nine, six, and four. Mark and I had the bountifully ambiguous plight of having about six relatively full-time jobs between us—two jobs left behind, two new jobs ahead, parenting, *and moving.* We wanted to include our children in the decision—a gesture, however limited, of our budding hope to "do justice" within our family by involving them in choices that shape their lives. But house shopping with three active boys under ten? These guys could barely stand in the grocery line without breaking into a game of tag, or shop for clothes without hiding inside the circular shirt rack. Exposing a real estate agent to our ineffective attempts at discipline didn't sound like much fun to me.

Nor did the ingenious idea, suggested by friends, of moving twice—first to get the lay of the land and then to a more permanent home. Showing our kids a home video of the places and neighborhoods we saw sounded like a much better idea. So we settled for that.

We soon discovered that choosing a house wasn't just a decision about location, size, and school district. Instead, it plunged us into much bigger questions. A few years earlier, I had observed that "becoming a parent requires nothing less than the clearest truth about

Doing Justice and Walking Humbly with Kids

one's deepest values"—and now I was experiencing how painful that could be. I first wrote those words in response to the powerful testimony of Mary Guerrera Congo about how becoming a mother had forced a "total reassessment" of her identity, requiring of her "nothing less that the clearest truth about my deepest and most protected feelings and hurts." For Guerrera Conga, a self-identified feminist Catholic, this realization came as she tried to balance her work and the needs of her children, an effort she saw as the "ongoing and nagging and unresolved puzzle in my life."

Moving across the country with kids, I realized, was forcing me to relive a similar conflict of commitments. Deciding where to live, which itself is a privilege not extended justly to all, marks one's fundamental convictions and forces one to put one's values into action. For me, this included my belief that Christian parenting means not only balancing our own needs and those of our children but also the needs of our own children and those of other children. Indeed, I had begun to consider the tendency of privileged parents to lavish love on their own children in the privacy of the home, to the neglect of all children—a serious betrayal of deeper Christian commitments.

Choosing a house unexpectedly became one of the harder decisions of parenthood. Should we live in an area where people of different economic classes or races or sexual orientation would be our near neighbors? Or should we focus on good schools? The fact that we had such a choice as a result of privileges of class and race was itself a troubling reminder of the injustices we opposed. What does one do with that kind of choice? Without kids, Mark and I might have felt freer to express our commitment to diversity by living in a less secure area. What would we convey to our kids by choosing a safer route? If we made the riskier choice, how would we handle the extra demands it would bring when we were already so busy with other things?

Lots of us make a similar decision even without moving, when we choose a worshipping community. Do we consider a working-class congregation in a changing, poorer neighborhood, struggling to make ends meet but clear about its mission, like the one Mark and I attended before our move? Or do we go to an established church with ample resources to fund burgeoning children and youth programs in spite of its air of conventionality? If we choose the former, will we have the energy to hold up our end and do our share, and will our kids stay connected in a community with fewer kids? If we choose the latter, can we communicate to our kids alternative values about wealth, class, and consumerism relative to the values that surround them in the well-off church in the safe neighborhood?

People of faith don't talk about these matters openly or often enough. Trying to do justice as a practice in the family, particularly a family with adequate means, is unsettling. There are "hardly any forums, including church," says Bill Wylie-Kellermann, a United Methodist pastor who is the father of two, "for genuine vulnerable conversation" about such dilemmas.

Wylie-Kellermann loves being a father but misses the time earlier in his life when he could act boldly on his faith convictions and "not drag a family into the risks." "As a father, I struggle regularly," he says, "with how the girls endure the consequences of our family's commitments in Detroit." Until his daughters were six and two, they lived in the barrio of Southwest Detroit. Then, not long after a rash of neighborhood shootings, he overheard his daughter explain to her younger sister how to duck when she hears gunshots. The family moved, not far but still out of range of the poverty they were committed to relieve.

What cost were they "willing to exact" from their kids, Wylie-Kellermann asks, "for the sake of our convictions"? When their older daughter could no longer bear the isolation and conflict she faced as one of two white students in her class, they put their two girls into a private Catholic school despite strong allegiance to public schools. Many other children, he acknowledges, face harsher discrimination from birth with far less choice. "Needless to say, I agonize as a father about such stuff, tossing and turning in the dark hours of the night," Wylie-Kellermann says. "Ah, what a terrifying business this fathering is."

People of color and other minorities that face racism, sexism, and heterosexism every day have to make such choices in a context that is even more hostile and complex, as the testimony of black lesbian mother and writer Audre Lorde makes clear. Lorde raised her daughter and son in the "mouth of a racist, sexist, suicidal dragon."

Amid many perils, she tried to raise her children "to be warriors," able to "recognize the enemy's many faces"—while also steering her son away from the assumption of his peers that he must fight and dominate others to prove his masculinity.

If she and her children were to survive, Lorde had to teach them to "love and resist at the same time." Her children must not only risk loving others. They must love themselves dearly for all God created them to be, regardless of oppressive police, legal practices, and other social and political realities, and despite hostile messages from the media (and even from those who profess Christian love). Lorde's understandably heightened awareness of injustice reminds us that all children must learn to stand up for themselves, to deal constructively with injustice aimed at them, and to protect and defend the rights, dignity, and well-being of others.

A good part of Lorde's essay focuses on redefining power within her own family. She and her partner constantly monitor and evaluate how they divide power between themselves and between themselves and their children. Redefining power also means honesty. Lorde is deeply honest with herself and with her children about her own fears and struggles. "I give the most strength to my children by being willing to look within myself and by being honest with them about what I find there," without expecting a response beyond their years. Only such honesty will help redefine power as "something other than might, age, privilege, or the lack of fear." By confessing her own fears, this mother hopes to help her children to acknowledge and then look beyond their own.

Unlike Wylie-Kellermann and Lorde but like many other people, my family ended up in a homogeneous suburb, a place I never would have expected to live in back when I was a socially conscientious graduate student in an urban setting. Then, I had ridiculed the names of subdivisions. Now, our home stood right in the middle of one whose name evoked horses, meadows, and fields (as did the names of other nearby developments). Our previous home was technically suburban too, located in an older town on the commuter rail line, but at least we had lived in a town and been able to walk to the post office and library. Our new home was fifteen minutes by car from the nearest library and grocery store. Neighbors commuted to jobs in corporate America. Lots of mothers stayed home. The subdivision and the area as a whole displayed little racial diversity. Although not ostentatious, our house still loomed down from its spot on the hill and looked huge by comparison to the one we left and more modest homes we'd considered.

But we could see the middle school from our front porch, and the elementary school was just down the road. We could get to work quickly on the main road not far from our back door. Our oldest son wouldn't have to change schools three times in three years, as would have been the case in the urban school system, and our kids would initially all go to the same school. We could make the living room into a study, which would let us work at home and be around after school and on snow days. And the sunsets are amazing, a joy to behold after the flatlands we'd left behind.

Our decision on where to live ultimately came down to a question of vocation. It was one piece in a more complicated and ongoing effort to balance a variety of commitments. How might the kind of Christian discipleship to which Mark and I felt called best take shape? Just how far could we go in implicating our own children in the call? That is, how was I to negotiate a call to teach and write as a theologian, a commitment to my children, and a commitment to do justice? We could not negotiate the challenge of living in a less stable, more urban neighborhood *and* sustain our felt obligations to read, think, write, teach, and lead. So we gained stability and focus but lost exposure, risk, and a readier social activism.

Doing justice in families often becomes a complicated matter of negotiation and compromise—something that seems to go against the grain of genuine prophetic justice. But without repeated attempts to arbitrate the demands of all family members, no one in the family would have the energy or resources from which to act at all.

"How to be peacemakers both at home and in the larger world is quite a challenge." So James and Kathleen McGinnis, Catholic parents and peace activists well known for more than two decades of work on "parenting for peace and justice," admit on the first page of the tenth-anniversary-edition of their widely read book *Parenting*

Doing Justice and Walking Humbly with Kids

for Peace and Justice. They have refused to see parenting and doing justice as divorced from one another. But they have struggled. "For almost twenty years," they say, "we have wrestled with the challenge of integrating our family life and social ministry. . . . We have wanted . . . to be able to act for justice without sacrificing our children and to build family community without isolating ourselves from the world." The effort to raise children faithfully pushed both of them to a whole new level of what it means to do justice.

CONSUMING SPIRITUALITY (WHILE LEAVING JUSTICE ON THE PLATE)

Lots of spiritual literature today ignores this challenge. In the mail yesterday, I received a free CD advertising a "spiritual path to serenity and contentment." "Feel good inside no matter what happens outside," the label promised. I had had a terribly disruptive day, spinning my wheels, yelling at those around me and myself, and I saw the attraction of these words. But was feeling good inside no matter what happens outside the solution? Apparently plenty of people hope so.

In a large independent bookstore in the metropolitan area where I live, I notice that the Spirituality section has been moved to the most prominent position. I can remember when religion books were sandwiched between sociology and philosophy along a side aisle. Now a huge sign identifying the section greets the buyer who enters the front door. Spirituality books appear in other sections as well, including the section on child rearing. One that seems representative is Phil Catalfo's *Raising Spiritual Children in a Material World.*

Catalfo grew up a devout Catholic in the heart of the Italian-American district of Brooklyn. But he left all formal religion behind in young adulthood because a life revolving around Catholic feast days and unquestioned acceptance of catechetical truths felt stifling. When he became a father, he faced a new question. How should he and his wife, a lapsed Lutheran, raise their children? They didn't want to raise them in faith traditions that they themselves had been taught to accept "without question." But they weren't sure what other practice to put in their place.

So Catalfo became a quintessential *bricoleur*. (A bricoleur is someone who patches together the pieces of varied cultures to make something useful in the moment; the term was coined by the French anthropologist Claude Levi-Strauss and applied to American religion by the sociologist Wade Clark Roof, who uses it to describe people who piece together strategies for spiritual living from a variety of sources.) He shops around for spirituality.

One section of his book on the results is entitled "Entries from a Spiritual Shopper's Journal." It reads like a restaurant review, rating the menu items of various church offerings. Generally, Catalfo concludes that the local congregations "didn't speak to me," even if he respects them for engaging in multicultural worship or supporting refugees fleeing from oppression.

Being spiritual, according to Catalfo, refers to the free pursuit of higher power, while being religious (which is much less desirable) entails getting entrapped by doctrines and institutional mandates. Spiritual renewal is something one pursues on one's own for personal well-being, not the glory of God or the good of the neighbor. As the cover states, the goal of this approach is "whatever path will enrich your family the most." Raising spiritual children means "trying various prayers and rituals on for size" and indulging in the "Whole Spirituality Thing." Whatever moral implications might accompany this Thing are similarly free-form. For example, responsibility means "owning" one's choices and not harming others, rather than actively seeking to do good for others or the wider community.

"One need not be an adherent of a particular religious doctrine in order to find the sacred in life," declares Catalfo. But right after this, he makes claims with a distinctly Catholic flavor: his children are "sacraments," he writes, and God is a "Mystery," and other human beings are reflections of this "same mysterious source." In a sense, Catalfo is far more dependent on his own religious upbringing than he realizes. Even his promotion of tolerance and religious freedom, which are actually matters of justice, has roots in the Christian and Jewish belief that all humans are created in God's image and that each is worthy of respect.

A great deal of New Age spirituality stands in a parasitical relationship to Christianity and Judaism, while also missing their central social teaching about the obligation of families to promote the wider common good. Thus contemporary popular spirituality on raising children gives too little attention to questions of justice that adults who care for children face. Commitment to doing justice, central to most religious traditions, is left on the plate with the spinach and Brussels sprouts. Maybe doing justice is just too hard.

A Spiritual Mandate for Justice

Perhaps the most difficult challenge for the practice of faith in families comes directly out of the Jewish and Christian mandate that family love must not stop at the doorstep. Genuine family values—for Jews and Christians alike—are not simply about family commitment or fidelity. Family values compel love of one's neighbor. All children are God's children, including the orphan, the leper, and the widow.

As it turns out, to sustain the sacred in family life, one does need to be an inheritor of, contributor to, and participant in a particular religious tradition or community. Preservation of ideals such as human rights, care for the environment, and social justice depends precisely on the vitality of particular religious communities and traditions. Perhaps even more than other practices in this book, the strength to pursue justice within and beyond the family depends on faith communities. Adults who bear responsibility for children cannot do justice in a family without the mandate and support of such a community or tradition—and, ultimately, the promises of grace, forgiveness, and redemption the community or tradition remembers and proclaims.

"What does God require of you" asks the eighth-century prophet Micah, "but to do justice, and to love kindness, and to walk humbly with your God?" (6:8). Here in one sentence, says the notation in my *New Oxford Annotated Bible,* Micah "sounds major notes" of other prophets—Amos, Hosea, Isaiah, and Jesus—and of Jewish law. In one fell swoop, he "sums up the legal, ethical, and spiritual requirements of religion."

This commandment is a zinger. God wants neither confession nor ritual. Rather, we are to "do justice" in our walking, talking, living, loving, moving lives. We are to make our spirituality visible and manifest in just action.

The prophet Micah knew that what God asks is no easy undertaking. The people of Israel had tried and fallen short for several generations. God sent fresh instructions, offering one more chance. No longer does God want "burnt offerings," says Micah, or sacrifices of newborn calves or rams or oil. God doesn't even want the promise of our firstborn, the "fruit" of our own bodies, an act that had heretofore assured further blessing among the people of antiquity and served as a powerful demonstration of faithful commitment (see Exodus 13:1). What God wants—which may be more demanding than any of these—is simply justice and loving kindness.

LOVE ONE'S CHILDREN, OR LOVE ALL CHILDREN?

When Micah composed this litany of outmoded sacrifices—calves, rams, oil, and firstborn sons—did he notice, I wonder, that he touches on one of the hardest aspects of seeking justice? Don't sacrifice the first-born, he says. That sounds easy; but how exactly does one seek justice in the world without sacrificing one's family?

So often just this kind of trade-off (do good for others *or* care for your children) arises, oh so intensely, in family life. Even the most amazing and admirable justice-seekers (Mahatma Gandhi and Martin Luther King for starters) left hurting family members in their wake. Knowing this casts a shadow on their otherwise bright legacies.

Does following Jesus mean leaving not just one's boat, fish, and the "dead to bury the dead" (Luke 9:60; Matthew 8:22) but also one's children? Does the God whom we worship ultimately force us to choose as God did with Abraham and his son Isaac: love one's child, or love God? Does the very passionate attachment to specific children (about which we've talked all the way through this book) make passion for social justice more difficult? People who know how much they would fight to preserve the life and welfare of their own children worry about this. People who know just how much energy, focus, time, and money it takes to raise their own children well wonder how to do both.

Bill Wylie-Kellermann, as we have seen, is one who tries to do both. He also tries to nurture in his well-loved children a passion for justice beyond their home. This latter effort, however, often gives him pause. In his experience of the baptismal liturgy, Wylie-Kellermann says he has no problem celebrating God's grace that invites all into faithful community. But what about obligating his children to the "path of discipleship"? He pauses at each child's baptism when he is asked to "live a life that becomes the gospel."

Living the gospel requires renouncing the "spiritual forces of wickedness, the evil powers of this world," resisting "evil, justice and oppression," and opening the church to "all ages, nations and races." These are, Wylie-Kellermann knows, "no idle queries but risky and costly matters." To reaffirm them before the lives of his children "was not merely to pass my faith along as some fatherly responsibility, but to draw them unwittingly into the path of discipleship. Did I really want to be the one giving them their first nudge down the path to the cross?"

CARE OF ONE'S OWN CHILDREN

At a workshop on children's spirituality, a new grandmother who is also a teacher spoke movingly. Her words brought a poignant pause to the chatter of our discussion about children's spirituality. She said her daughter had just given birth. She had held the child in her arms. She felt forever changed. Seeing this child, a child in her own lineage, awakened her to the childness, the child-hood, the reality that every person is a child of another, a child of God, and worthy of such love, admiration, and care. If she felt this way about her own child, then all children deserved as much. This kind of love spoke volumes to her about God's love and her own place in passing God's love on. It renewed her commitment to care for other children.

It is important not to see the care for one's own children and care for the world's needy children as necessarily antagonistic. Love of those within our own family and care for the neighbors beyond the household are not mutually exclusive. There is an intricate connection between home and world, love of one's own children and care of all God's children. They are potentially complimentary and mutually enriching.

How can this be? Or how can it be actualized? I can think of at least four rudimentary ways. We learn from the love of our own children, as this grandmother did, to love other children. We care well for our own children for the sake of a better world. We teach our own children to seek the good of others and work toward broader social justice. We model just love within the family.

Caring for our own children can elicit a new way of seeing each person as someone else's child and tie adults into life in a new way. One mother and poet argues that the "carrying and laboring for my children . . . forever altered" her. Her children "worked a profound change in my ability to care for others." "Slow learner that I am, it took the birth of my first child to see each person as someone else's child, someone else's pain and joy. This radical restructuring of my world left me unable to bear some of the misery we inflict on each other."

To learn to nurture through parenting can potentially teach essential human virtues of patience and care, deepening one's life of faith. In fact, the Christian tradition asks us to generalize our intense love of our closest family members to include our farthest and most marginalized neighbors. With my children, something propels me at times to extend myself at greater cost and to a greater extent than I might once have thought possible. It is precisely this impulse of self-extension for our most proximate loved ones, those most closely related to us, that Christianity has commanded us to extend to our neighbors at large. We are to build on such passion, not reject it. In all three Synoptic gospels, Jesus upholds his own Jewish formation and argues, echoing the Shema as his own parents must have taught him, that the "greatest commandment" is to love God with all one's heart, soul, mind, and strength. The second, he continues, is like it:

Doing Justice and Walking Humbly with Kids

love your neighbor as yourself (Mark 12:28–34; Matthew 22:34–40; Luke 10:25–28).

Caring well for one's own children for the sake of the wider society, including raising them to love justice, can itself be an act of faith and public service. Contrary to modern assumptions, raising children is not merely a private matter of personal gratification far removed from the larger world. Children are in fact our closest, most vulnerable, and most valuable neighbors. Their neglect is a grave transgression. Their welfare is a rich benefit for all the other people they will deal with in their lives, and for society as a whole. This includes basic provision for children economically, materially, and beyond. No family stands alone in meeting this obligation, and families without sufficient means need our social and economic support. There are even times in a family's normal life cycle that make outreach to other children difficult, but this need not negate the family as an arena of public service.

A "whole and healthy family *is* a service to this world," says Presbyterian minister Marjorie Thompson. "The pastoral care that family members provide one another is the *principle* ministry of family life, preceding and undergirding all other forms of ministry." Martin Luther even calls siblings our "first neighbors." Sometimes they seem to be the very hardest neighbors to love well; perhaps for just this reason they are good ones to practice our loving on.

It is interesting that Luther even applied to the family one of the key biblical texts that asserts the importance of caring for those who are poor and in need, the Parable of the Judgment in Matthew 25:31–46 ("For I was hungry and you gave me food"). The King in the story commends those who have cared for the "least of these." In Luther's interpretation, this commendation also pertains to those who care for children. I find this comforting after years of listening to Matthew 25 with self-reproach because I have not made it out of the home to somewhere else—prison, hospital, homeless shelter, food pantry. But Luther boldly proclaims, "How many good works you have at hand in your own home with your child who needs all such things as these like a hungry, thirsty, naked, poor, imprisoned, sick soul!" He christens parents "apostles, bishops, and priests to their children." The adult who engages in the Christian nurture of children is carrying out, as historian William H. Lazareth puts it, "a far better work in God's sight than all the current pilgrimages, sacrifices, and cultic ceremonies combined."

This does not excuse parents from wider works of mercy beyond the household, nor condone overindulgence in one's own children. But it does sanction domestic work as one way to participate in bringing God's reign on earth. Those who attend closely to children may, through this very practice, quicken their receptivity to the divine. Maybe this is partly what Christian philosopher Simone Weil means when she writes, "A quarter of an hour of attention is better than a great many good works."

PARENTS AS A BRIDGE, HOME AS MISSION FIELD

There is, however, a slippery slope down which caring for our own children carries us, tempting us to put our own children first and foremost to the neglect of children in general. Human biology and psychology together ensure this. Evolutionary biology shows that humans are predisposed to preserve their own extended kin, those who look like them and carry their genes. Across time, human beings have been consistently less benevolent toward those who are not their relatives.

Psychologists suggest that our own narcissism, our pleasure in seeing ourselves reflected in our own children, ensures our care for them. Sigmund Freud even claimed that "parent love . . . is nothing but parental narcissism born again." We are, in Freud's words, "impelled to ascribe to the child all manner of perfections. . . . The child shall have things better than his parents." So our love for our children loses all perspective. The child turns into the "center and heart of creation, 'His Majesty the Baby.' "

We love our children because they look like us, and we love them because they perpetuate us. Both factors foster a proclivity toward distorted, immoderate parental narcissism that can lead to obsession with and lauding of the accomplishments of our own children without care for other children. When unchecked, the hope for love of all children as God's own is itself perverted.

Religious tradition has worked to check this. "Those who would serve God," insists Catholic ethicist Julie Hanlon Rubio, "must resist the temptation to make caring for kin their only mission in life." The Jesus of the Gospels sees family like money and power, all dangerously tempting us to turn in and away from others. Luther, Weil, Thompson, and maybe Jesus himself would adamantly reject one of the most troubling developments of our day: the overindulgence in the care of one's own children as an end in itself. This is an especially egregious temptation among today's middle class. But it was also a distortion observed by John Chrysostom, a fourth-century theologian in the Eastern Roman Empire.

Chrysostom was a prominent preacher who lived during a time when most church leaders looked to monasticism as the best way for Christians to live. Chrysostom, however, turned from applauding monasticism to praising family life because of his concern for families caught up in a materialistic pagan society. While monks lived holy lives in the desert, married people in the cities were joining the church for all the wrong reasons, especially to procure its social prestige and seek worldly advancement for their own children. Practicing virtues of hospitality, neighbor love, and charity to the poor was not reserved solely for monks, he realized; rather, these practices were profoundly relevant for parents and children as well. In a homily on Ephesians, he actually claims that it is possible for "good husbands and wives" to "surpass all others in virtue" as they do such work. He called the family a "domestic church"—a view now under rejuvenation in the Catholic Church—precisely because he was convinced that parents must teach their own children to seek the good of others and work toward broader social justice in a society gone bad.

A woman with two young children of her own once went to stay with a friend who had just given birth to her first baby and who was in need of company and support. Even though it wasn't easy to be away from her own family, she was glad she could come to her friend's aid. But what most astounded her was the reaction of other people. Almost everyone was surprised, but some went further, conveying a thinly veiled disapproval that she would leave her own home and children to welcome another baby into the world. It brought home to her just "how narrowly we define the nurture of children." We have so isolated care of children as an almost exhaustively private concern of individual parents rather than an obligation shared by a wider circle of friends and community.

Isolated care of one's own children is not the Christian message. Although families naturally seek their own well-being, the "most distinctively Christian moral virtue," Catholic ethicist Lisa Cahill insists, is seeking the well-being of those beyond natural family boundaries. Others, like Rodney Clapp and Cheryl Sanders, agree: the Christian home is, in their words, a "mission base."

At our first housewarming many years ago, we received a gift from our church soprano, a Jewish woman who married our choir director (and whose voice I hear every time "Oh Holy Night" is sung on Christmas Eve). She gave us a Mezuzah to nail on the door post at the entrance to our home. Inside the gold oblong container sits a small scroll with the Shema, the great commandment to love God with all one's heart, soul, and might (Deuteronomy 6:4–5). Torah commands Jews to etch these words on their hearts, binding them to their hands and fixing them on their forehead. They are to post the words on door and gate (Exodus 13:9; Deuteronomy 6:8–9).

Throughout Jewish scripture, the mandate to love God is repeatedly linked to the mandate to welcome the orphan, the widow, and the stranger. This great commandment is the source and foundation of love of neighbor. What does God require, asks the book of Deuteronomy at the climax of its review of the story of the Jewish people? To love God and to love the fatherless, the widow, and the sojourner (Deuteronomy 10:12, 18–19).

The Mezuzah on our door post reminds me of the challenge before me. It sits there on the door, the turning point between inner and outer, mine and not mine, familiar and stranger—precisely the point where one's heart might turn away, might curve in on itself. On the doorstep, at the gate, from the center of one's most primal, passionate, intimate love of our children, we are called to realign our passions and help our children do likewise. The words commanding love of

Doing Justice and Walking Humbly with Kids

God and neighbor are the same words the faithful are commanded to recite diligently to their children and their "children's children," talking about them "when you are at home and when you are away, when you lie down and when you rise" (Deuteronomy 6:2, 7). The Mezuzah's placement on the doorpost is so similar to a parent's station with children in the family, standing between home and the wider public, loving children inside the home and helping them learn to love others outside the home.

Parents must negotiate the odd position of standing on the border, a bit like the Mezuzah, between inside and outside, God and other human beings, intimate attachment and the wider common good. They must shepherd children back and forth across this threshold. This is why practices that bless the coming and going across this border as one begins a new venture with the world, such as school or travel, are so significant. Such practices of sending forth are most powerful when they send children into the world to do justice, love kindness, and walk humbly with God in their own small way.

Perhaps not by coincidence, the commandment to honor one's parents falls in the middle of the Ten Commandments. It comes right between commandments that concern our relationship with God ("You shall have no other gods," "You shall not make a graven image," and so forth) and the final commandments that govern our relationships with each other ("You shall not kill," "You shall not steal," and so forth). The commandment to honor one's parents functions as a turning point, a hinge, or a "bridge between God and human beings," according to the great first-century Jewish philosopher Philo. As Jewish ethicist Elliot Dorff observes, parents are to teach children "both how to behave in human society and how we are to think and act toward God."

DOING JUSTICE FROM HOME TO WORLD

In the ten years since we moved to our house on the hill, Mark and I have tried to develop mundane, daily routes to the practice of justice. Sometimes this happens through table talk. At the dinner table or in the car or on the run, I find myself explaining why, in contrast to the home we just visited for the end-of-the-season team party, we wouldn't have a television in every room (including the bathroom) even if we had the money. Or why we're driving a fifteen-year-old van yet another year. Or why using "gay" as a derogatory adjective is wrong and puts down gay and lesbian people and families I know, like, and admire. Or why composting makes sense or why there's no longer much excuse for throwing plastic or aluminum into the regular trash. Or why my sons as siblings must treat each other with respect and are not allowed, as I would often say, "to put the other person down to feel better about yourself" ("It doesn't work anyway," I'd add). Or why a longer history of racism and poverty stands behind the conflict and unrest that continues to surface in the high school hallway. Or why racism justifies people of color's distrust of police, medical professionals, the courts, and even the university where I teach. Explicit, self-conscious attention to our unreflective perpetuation of racism is especially important.

Are these small, daily efforts to do justice gestures in the night? I hope not. It's hard to know for sure. But affirming mundane, routine conversation as a small act of doing justice essential to the faith life of the family is certainly a step in the right direction in a culture where spiritual often means inner peace, personal enrichment, and escape from the world's injustices. Attending to these small acts with children has certainly intensified our own awareness about how intricately matters of justice infiltrate our lives and shape daily living.

Doing justice can enter routine, daily life in a variety of ways. McGinnis and McGinnis delineate three of them: lifestyle changes that contest dominant cultural values, "works of mercy" that minister to those in need, and "works of justice" that advocate for wider social change. They also identify obstacles that arise on each of these fronts. In addition to the limitations of time, energy, and resources, they add three others: a social context inhospitable to raising children, especially for poor families; isolation of the home and parents from community; and lack of imagination.

How then do parents work for peace and justice at home and in the larger world? The answer is at once simple and complicated:

Doing Justice and Walking Humbly with Kids

involve children every step of the way. The McGinnises lift up six areas—violence, materialism, racism, sexism, social action, and prayer—and in each case move from a rationale for action to lists and examples of concrete practices for doing justice and seeking peace (how to eat, dress, play, use money, consume energy, celebrate holidays, serve the homeless, march in protest, and so forth). The multiplicity of suggestions, they are careful to insist, are "not meant to overwhelm people" but encourage them to take "one step at a time."

It is hard not to feel overwhelmed. After reading the McGinnises' book with a group, one participant quietly confessed it intimidated him. Another person seconded this. So many ideas and choices, so little time. Almost everyone agreed: it was hard to read through all the constructive suggestions without guilt, remorse, and a sense of repeated failure. The people in the group did appreciate the McGinnises' honesty about their own difficulties, however. After reaching high school, their children were not "models of social involvement" but rather "typical adolescents"—and the McGinnises' own energy and resources as parents were greatly stretched.

One son wanted to stay home from a peace rally, something that seldom arose when the kids were little. In another situation, they made a joint decision to seek professional counseling. They describe a family meeting where they all recognized for the first time the gross sexist inequity that still characterized their practice of who makes dinner. Stewardship of material goods "has been the most difficult." When it comes to clothes, shopping, and television, they admit that there is "constant tension" and a need to compromise "between our values and their world and needs." What do they now recommend? They must "lighten up," choose "battles" carefully, negotiate, make "nonnegotiables" clearer, and otherwise let their kids become fuller participants (or nonparticipants) in doing justice. They try to take needs for peer acceptance or beauty or comfort, and even money, "into consideration and not simply to impose our values on our children."

This constant finely tuned negotiation in the doing of justice hones and refines the faith of the adults who attempt to achieve it as much as the children themselves. It forces adults to consider and change their ways, more acutely aware than ever of how their most mundane actions and choices shape justice and the next generation's ability to do justice. One does justice even in the presence of the powerful passions felt toward one's children by teaching, learning about, and indeed struggling over justice with them. Adults raise their own social awareness as they strive to raise socially aware children. In this practice, they turn the private task of raising children into an important public ministry.

Doing Justice at Home

So the family is, as one scholar argues, a "school for critical contribution to the social good." But it is more than this. It is also a "school of justice" unto itself. That is, the family is a school of justice not merely as parents work with children to reach outward to those in need but in its own internal dynamics. Families teach justice by the very way they structure the work and love of daily life.

Our common arrangements of work and love often impede justice, sometimes when we are least aware of it. Consider a few of examples identified by political scientist Susan Moller Okin: "What is a child of either sex to learn about fairness in the average household with two full-time working parents, where the mother does, at the very least, twice as much family work as the father? What is a child to learn about the value of nurturing and domestic work in a home with a traditional division of labor in which the father either subtly or not so subtly uses the fact that he is the wage earner to 'pull rank' on or to abuse his wife?" When parental relationships are unjust—when one person has the final say in decision making, greater economic and social opportunity, or ultimate responsibility for labor in the workplace or home—children learn injustice. When the "first and formative example of adult interaction" is "one of domination and manipulation or of unequal altruism and one-sided self-sacrifice," rather than "one of justice and reciprocity," children are considerably hindered in learning justice.

"It is within the family," Okin argues, "that we first come to have that sense of ourselves and our relations with others that is at the root of moral development." The family must be just, she asserts, if we are to have a just society.

Major Western theories of justice have almost always ignored the family. People ordinarily view family life as simply a matter of love. Over the last two centuries, as the separation between the public and private spheres grew, so did the ideal of the family as a "haven" of affection, intimacy, and love. One fights for justice in the wider society; one seeks love in the privacy of one's home. This dualistic perception has made it extremely difficult to establish relationships of justice within the home.

Feminists of the last two centuries have worked hard to counter this, especially second-wave feminists of the midtwentieth century. Whereas earlier movements focused on changing women's public status and rights, second-wave feminists turn to a new front: justice in the sanctity of the home. In the last several decades, people have tried all sorts of ways to foster greater equality between men and women, from legislating social reform (day care and leave policies) to encouraging individual women to become better negotiators with their domestic partners.

Ultimately none of this will work, argues political philosopher Pauline Kleingeld, until we reconceive the cultural institution of marriage itself. Marriage must be redefined culturally not only as a love relationship but also as a matter of "interpersonal justice." This redefinition does not rule out genuine acts of sacrifice, affection, and passion but invites the intentional pursuit of "fairness and reciprocity in the recognition of each other's interests" and a "just distribution of benefits and burdens." "Just love" is another phrase, similar to mutuality, that many have used to rename love in family life.

Children also learn injustice when they are treated unfairly— something Okin and Kleingeld don't mention. In fact, as we saw in the last chapter, it is not uncommon to overlook what just love may mean for children in attempts to reconfigure the family. Failure to include children as fully as possible, with consideration for their developmental abilities, underestimates their role in just love and household economics.

In the Midst of Chaos

The glorification of maternal sacrifice in family life has been part of the reason children's role in just love has gone unnoticed. Reevaluation of such sacrifice reveals that love for children is never completely selfless, disinterested, and detached from a desire for a return of such love. All parents, if they are honest, hope that over time the love extended to children will become more equally shared. From the beginning our children give to us not only of themselves but also by turning us into new, different, and potentially richer people. Our own parenting efforts "rebound to our credit," observes Catholic ethicist Christine Gudorf. "Failure to provide" for them discredits us. Gudorf and others (including myself) make a theological case for the validity of children's fuller participation in families, suggesting a new meaning for Christian love as Jesus embodied it not in sacrifice but in his invitation to embrace each other in expectation of God's reign.

A similar argument has arisen within psychology. "Babies control and bring up their families as much as they are controlled by them," the famous life-cycle psychologist Erik Erikson observes. "In fact, we may say that the family brings up a baby by being brought up by him." His observation here is part of a broader discussion of the "mutuality of functioning" at each stage of life in which meeting the needs of children (for care, for example) matches the developing needs of the adult (to give care, for example). Mutuality or a "just love" is built into the very structures of healthy growth.

This redefinition also has implications for children's place in household economics that have gone largely unconsidered. A lot of negative comments are made about children of divorce these days. In all this bad press, an important finding goes overlooked. Children with one parent in the household learn quickly what it takes to run a home and quite often how to pitch in. They often learn this because they must. In some cases, the need for their contribution to domestic welfare fosters a greater sense of participation, responsibility, and maturity.

I see this when Mark is away. I ask more from my kids, and they usually come through. I realize then that I have let them down in not regularly expecting more (even though I doubt they would immediately agree!). Distributing the work of the household fairly is difficult,

Doing Justice and Walking Humbly with Kids

however, and sometimes it seems easier just to do some laborious chore than explain and supervise it or argue about it. So I let it slip—and I do a small disservice to my kids, my principles, and myself.

Years ago I talked about this in terms of a new kind of "pitch-in family," borrowing this phrase from a good friend who has asked and expected more of her children in the daily round of family maintenance. For just love to flourish, everyone has to pitch in. "Is not the narrative of the 'pitch-in' family more wholesome than the 'cookies and milk' narrative," I ask, "even if it conjures up images of overt conflicts rather than temporary tranquility? Embodied in this pithy phrase is the idea that given love, children also need daily exercise of the practice of loving others as they love themselves, and this means a family system in which their pitching in is also essential to the family's functioning."

Children need family duties, Rubio says, "not just because they will learn discipline by doing so, but because through this work they will understand that no one in the home exists just to serve them." Even though her children are still young, she tries to tell them that "we work because we feel called to, not because we need the money, that they have to help because we are a team, not because we cannot do it alone, that we expect a lot of them because they have an obligation to engage in loving service, not because it will teach them to be tough." Sometimes God's grace itself inspires our fuller participation in the work of the household.

Both Mark and I cut corners at work and home, giving up our chance for a "good-housekeeping" award as well as the professional eighty-hour work week, but we also expect more of our children. Years ago this meant that "cookies are store-bought, baked at odd hours, or more likely, our kids drag their own stools over to the stove and 'pitch in' . . . to make them, or even the main course." Today, when it means asking our kids to take up less appealing chores, it is harder to recruit them to the tasks we need them to do. Grocery shopping and weeding are not half as much fun as making cookies. But the principle still stands even though it is harder to implement: children need a gradual, incremental transfer of power and responsibility for family welfare as appropriate to age and situation.

Of course, life isn't as harmonious as many of us would like to assume. Just love in families is incredibly sloppy. Family members are not the static, independent, and mature people often presumed in many a discussion. They are children who have needs and cannot fully reciprocate, and adults who in their care for children need the support of others and appropriate means to meet their own needs.

Ultimately, both the impetus and the grace to persist in doing justice within the family and beyond rests on baptism into the Christian community of justice and grace. In the end, Wylie-Kellermann's connection to the Detroit Catholic Worker community sustains his family through long hours of difficult deliberation. They could live where they lived partly because they were close to other faithful families whom their children had known from birth. Parents need the grace of the gospel message and the community's resources, reflections, and encouragement if they are to respond boldly to the imperatives to do justice, to love kindness, and to walk humbly with children before God. These risky, costly commitments are possible only by standing in an immediate relationship to such a community and sharing with it the freedom and promise of resurrection.

Doing Justice and Walking Humbly with Kids

Chapter 7

PLAYING THE FIELD

Xbox, Soccer, and Other Fun Family Games

I had no business running that fast or hard. When I finally stopped to recover in a dark corner, I wondered if this was how people had heart attacks. I was hiding in the interior maze of a local laser tag facility, aiming a gun with flashing lights I didn't really understand and sporting a vest that beeped when I got hit. I had joined one of my kids and his birthday party buddies in the second round of a game the whole concept of which I had adamantly opposed when I first heard about it a few years earlier.

My boys had long since proven the truism that if parents don't allow them guns they'll make them out of just about anything. We'd tried a few ground rules of moderation ("a squirt gun is better than a metal pistol"). But even these had become increasingly hard to enforce. The irony that we struggled to promote nonviolence by keeping fake guns out of our kids' hands while children's exploitation and mortality in real warfare escalated worldwide had not escaped me. I clearly had work to do on many fronts.

Still, there I was, signed in as "Cruella de Ville," hoping to kill more than get killed. I was doing pretty well, second place, to be exact (I should have kept the scorecard; my kids say they don't remember this). More important, I didn't have a heart attack. I had a great time.

This is just one glimpse into the complexity of "play" today. For some, it might be evidence that play has very little to do with faith. Hasn't play moved so far out of the orbit of spirituality—not only in our technological, economically stratified world but also over the long history of Christianity's subtle disdain for embodied fun—that attempting to make this connection is ludicrous?

Playing well, much less playing as a form of spiritual practice, is fraught with challenge. Puritans and modern evangelicals are among the many Christians throughout history who have condemned certain forms of play, such as dance or cards, along with their sensual delights and predictable entanglements. An "obsolete" definition in *Webster's New Collegiate Dictionary* for the noun "play" is, not surprisingly, "sexual intercourse" and "dalliance." Today time pressures, modernity, and adulthood itself present their own unique impediments. Children's play especially has been co-opted by mass media and organized sports. Play is perhaps one of the most fought-over arenas of human activity, yet also one we seldom consider in depth. I am particularly at a loss when I try to think of a recent theologian who has paid much attention to it as a realm of the sacred.

I am struck nonetheless by the life-giving potential of play. My oldest son is upstairs playing drums. He plays well. Years ago I doubt I would have recognized "plays well" as a goal toward which I strive as a parent. But now I see its rich role. Play deeply shapes the texture of our daily life. In the best moments, it opens up space for encounter with God. Figuring out just how and why family play is so important to the life of faith is my task now, a task made more important by the challenges families face.

THE BATTLE OVER PLAY

Families that care about both faith and play face unique problems today. "If the nineteenth-century paradigm of domestic life was the Victorian patriarch at prayer with his wife and children," historian Margaret Bendroth observes, "a century later the dominant image of middle-class family life is a heavily annotated kitchen bulletin board next to a busy telephone." She continues, "It was one thing for Victorians to raise godly children in a relatively static, sheltered institutional setting, with the prospect of daily reinforcement from school and church. But what of parents who compete with schools, sports teams, television sets, and toy manufacturers for their children's time and attention?" The landscape of play has changed immeasurably.

When I talked with a group of people about play as a practice of faith, we had no trouble naming impediments. People shared readily their arduous journey through competitive sports with boys and girls alike: failed attempts to moderate them, loss of weekend and family time, endless practices, obnoxious parents, overly ambitious coaches, and overblown aspirations to play at the "next level." Some had experience with other highly organized "play": drum line, community orchestra, chess competition, even a national bubble gum blowing contest (I am not making this up).

After we moved several years ago, we followed what seemed like good advice, to "enroll your kids in recreational sports; it's a great way to enter the community." So we did. We spent almost all day every Saturday for the next three months at the soccer fields, watching our four-, six-, and nine-year-olds' teams. Life hasn't been quite the same since. Sports took over, you might say. Whether this was faithful play is debatable.

With each child, we faced further decisions about travel teams. Often enough, we caved in. Competitive play consumed more and more time and divided the family, sending Mark and me and each of the boys in different directions to separate events. When we finally had a free weekend one fall several years ago and wanted to do a family camping trip in one of the many state parks that surround us, everyone was too tired. We haven't gone camping since then.

I have often said that I let my son play travel sports for fun and friends. But research suggests my intention is foiled. Pleasure and friendship—elements central to good play—are often superseded in organized sports by the pursuit of skill, personal advancement, and a chance to play at a higher level. These goals become so important, in fact, that we don't even recognize other values any more. Saying that one plays soccer—or, similarly, a musical instrument—just for the fun of it seems to lack seriousness. It suggests that one isn't among the better players who play to compete, dominate, and win.

This may not be what kids want or need. "Clearly there is often a gap" one study reports, "between what players think is fun and what the coaches try to convince them is fun." Coaches often say that hard work will lead to fun in the long run when the team wins, or that drills designed around competition and competence are fun in themselves. But when the researcher asked fourth through eighth grade players themselves why they played, none identified a desire to improve or learn self-discipline. They all said they played for fun. Kids, the report concludes, have "numerous concerns and interests that go beyond what adults have in mind for them." Most enjoyed playing more when coaches and adults left them alone.

Play is often controlled by adults, however, and structured to promote the success of individual children. It absorbs an inordinate amount of time, but this time is spent less in imaginative, creative play than in activities that require the work of both child and adult, such as purchasing proper apparel and equipment, getting to events, raising funds, and performing publicly. Winning and losing, as one parent noted, are no longer woven into the larger fabric of ongoing community. Instead the "parents and kids don't even know each other and they go their separate ways immediately after the event." So the loss or win is "never balanced out over the long haul, with everyone taking turns in each role." Kids don't learn larger life skills of gathering neighborhood friends together, negotiating rules and boundaries, beginning and ending the game, discovering other values besides a win or loss, and so forth. Nor do adults have time to play with their kids or with other adults. We mostly watch, applaud, and in our worst moments become belligerent toward other adults, whether the opponent or those refereeing, judging, or otherwise overseeing the "play."

When values of competition, domination, and winning color children's play, other temptations arise for adults. I have to fight the inclination to measure the playing time and success of my sons versus those of other kids. I try to stay calm as I sit near parents who yell only for their own kid, and then I try to stop myself from doing the same.

I watch parents chide their kids in a relentless attempt to get "better play" out of them and try to resist such tactics. I am tempted to believe that the higher the level at which my kids play the better they are (or I am) even though I know this isn't true. I have sat on both sides of the fence, as the parent of a child left on the bench and the parent of a child (sometimes the same child) who gets lots of time on the field. I know the insidious way both experiences pervert the healthful benefits of genuine play and foster obsessive patterns of anxiety about a child's success. Distorted motives, especially promotion of one's own kid and oneself through a child, distort play and prevent play from serving any positive role in fostering joy, freedom, or faith.

Sports teams often compete directly with time that might be spent in a better way. Ironically, just now, as I make final revisions to this chapter, my husband calls. We have the high school basketball schedule in hand and we see, with dismay, if our son wants to be serious about playing he will miss church camp, and at one of the most important times during the first years of high school. Travel sports have already kept him from regular attendance at church and youth group. We wonder, as do many parents, about the long-term trade-offs. Play is ultimately no substitute for worship.

Equally challenging, nearly every parent of a boy with whom I've spoken in the last several years has stories to tell about staving off mind-numbing hours of video games—Nintendo, Play Station, or Xbox—or about forbidding violent games, only to have kids play them at someone else's house instead. Of course, we adults tend to ignore our own comparable technological play habits. We have the prerogative of overlooking the amount of time we ourselves spend on the Internet, e-mail, and computer. Once I watched a mother tell her son to turn his Gameboy off at the beginning of Sunday morning worship—and then spend the rest of the service on her own Palm Pilot.

At some point, I realized we are no longer talking about minor incidental choices but an entire pattern of life gone awry. As a father of four children and professor of systematic theology, Richard Gaillardetz has observed a similar major change in his own family life. "As our family began to grow," he writes, "and our lives became more hectic, I gradually sensed a change in the 'ecology' of our home: Was it the purchase of a second TV set, a second VCR, the 'family' computer, or, first one, then two cell phones? I do remember ruminating about my purchase of a cookbook entitled *Thirty-Minute Meals* and feeling relatively guilty about saying that I baked bread when in fact I was using an automated bread-making machine! All I know is that in spite of the shared commitment of my wife and me to our vocation as parents, something precious in our lives seemed to be seeping out of our family life."

One does not have to read too far between the lines to guess that he probably marched into the family room, tripped over all the Xbox control cords, and lost it. Or at least that's what I imagine him doing—yelling "turn it all off!"—because this is what we have done, usually after forgetting to proactively deliver our more reasoned speech on the ill effects of too much computerized gaming and the need to set a time limit.

Drawing on social philosopher Albert Borgmann, Gaillardetz traces how technological "devices" have reshaped the very texture of family life. A modern device is something created through technology, such as fast food and electric heating, to expedite satisfaction of essential human needs. But such devices meet our needs for sustenance and shelter in a way that disconnects us from the finely woven fabric of the natural and human world.

Devices "commodify" the goods we need—heat or food, for example—by allowing us to purchase them without getting involved in their production. To get more heat, we merely adjust the thermostat; we don't leave the house, find wood, learn from others how to chop it, join others near the fire to stay warm, and coordinate meals and bedtime around its available warmth. Heat thus becomes an "abstraction," argues theologian Vincent Miller. Miller finds this pattern disturbing because it hides from us "consumers" some important truths about our human need, our place in nature, and our dependence on the labor of others. "Commodities appear on the scene, as if descended from heaven, cloaked in an aura of self-evident value, saying nothing about how, where, and by whom they were produced." Needs are satisfied without engaging people and the world from which each good arises. We now have access to food without preparation, stereo music without musicians, Internet information without librarians, and treadmill exercise without setting a foot outside.

Play itself has also been commodified; that is, it has been extracted from its relational context and transformed into something that can be controlled, packaged, bought, sold, and exchanged. In many cases, it has become one more consumer product available only to those with money. If you go into a major athletic store, you'll notice sportswear is now segregated by activity: bike gear, tennis attire, running clothes, etc. One cannot play, the market seems to decree, without the proper accouterments. Real play costs.

Play is commodified in other ways as well. New play devices, such as laser-tag centers, video games, and even organized sport leagues, seem to have a mind of their own, invading our lives and operating like a machine over which we have little control and to which we often feel we have to submit. Television and video games are also prime examples of "abstraction" as Miller defined it: by the simple turn of a switch we enter a "reality" more vivid than the one that actually surrounds us, a reality that places no demands on us and creates no authentic human interaction. It is particularly troubling that violence is so often rampant within these abstract worlds of so-called reality. My sons and I regularly debate just how much watching violent movies or playing video games designed around shooting an enemy shapes them. Even if they think they can resist its influence, game and media violence has had adverse effects on kids, including an impact on the rise in horrific school shootings.

Repetitious ritual, whether game playing or doing e-mail, forms us and our spiritual lives, and not always for the good. When I look at my three sons, I see a difference in the range of interests among them that goes beyond personality difference and is based, at least in part, on the age at which each one first encountered video games as a regular part of his daily diet. The son who started playing games later plays them less and innovates more. He is, essentially, less "addicted" (though Mark and I hate to put it this way). When he plays video games, he doesn't play long because he usually has other activities and friends awaiting him.

This pattern of play has a longer history. When he was in elementary school, he and another friend spent hours hovered over notebooks of basketball cards and Pokemon cards, creating fictional narratives and figuring out fair trades. They'd drift from that to escapades in the neighborhood on bike, rollerblade, or skateboard. Later I'd find them hunched over their Lego and Playmobil sets, creating imaginary scenes of cities under construction, search-and-rescue missions, and cowboy adventures. He made steady use of an art supply box filled with sequins, glue, ribbon, fingerpaint, chalk, buttons, doilies. When it snowed or poured, he was often the first outside to sled, dam up the stream, or skim a board across the puddles, and just as often the last to come in. He still engages in a rich range of creative play, from hiking up the wooded hill behind our house to composing music to recording humorous video acts with his good friends. It is hard not to worry that my other two have missed the opportunity to develop less damaging, more faithful and creative ways to engage each other and the world in play, a plight that weighs on me, raising questions about my own beleaguered patterns of play.

Transforming Play from Within

Once when I expressed frustration to one of my best friends about my constant battle against all the cultural pressures that seem to work against parents (dart guns, organized sports, video games, scary Disney movies), I was surprised by her response. "I never expected support from society," she remarked, a bit amazed by the confidence with which I did.

Later that year, I learned why not. For the first time, I experienced the Christmas season through the eyes of her five- and two-year-old Jewish daughter and son. Christian symbols and their aberrations were everywhere. Piped-in carols, wreaths and shining stars, shopping day countdown, and honey-baked ham filled stores, schools, streets, and homes. One night after our families had eaten together, she suggested singing a few common Christmas hymns. She knew all the words, sometimes better than I did. How did she manage to convey the richness of her own Jewish tradition and its holidays, beliefs, and practices to her kids? It wasn't easy. But she was "used to" battling culture, she said. I realized then how much I presumed—wrongly as it turns out—that wider culture would bolster my efforts to raise my children.

Many people are surprised to discover that society does not support their efforts to raise faithful children. But even those in communities versed in protecting their children from social hostility and marginalization—Jewish, Catholic, and African American, for example—now struggle to sustain faith commitments. Some say adults are trying to raise children in a toxic environment or a society that wages war against families. Although disease and war imagery seem extreme, parents often feel under attack.

A common reaction is to reject culture entirely. "We simply got rid of our television," one woman said. Others opt out of organized play entirely. It is tempting to react to distortions of play by defining culture as the enemy.

Moves to eliminate television, video games, and organized play will not fully resolve our problems, however. It is hard to reverse the tide and go back in time. Besides, as contemporary people we benefit greatly from the same technological advances that create these problems. So we need to ask, Is there another way forward short of opting out?

A typology in a classic text of the midtwentieth century, *Christ and Culture,* offers a suggestive road map. Protestant theologian H. Richard Niebuhr identifies five answers to the perennial challenge of living one's faith within culture. At two ends of the spectrum are "Christ against culture" and "Christ of culture." The former sees human culture as opposed to Christ and withdraws from it (monastics, modern-day sectarians). The latter affirms culture as compatible with Christ's truth and embraces it (Enlightenment Christians). By contrast, three other types "mediate" or try to put the two often-conflicting authorities of faith and culture in some kind of deeper relationship. Niebuhr summarizes these types as "Christ above culture," "Christ and culture in paradox," and "Christ transforming culture."

It is ultimately the last—the conviction that God saves both in and through a grace-filled conversion of mundane, fallen existence—

that provides a guiding light for rehabilitating play as a potential realm of faith. The model of Christ transforming culture suggests a way to be in the world but not of it, a way to practice faith within (rather than moving outside) the culture within which we live—including even its distorted forms of play.

For many people with whom I talked, simply airing their turmoil and frustration was itself a healthy first step of mediation and moderation. As with consciousness raising in political movements, it dispelled the feeling that this was a problem with no name, that we are alone in our bewilderment, and that there is no hope or recourse. "Technology's ability to influence us so profoundly," Gaillardetz contends, "lies in its pervasive 'hiddenness'; we are often blind to the subtle ways it shapes our view of, and interaction with, our world." It helps to become aware of what he calls our "silent and generally unreflective conspiracy" with the very technology that troubles us. The same can be said about contemporary forms of play. Talking about the way today's play subtly shapes our view of the world challenges the notion that how we play has nothing to do with faith.

A second, equally important step is to revitalize forms of play capable of resisting the destructive patterns of contemporary devices. They are not bad in themselves. Problems arise when they crowd out the things, events, and practices that draw us into any deeper realm of meaning and relationship. Borgmann and Gaillardetz use the term *focal* to describe these valuable centers of meaning.

Focal practices, such as tending a wood-burning stove or preparing a meal, meet the same physical needs as devices: they produce heat and nourishment. But they also invoke a rich set of skills and practices—collecting wood, stoking the fire, cutting up vegetables, and setting the table, for example. These bring us into interaction with nature (to gather wood) and other people (to learn how to chop wood). Such practices enforce a shared rhythm of life for a family (maintenance of the fire determined when people gathered together and when they went to bed). Focal practices also honor "more mundane human activities"—the very daily chores and burdensome interactions that technology itself devalues and tries to eliminate—"as a possible arena for experiencing God's presence." Through the "positive and intentional

IN THE MIDST OF CHAOS

cultivation of vital focal practices," one recognizes the negative impact of technology and also learns to resist it, "even as we make appropriate use" of it. A family's efforts to share meals, for example, might be enhanced by a gas range and electric dishwasher but destroyed if each family member orders pizza or runs out for fast food whenever they feel like it.

A few years ago, we remodeled the family room that adjoins our kitchen, replacing some of our furniture from graduate school days. We had a television in a back room. Did we want to put one here? Now was our chance. After much deliberation we scrapped the idea and held out hope of reserving this room for conversation and reading. This turned out well. It didn't stop us from watching television or the kids from playing video games. But it set limits on both and preserved space for other valued practices.

Revitalizing play as a practice of faith today calls for a steady and demanding discernment, moderation, proactivity, and repentance. These four steps constitute the recovery and transformation of play as a focal practice of faith. What Gaillardetz says about technology can basically be said about play itself. We must discern its negative impact so we can resist it "even as we make appropriate use" of many forms of play. We must seek the fine line of moderation between addiction and complete rejection, limiting the time spent playing video games or the number of organized activities per season. We must proactively and conscientiously pursue alternative forms of play that shape a richer household ecology and work against those that breed isolation, self-centeredness, and violence. Ultimately, we must repent and acknowledge our tendency toward perverting the best qualities of play, whether in response to social pressure or as a result of our own brokenness.

RECLAIMING PLAY AS FOCAL PRACTICE

When I first began thinking about how to sustain faith amid the chaos of family life, neither play nor reading (the next chapter) came immediately to mind. It took a good friend to point out what seemed

Playing the Field

second-nature to me: "People in your family," she said, "play and read a lot." I hadn't really stopped to notice.

Few Thanksgivings go by when I don't think fleetingly that I'm late for the "turkey bowl" and then realize, a bit deflated, that we don't play turkey bowl any more. I wonder if my two brothers experience this. Like the stimulus-response of Pavlov's dog, when my family got together with the Olcotts, our close family friends, we played. We—adults and children together—played Hearts and Oh Hell, we played Wiffle ball in the side yard, we took joint trips to major league baseball games, theme parks, and zoos. And we played turkey bowl. Even though I don't like football, touch or tackle, I'd show up in sweats and mittens with my brothers every November, rain or shine, to divide the Miller-Olcott brood and any welcomed interlopers into lopsided teams.

All this playing filled many good purposes. We never dwelled on them or even spelled them out. But we knew deeply and thoroughly, without having to define them, the lessons of fun, vigor, joy, happiness, defeat, recovery, conflict, arbitration, reconciliation, camaraderie, sensual energy, touch, tackle, and roll.

Born and raised a Hoosier, along with other Indiana soulmates I believe in basketball. My brothers and I went to Big Ten basketball and football games with my parents about as regularly as church. I've weathered more than my fair share of dinner conversations (family members, are you reading this?) on NCAA score predictions or, for a big change of pace, the play-by-play of the seventh (or eighth, or ninth) golf hole. Some kids take a break from church during their college years. I took a vacation from sports.

Then I had three boys. I'm back scoring runs, hits, outs, baskets, assists, and rebounds, a skill acquired under duress (how else to get through one more game?) that I never expected to be in such high demand from my kids' coaches.

By preference more than protest, I branched out. I drifted to less competitive play as early as I saw the opportunity, and I'm still exploring. I designed elaborate living quarters in cigar boxes for my "wishnicks" dolls or in the field behind our house for my friends and me. I swam, biked, and went to every wilderness, canoe, and backpacking camp our regional church youth program offered. I had my most vivid experiences of God through the practice of playing outside at various church camps, whether on prayer walks with "morning watch" booklets to guide us, hiking through old established forests, building a fire to make dinner, or singing together at night's end. Such play invoked God's presence without pretense or superficiality. It brought us into conversation about life's meaning and put our minor troubles into proper perspective.

I hear only episodically about what my kids do at their church camp now: skits with outrageous costumes and jokes, mud football when it rains, an educational role play about world wealth and hunger in which each unit portrays a continent. But I suspect they find God within the alternative practices of play that church camp inspires, just as I did.

Shortly after Mark and I got married, his mom asked him to clear the last box of his stuff out of her house. Rummaging through the box, he found a picture from one of the church camps he had attended in high school. He handed it to me. When I looked at it, I recognized the picture immediately. I was in the same picture.

Although it might be extreme to put it this way, I fell in love with my husband because I saw him as someone who knew how to play. Mark's play ran the gamut. Only a few days ago, he regaled our boys at the dinner table with decades-old stories of his antics on a beleaguered Divinity School intramural baseball team. This was better than his tales of boyhood pranks I worried my sons would replicate. He used to subscribe to *The Funny Times,* a magazine of jokes and humor, and he still regularly reads comics (all references to "Zits" cartoons I owe to him). I'd hear peals of laughter from the back room when he was watching *The Three Stooges* with our three boys (a male bonding experience, I decided). He also plays around with a guitar, a mandolin, and several (too many?) banjos, and he likes some of the same outdoor activities that I do. His mom gave him a canoe on his birthday after we moved closer to so many navigable streams. He taught our first cat to fetch a wad of paper (and worried I'd be a poor mother because I wasn't entertained). He invented "stairball" when our kids were young enough to find it challenging to try to block his shot up the steps past them (you'll have to ask them the rules).

I, in turn, have kept dabbling. Right after we moved, my youngest son and I signed up for ice skating lessons (I needed a cold fix in the snowless midsouth, and I needed time with my son who was spending longer hours in child care). I have toyed with horseback riding, followed my oldest son and church youths onto the ski slopes (and fell in love with the speed, cold, mountain views, and bodily thrill), and will try to run my first half marathon next weekend (although I'm not sure I'd call that play).

When I told Mark about this chapter, he asked whether I would describe "underdog," a sing-song game of duck-and-run-under-the-swing that I made up as I sent our kids soaring during our many park outings. We loved the many small parks where we lived when our kids were young, theme parks when our children grew older, and Lake Michigan and Florida beaches. All of them served a similar purpose. They have been wonderful places to renew family bonds, exert energy, and spend time in fun and enjoyment with the hope of a glimpse of joy and grace. They have been places of creation, re-creation, and even resurrection, vanquishing woes and worries and freeing us for better, more faithful living.

I don't think we're unique in any of this. All children and adults—across time and culture, and under harsh circumstances—play. Nor, on the other hand, is our family exemplary. There are forms of play we've neglected—dressing up, putting on plays and musicals, acting out imagined stories or stories from books and movies—perhaps partly because I've lived with brothers and sons. Sometimes our children don't play well when they could or should. As adults Mark and I too often forget to play, and playing together has gotten increasingly harder as our kids grow. I don't have time (or think I don't). I don't like what my kids play (video games rank right up there with guns). I can't play with them because I don't understand (laser gun, computer game, remote control machines) or they have far exceeded me (basketball, guitar, skiing).

Nonetheless, even if our play isn't optimal or the only kind of good play, I recognize deeply embedded in the sheer mechanics of family life just how play serves as a rich practice of faith. Defining play—much less, faithful play—is no easy task. I turned to the dictionary for a snappy definition when I began this chapter and discovered that *play* occupies a rather large space. But no definition hit the nail on the head so that I could say, "Ah, yes, that's play!" or "That isn't."

Play involves immense pleasure, even joy, of a holistic sort. Mind, body, spirit—all are engaged together. Sometimes play results in the visible, tangible sensations of a smile, laughter, muscle ache, or cleansing breath. Play has rich interpersonal and intergenerational potential, connecting us deeply to others, and is wonderful when done together in a communal or cooperative context. But play also involves activity done by oneself. One must be able to play well alone in order to play well with others. Play sparks and fuels imagination and creativity. It suspends reality but doesn't supersede it. It can transform reality. It involves an attitude of delight and enjoyment—an embodiment of joy—as much as specific activity. In fact, any playful act can become work if the pleasure dissipates. Everyone should have equal access to play, regardless of talent, wealth, or the right outfit. Genuine play does not harm those playing or others around them.

I didn't develop these criteria to judge video games or organized sports or any other form of play. But in each case they furnish a means for assessment. They suggest why I am less enamored by play that resembles a commodified device rather than a focal practice. These criteria criticize play that heightens our inclination toward violence, as some video games do; or that disconnects us from our body, each other, nature, and reality, diminishing or even destroying the rich potential of play as a practice of faith.

This, of course, is not always the case with video games or organized sports. Lasting friendships can arise through travel soccer—as one parent attested, forming for her family a genuine network of support. One of my sons has built a large circle of friends by playing on teams together. The church youth play on a basketball league because playing together cultivates fellowship and offers renewal of faith. I myself have witnessed creation of community when kids haul televisions to our house, hook them up to each other and several video consoles, and enter into a huge boisterous game of video hide-and-seek, otherwise known as "Halo," a battle strategy game. Critics have overlooked the extensive cooperation, collaboration, and companionship between kids trying to beat a game as well as the mastery required and the self-esteem it offers kids.

Keeping an eye on the deeper values of play, however, helps reveal where and why games like Halo often fall short (just in case my sons read this someday and want to know why I yelled) and how we can redeem play's best practices. Because play deeply shapes the habits of our daily lives and because our ordinary proclivity to play is deeply connected at so many levels to our religious capacity and need, identifying play's faithful components becomes all the more important.

Play as a faith practice involves the whole person in body, mind, and spirit; it brings meaningful connection to nature and other persons; it allow us to confront life's limits and failures; and it offers a glimpse of grace. In its unique power to create, re-create, and resurrect, play embodies essential facets of God's relationship to the world and of our relationships with God and each other.

PLAY AS CREATION

When I was a new mother, I spent what seemed like hours with my five-week-old son making faces simply to elicit a smile. I'd lay him face up on my knees, lean over, and smile. He'd smile back. Miraculous! I thought. But now I see, gladly, that this play is nearly universal.

All life begins with play. Parents of newborns and adults who see babies know this. When adults spy a tiny infant, the first thing they do is make silly expressions to evoke a smile. Antics designed to evoke that smile, on the part of adults *and* children alike, are a fundamental form of play. Initial efforts to connect with each one of my infant children centered around play. Peek-a-boo, this-little-piggy, horsy rides, tossing in the air, rocking—all are primal acts of playful interaction that draw the child and the adult into life. These acts fall on a continuum with later acts of hiding, chasing, strolling, spinning, pushing on a swing, and turning on a merry-go-round.

Even animals know this. They practice play as an act of creation. Kittens pounce on string; puppies tussle. In play, they rehearse life's calling: hunting, fighting, mating, retrieving, herding. Play also forms us vocationally for roles we may assume and purposes we may pursue.

Our eighty-five-pound chocolate lab, Kelsey, offers daily lessons on pure sport. When I can barely rally enthusiasm for our two-mile nature trail circuit every morning, she bounces, bounds, prances, and pants with anticipation. So I try to cheer up, follow her, and welcome the day's play. She reminds me how integral play is to creation and to humans as part of God's creation and God's own being.

Various periods of religious history, however, have regarded this creative aspect of play with suspicion. "Pamper a child, and he will frighten you; play with him and he will give you grief. Do not laugh with him, lest you have sorrow with him, and in the end you will gnash your teeth" (Sirach 30:9–10). Such was the advice on play from an apocryphal or noncanonical book similar to Proverbs. Many centuries later, John Wesley, founder of Methodism, said pupils in his school "ought never to play," reflecting the tenor of his times (though it is worth noting that he himself did not see a problem with enjoying all kinds of games as an adult). Not surprisingly, few theologians over the course of history have considered play a component of creation and a practice of faith. This is a shame, perhaps owing to the association of God with rest or stasis and play with forbidden sensual pleasure or indulgence and pampering.

Contemporary research offers a helpful corrective. Cultural historian Johan Huizinga, a modern master scholar of play, argues that to be human is to play. In fact, he renames our species *Homo ludens,* or "man as player," because he sees play as foundational to human creativity and growth. From child play evolve adult forms of law, politics, art, and religion. Practices of faith, even the liturgy itself, exist in direct continuity with play.

Contemporary psychologists have also noticed this. The play of early eye contact between parent and infant creates a trustworthy world for both participants. This playful ritual actually enhances our potential to experience religious transcendence later in life and shapes our images of God. A positive view of the creative role of play was an important leap beyond the approach of Sigmund Freud, father of psychoanalysis. Where Freud viewed play as closely linked to masturbation and instinctual drive, life cycle theorist Erik Erikson believed that children used toys and play to act out "much more than they could possibly say or probably know 'in that many words.'" Where Freud saw dreams as the "royal road" to the human psyche, Erikson saw play. Children "express and confess" a great deal through their play, he argues. Health itself, British psychoanalyst D. W. Winnicott says, is a "state of being able to play." Illness is "not being able to play."

I once watched a video made by a friend who, in Erikson's legacy, teaches play therapy. She had asked permission to video my four-year-old son to demonstrate play techniques. With only Play-Doh, she learned more about his struggles with our recent move across the country than I could ever have suspected. If I had stopped to listen more closely to his play, I realized, I might have learned a great deal—maybe more than I wanted to know at the time.

Play creates "protected space," or a smaller and more "manageable world," which is particularly important for children's development. Children need this "intermediate reality between phantasy and actuality" to dramatize and master problems. Play is especially important for learning language. One cannot begin to acquire language "with intelligence or confidence," says theologian Rowan Williams, without play or the freedom to "make utterances that I *don't* have to answer for." He continues, "We do not treat children as adult speakers whom we expect to take straightforward responsibility for what they say according to recognisable conventions: we accept that there is a *sphere of legitimately irresponsible talking,* of fantasy and uninhibited role-playing, language without commitments beyond the particular game being played."

Adults also need space and time in the intermediate place of play between fantasy and reality. They need spheres of legitimate irresponsibility too. The boundaries of play create a space where we do not have to answer for all our words and actions, or feel paralyzed by fear of making a mistake or of being bound by thoughtless or ignorant actions. It prepares us for a more serious staking of our claims.

Play constitutes the very building blocks of growth and faith. To grow and thrive, healthy children create "transitional objects," Winnicott observes. A transitional object is a playful, imaginative way of embodying the loved parent. The child plays with reality in order to endure its frustrations, disappointments, and limits. He creates from a blanket or a teddy bear an object of love and solace that lies somewhere between baby and mother and is neither completely reality nor completely illusion. This major developmental achievement, occurring between four and twelve months, serves a fundamental creative role throughout adult life. We move from infantile play with transitional objects, asserts Winnicott, to "shared playing" in adolescence to the creative play of engaging in cultural life (including religious ritual) in adulthood.

Play can also bring us to the edges of life. There is often a fine line between playful connection and destructive aggression, as there is between laughter and ridicule, sport and torment, or competition and combat. Kids and adults often use creative play and games to simulate a cosmic struggle between good and bad or life and death. Play exposes us to failure, loss, finitude, and destruction without serious risk. So sometimes it is possible that even laser tag has a certain relative place, as controlled play with risk, death, and triumph.

GODLY PLAY AS EXAMPLE

Today another kind of proverbial wisdom issues forth from one corner of the theological world that runs something like this: "Play and laugh often with your children, lest you have sorrow. Playing creates meaning and makes space for God." Jerome Berryman stands out for his innovative appreciation for the creative role of play in religious education. His approach, what he calls "Godly play," is a way of engaging children with faith through play. Berryman, who is a trained Montessori educator, has been powerfully influenced by the extensive work he did in Rome with Sofia Cavalletti, one of the first to apply Montessori methods to religious education. He first saw her demonstrate how young children might encounter God through story, parable, and symbol in 1970, and this has been his life work ever since.

In "Godly play," children are greeted at the door and invited into a circle. On the shelves around the edge of the room are carefully arranged boxes, baskets, and trays filled with many intriguing things: articles to be used in telling biblical stories, art materials, candles, colored cloths, materials representing the liturgical seasons, symbols of baptism and communion, and so forth. A single lesson might focus, for example, on the parable of the mustard seed. After introducing the lesson, the adult leader retrieves the parable box and slowly reveals the articles from which the story will unfold: a yellow cloth, a green felt tree, a cardboard figure, some birds, and a mustard seed so small you can't see it. The leader speaks calmly, slowly, leaving lots of room for kids to enter into the story imaginatively, add to it, ask questions, and in essence play with it. The leader then invites each child to choose a way in which to play with and engage that or any other lesson, making something about its felt importance with paints, clay, wood scrapes, cloth pieces, or other materials. The play concludes with a "feast"—cookies and juice celebrated with simple prayer. Laughter, playfulness, wonder, mystery, freedom, and living deeply in each moment are constants of the entire process.

Play is an avenue through which children can create meaning and find language to communicate their religious ideas and hopes. Given the chance, Berryman believes, kids will play with four big-picture questions: death, life's meaning, freedom, and aloneness. In its "direct, active encounter with the Creator in the midst of real nature, real people, and the real self," such play offers a needed alternative to dominant forms of play that allow little room for creativity and interaction. With story, figurines, symbols, art supplies, space, and time, children explore their own answers and encounter God through laughter and play.

PLAY AS RE-CREATION AND RESURRECTION

The guru of the "hurried" child, psychologist David Elkind, says children, like adults, now "work much more than they play and this is the reason that they are so stressed." I agree with him that adults often overprogram children's lives and ruin their play. But I also think that this nostalgia for a time when "unhurried" children "played" perpetuates an unhelpful portrait of play.

Western models of play of the last century have romanticized children's activity and created a false bifurcation between playing children and working adults, and even more broadly between work as "productive" and play as "unproductive." Such definitions are a problem for both adults and children. The view of work as valuable only in what it produces and play as valuable in itself distorts the complexity of hard productive play and satisfying unproductive work. Play is both unproductive and productive, done for its own sake but also rich in consequence.

Since we don't live in the best of all worlds most of the time, however, there is indeed a difference between play and work. Play does have its own distinctive contribution. Although sometimes my work is my play, at a certain point I also simply have to work on this chapter, for example—through the drudgery, tedium, frustration, and real labor, hoping for the next oasis of play.

These oases afford a quality of freedom and renewal where I forget myself and enter into the task more fully. The game takes over. I lose track of time. Cultural theorist Mihali Csikszentmihalyi dubs this experience in which one is focused, even transfixed, "flow." Flow is the "holistic sensation present when we act with total involvement" or a "state in which action follows action according to an internal logic which seems to need no conscious intervention on our part." Flow happens when my husband, kids, and I build mountains and tunnels in the sand at the beach or ride the waves. Flow is what captivates me about skiing despite its extravagance and expense.

The experience of flow is not exactly within our control, though people have found ways to nurture it. In this evasive quality, flow and play are a lot like grace as Christians have long understood it. Sometimes flow (and maybe grace) comes after long hours of mastery of the skills characteristic of a particular activity, whether rock climbing, writing, or praying. Sometimes flow is fostered by good ritual that suspends time temporarily through careful creation of sacred space and time. Mostly flow surprises us.

In the flow of play, Huizinga argues, the awareness that we are "embedded in a sacred order of things finds its first, highest, and holiest expression." The experience of disclosure in religious revelation, observes philosopher Hans-Georg Gadamer, is also like the act of playing a game. When we truly enter into a game, we lose our usual self-consciousness. As the game "plays us," we find ourselves gripped by a "happening, a disclosure" that has the power to transform and renew.

In fact, on one level all liturgy is play. Effective liturgy invites us to enter another world and story, resist the power of death, practice the reign of God, and return to life rejuvenated. Particularly "when we celebrate the Eucharist," says Irish theologian Anne Thurston, "we act out and momentarily are a risen people." Play lets us "live the life we desire. Play prepares us for the future. Play believes in the resurrection. . . . Play, and liturgy, give us a different time-scale as we brush up against the timeless moments of eternity." In play and liturgy, sacred space and time is marked out and inhabited.

One of the powerfully transformative aspects of play is its liminal character. The one who plays is so completely immersed in the created world of the game or the activity that one loses a sense of time, place, boundaries, and rules. Anthropologist Victor Turner coined liminality to talk about the middle or transitional phase of significant rites of passage, such as coming-of-age rituals or weddings. But he also recognized that liminality appears most powerfully today in play, an arena not conventionally seen as sacred or religious.

Games, whether football or fantasy, are often structured so as to put the player on the boundary or threshold. Play epitomizes the human capacity to mark off an imagined scene in a circumscribed sphere (card table, field, stage, court, sanctuary) as a place to encounter the sacred. Play allows us to endow ordinary objects—deck of cards, ball, piece of clay, musical instrument, or bread and grape juice—with specific, symbolic meanings that represent far more than the objects themselves. The practice of play—the creation of designated boundaries, the special place for players only, particular dress and pageantry, control over the clock and time, specific physical exertion and concentration—all simulate and create feelings of liminality.

One finds oneself in the liminal "betwixt-and-between, neither-this-nor-that," a place often suggestive of and open to transformation and encounter with the sacred. After we genuinely play, we feel different than before, refreshed, renewed, born again. We are often freed from what constrained us to live an alternative story glimpsed in our play.

I remember attending parent day in the elementary school gym class one year. The teacher's chosen game was "battle ball," better known to old-timers like me as a combination of dodge ball and capture the flag. Parents were expected to join in. So I did (though only for my son's sake, of course). I didn't really feel like playing, or so I thought. Soon, however, I got caught up in the game with (once again) heart-attack-threatening abandon. I had forgotten just how much fun it is run, jump, throw, dodge, and move. In its re-creative capacity, play not only "matures us when we are young"; it can make "us young when we are old," as Berryman observes.

Living with children keeps play alive, and we adults are fortunate when kids invite us to run in this direction. Sometimes my son says, "You *never* get *in* the pool." He implies that I have sadly forsaken play and all its gifts. That *is* a sad development. I used to love to swim. Trips to the public pool, my mom recalls, served as her chief summertime relief from three small kids. I spent many happy hours submerged. In college I swam laps, succumbing to the adult tendency to regiment play. Now the water just seems cold. Adulthood and age can inhibit play. Adulthood by definition involves growing up, out, and weary of play. Adults outgrow some of the best kinds of play, in much the same way that our capacity for wonder fades, as part of living longer and growing older, assuming responsibility for others, or maybe as part of human fallenness itself. But then along comes a child, not simply reminding us but *inviting* us to play.

In other words, playing draws us into creation, heals, and resurrects. It re-creates. Play demonstrates the "capacity of the ego to find . . . self-cure," says Erikson. "Playing is itself a therapy," Winnicott remarks.

Scripture also envisions play and child play in transformative roles at the beginning and end of time. In hymns of creation, the Psalmist pictures God as a God of play, a God who laughs, plays, and cavorts, not just a God of "rest." In Psalm 104, God creates the sea animal Leviathan for no other reason than pure "sport": "There go the ships, and Leviathan that you formed to sport in it" (104:26). In other places, the Psalmist invites us to praise God through play—singing forth a "new song," playing "skillfully on the strings with loud shouts" (33:3).

Wisdom itself, personified as a divine female force, plays "like a child," acting in creation right beside God as God's "delight, rejoicing" in the beauty of the world and "delighting in the human race" (Proverbs 8:30–31). In turn, the prophet Isaiah depicts God's reign to come, paradise regained, through the image of a child at play in ultimate vulnerability and extreme safety: "The nursing child shall play over the hole of the asp, and the weaned child shall put its hand on the adder's den" (Isaiah 11:8). Is it possible that Jesus himself welcomed children precisely because they play? Doesn't the imperative to "become like children" (Matthew 18:3) have something essential to do with prizing playfulness as a part of rejoicing in God's love? With children in play, we practice the freedom of the Garden and the laughter of resurrection, imaginatively resisting the powers that seek to define, capture, and destroy us.

Chapter 8

TAKE, READ
From Seuss to Scripture

"I'm not going to bother to read the book," my nephew announced. "I'm just going to wait until the movie comes out." An avid reader myself, I didn't exactly gasp when he said this. But I did laugh. It spoke a thousand words about today's temptations *not* to read.

The latest Harry Potter book had just appeared. Several cousins were talking about all the hype and seeing who had read the furthest (and knew the secret of which character dies). I was happy to see that reading was not a completely vanishing art. All these children, youths, and adults reading Potter had impressed me. Book sales in general have been rising in recent years.

Yet my nephew spoke for lots of people when he said he'd just wait and watch instead of read. The same factors that disrupt the practice of play—technology, fast-paced living and lack of time, consumerism and the consumption of highly desirable alternative forms of play, and poverty—now challenge what seems like the solitary, slow-paced, old-fashioned, elitist practice of reading. Reading becomes a chore, narrowly associated with school and privilege.

Why did my heart sink just a little when I heard my nephew's remark? The Harry Potter movies and lots of other book-inspired movies are wonderful (not to mention those special effects—they're something). What, then, makes reading a book sometimes better than watching the movie? Why do I want my kids to love reading and always have a book they've just started or finished? Why do I see helping other kids and adults read as a ministry of sorts?

If you have gotten this far, then it seems you like to read. You likely agree with my conviction: the practice of reading forms and changes lives. But how does it do so? More important, what characteristics make reading a rich practice in an active life of faith? Are there particular strategies of reading as a faith practice within families?

PEOPLE OF THE WORD

Tolle, lege; tolle, lege. "Take, read." These words mark St. Augustine's conversion in 386, as he himself tells the story in *The Confessions.* These words—"Take, read"—shaped not only his life; they have also shaped mine. They planted a seed of spiritual truth for Western Christianity: in reading, one may hear God's voice.

Augustine was tormented, struggling to discover what to do with his life. He studied, traveled, talked, took classes, read widely, sought wisdom, joined groups, pursued pleasure, listened to brilliant speakers, considered retreat from the world—and he was still floundering. He drifted from one self-help theory to another. But his life still seemed like a failure. Close to despair, he turned from his good friend, Alypius, in anger, frustration, and tears, fled to the garden, and flung himself down under a tree.

Then he heard a child's playful voice, drifting over from the neighboring yard, repeating again and again, *Tolle, lege; tolle, lege.* "Take, read. Take, read." Believing the child's voice conveyed God's will itself, Augustine picked up the Bible and read the words on the page where it fell open: "Let us live honestly as in the day; not in reveling and drunkenness, not in debauchery and licentiousness, not in quarreling and jealousy. Instead, put on the Lord Jesus Christ, and make no provisions for the flesh, to gratify its desires" (Romans 13:13–14). God was asking him, as he heard through the text then and there, to walk forward in a life of commitment to Christ and Christ's church. So he did, eventually becoming the bishop of Hippo, a city in northern Africa, as well as one of the most influential theologians in history. When he died forty-four years later, he was reading the Psalms posted before his bed.

Reading "was nothing short of salvific" for Augustine, asserts historian and Augustine scholar Margaret Miles. When, as a young adult, Augustine desperately sought a philosophical and psychological position to orient his life, he turned to books, "never doubting that books possess the capacity to heal and transform." Shortly before his conversion, Miles continues, he "found the books that would excite and incite him—several accounts of people who had abandoned career and family to follow Christ in passionate celibacy." He says he was "on fire" as he read.

On fire. His use of this image echoes the prophet Jeremiah, who proclaimed that God's "word" is "like fire" (23:29; see also 5:14). Reading burns. It turns things to ashes. It refines. With the "right books" and a "fruitful method," Augustine was convinced, "truth could be found." Earlier in this book, I told the story of my own discovery of the spiritual power of words, a story that featured a babbling toddler in the bathtub. It too was a powerful reminder of the place of ordinary words in Christian life, supplementing and enriching the practice of silence, solitude, and private prayer. Reading aloud, reading silently, reading together, reading alone, meditating on words, meditating on the Word, listening for the Word among all the words—all of these deeply spiritual practices immensely enrich our daily life. If words are important, and if the Gospel of John pictures God's own beginning as "Word" (the "Word was God"; John 1:1), then not surprisingly reading and its companion practices of writing and telling stories—the art of seeing and composing a life through words—have rich potential for faith. Christians are "people of the Word."

Even so, reading has waxed and waned over history. The illiteracy that plagued Augustine's era still impedes the practice of reading today. Those who are poor are denied access to education, and illiteracy in turn perpetuates poverty. Those who are rich are distracted by the diversions and power their wealth grants them. Even those who read quite often do so in a mode that is hardly spiritual, reading to consume or "extract what is useful or exciting or entertaining . . . preferably with dispatch," as religion scholar Paul Griffiths says. We read for speed, not to savor, scavenging quotes for a research paper or trying to keep up with the news. Schoolwork itself often encourages this consumerist kind of reading.

Yet it is also clear that reading can cultivate deeper self-reflection. During Augustine's time, the common practice was to read aloud rather than silently to oneself, so the illiterate majority could hear the message. He and some of his contemporaries, however, were part of a shift toward private, silent reading as a primary spiritual practice. His own story of conversion presumes and perpetuates the idea that reading is aimed at the individual's interior reflection.

Reading can never be limited to solitude and the inner world, however. Reading aloud together is one of the most satisfying and mutually transformative experiences adults and children can share. The text can become the focus of a relationship for a time and foster community among readers. It can also create a powerful connection between readers and the wider world and its transformation. Reading aloud together is also, of course, something Christians do in worship, Bible study, and Christian education. Christian faith has been deeply shaped by story and narrative, which Christians have shared in written and oral form for centuries. Behind this is the conviction that reading and telling the story can subvert and transform the world we live in.

I know someone who always learns the scriptural text for his sermon by heart before he preaches. Then he speaks the text, looking each listener in the eye, letting the words flow from memory, hoping to recreate the initial manner by which people passed on the tradition orally. When I heard him do this, I was astounded by how I heard the scriptural passage anew. The text became once again a living word.

PEOPLE OF THE BOOK

The love of word, story, and text, as well as the conviction that they have transformative power within the world, is not unique to Christianity. Christianity grew out of Judaism and Judaism's own textual passion. "At the heart of Shabbat worship is a text," observes children's author Sandy Sasso, "the reading of the stories of the Torah over which we say a blessing." Each week the Torah scrolls, the living testimony to God's covenant, are taken out of their sacred place and carried around among the worshippers, where they are touched or kissed by children and adults, who pass their hands or prayer shawls over the Torah and kiss them as well. The entire Torah (which includes the text of the first five books in the Bible) is read each year. In Jewish belief, the annual, ritual reading of the many stories of faith supports the "cosmic repair of the world" and even has the "power to bring the Messiah."

Jews are "people of the Book" with a long history of storytelling. Their revelation itself is "heard and not seen." Sasso continues: the "central affirmation of faith, the *Shema,* is about listening." "Hear, O Israel . . ." (Deuteronomy 6:4). "What is crucial is voice not image, words not pictures." Sasso cites Susan Handelman, a Jewish studies scholar, who observes that for Christians the "word becomes flesh." But for Jews, the "word becomes more words." "God's presence is located in a text, not a body; in language, not person—in other words, in story" and its ongoing interpretation. The practice of Midrash, an interpretative method and body of literature creating new words where the text is silent, invites people to engage the text deeply. Children and adults must "make the story their own" and let it transform them. The text calls to us: "Come live in me, stretch me, breath into me, find where you are in the story. Only then will it have power to change your life."

Take, Read; Take, Eat

I have worshiped since I was born in a church that also deeply engages a text, though in a different way. My tradition includes celebration of communion every Sunday. Week in and week out, we tell and act out the story of Jesus' last meal with his disciples, hearing again and again the words from scripture that all Christians hear, with slight variation, when they share the bread and cup of holy communion, or the Mass, or the Lord's Supper: "While they were eating, Jesus took a loaf of bread, and after blessing it he broke it, gave it to the disciples, and said, 'Take, eat; this is my body.' Then he took a cup, and after giving thanks he gave it to them, saying, 'Drink from it, all of you; this is the blood of the covenant, which is poured out for many for the forgiveness of sins'" (Matthew 26:26–29).

"Take, eat, this is my body." These words—so like "take, read"—have shaped my life.

Take, eat. Take, read. Who knows if Augustine noticed how closely these phrases mimic each other? But the parallel between the "central words of the mass, familiar to Augustine from his boyhood" and the words he heard in the garden was probably not accidental, Miles suspects. To read was for him "to ingest, swallow, digest and incorporate—to *eat* the text."

Over the years, but especially during the Middle Ages, Christians drew a close parallel between nourishing oneself through food and nourishing oneself through text and word. In the Middle Ages, reading scripture was often described using vocabulary "borrowed from eating, from digestion, and from the particular form of digestion belonging to ruminants," animals like cows, camels, and sheep that digest tough materials many times, asserts Benedictine monk and scholar Jean LeClercq. The reader usually pronounced the words "with his lips" in a low tone and memorized the text, trying thereby to implant the text in muscular facial movement and to learn it "by heart." The scriptural lesson was impressed into the "very viscera of a reader's body." *Lectio,* or reading, meant "carving up the text," according to medieval historian Mary Carruthers. *Meditatio,* or meditation, involved "imbibing and absorbing" it. Like a cow chewing its cud, one tastes, chews, ingests, digests, and rests. Scripture itself contains powerful images of eating the word and likens God's word to honey and its sweetness (Psalm 119:103; Ezekiel 3:1–3).

Just as food determines the state and shape of one's body, books can form the soul. Reading, like eating, provides essential nourishment and communion. We cannot live without eating. We cannot live fully without reading. Take, eat. Take, read. Reading is this elementary, this basic to life and faith.

TASTING: READING AS
PLEASURE AND JOY

Not one more time; did we have to check out another Beatrix Potter book? He hadn't even wanted to read them last time we came home from the library. For some reason, neither Mark nor I liked Potter's Peter Rabbit series, except maybe the beloved tale about Peter lost in the cabbage patch and threatened by Mr. McGregor. But when our youngest son was just barely a toddler, he'd pull the library chair from its table over to the wall to reach up to the top of the corner shelf where the little books were displayed. We were destined to check out as many as he could talk us into. He didn't much like the stories either. They were too long and detailed. He liked *how they felt*.

Reading is a sensual affair. Go to a good bookstore for a few minutes and you are sure to see someone pick up a book, crack it open, stick a nose in, and inhale. We breathe books in, like creatures seeking the breath, life, and spirit that God breathed into the first human being (Genesis 2:7). A book's cover, its size, its print, its chapter illustration—its feel—make a difference. My son liked the Peter Rabbit books because they were small and solid. He liked tiny hardback books. He just wanted to hold them.

Over Christmas break, my almost-twenty-year-old son wanted to read *The Hobbit* again. He searched our house but couldn't find our tattered old copy. We figured it was lost or lent, or had finally just disintegrated. So he headed to the bookstore and returned with a cheap paperback. He'd passed over a "really nice" hardback with a "real cool cover," he said, with a little note of longing. I understood his longing.

"My mom always bought a book for each of us at Christmas," declared my mom one more time this year when she and my dad joined our family around the tree. "When we were done unwrapping, that was the first thing I would do: curl up and read."

"Curl up." Now, there's a sensual image usually reserved for what we do with loved ones. Reading and memories of reading can convey connection of the most visceral, tactile sort. One writer confesses that his images of the "perfect environment for reading" are "merely displacements, sentimental attempts to replicate the warmth and snugness of my mother's lap." His mother created a "sensual transport," he says, "that I have yearned to feel each time I pick up a book." For many of us, our lives take shape, as another author says, "under the curve" of a parent's arm or surrounded by the "calm caress" of a parent's reading voice. My own mom's repeated hint is not too subtle, then: buy her a book at Christmas so she can embrace once again the gift of love, life, and connection.

I smile when I remember the warmth and smell, the touch and tug of kids fighting for my lap, leaning into my side, intent on the book stretched between us. When my kids were young, we could read at almost any time of the day. But the favorite time was bedtime. It started with the baptism of a nightly bath, three in one tub. Since our only bathroom was grand central station upstairs between the bedrooms, we often stayed up there, piled on our queen bed as if it were a gigantic extended couch, and read together, flushed and clean, kids tucked into pajamas with soft plastic soles on the bottom of the feet. Mark and I took turns each night, and our two youngest boys, twenty-two months apart, traded off sitting in the favored position on my lap or Mark's.

Having children rewards an adult with the privilege of reading just for fun. It gives us permission to read children's books, read aloud, and read with a warm body or two or three pressed close. Children are a gift. Books are a gift. Engaging both can be an immense pleasure in life.

Only recently has pleasure itself, including tactile pleasure, become a viable rationale for reading with children. Some books, like *Pat the Bunny* and pop-ups, even incorporate the tactile right into the text. Three centuries ago, reading with children as a religious practice meant reading scripture and catechesis. Reading for fun was suspect. Tutoring children in faith, notes an editor of a publication on children's literature, was the "only existing rationale" and the Bible the only text for reading to children "whose souls were thought to be in need of saving from the moment of birth."

Mark and I did buy good children's versions of Bible stories. We especially liked Tomie DePaola's hefty, beautifully illustrated *Book of*

Bible Stories, The Parables of Jesus, and *The Miracles of Jesus.* We also discovered his smaller paperback treatment of heroes and heroines of the Jewish and Christian tradition, including the three kings, Mary, Esther, Noah, David and Goliath, St. Francis, St. Valentine, and Patrick the patron saint of Ireland. Regrettably we tended to read these more with our oldest son than with the others. But we gradually came to see that good children's books do not have to be overtly religious—about Jesus, for example—to be about Christ and faithful living. Everyday books about common life can also evoke faith. Moreover, fantasy and fun are important ingredients in the practice of faithful reading.

If I truly believe this, does it mean I have to read one more time *Captain Underpants,* or a Ninja Turtles book Mark and I especially despised (with an inanely repeated sentence, "My name, my name, my name is Crying Hound")? Some books are trivial to an extreme; I think we finally did toss the Crying Hound book. But we should be careful about making too-easy judgments. There is often more to a book than meets the eye, even if I will never know what proved so moving for my kids about this one except its fantastic tale and the common desire of children to hear the words of a familiar and well-liked story repeated.

My grandma bought books for me at Christmas, as she had done for my mom, and she spent lots of time reading herself. But she did not, my mom often stressed, like Dr. Seuss. Too nonsensical. Nor does my mom to this day like "fantasy" (citing J.R.R. Tolkien's *Lord of the Rings* as a leading example). Too ethereal.

Initially, editors agreed. The first book by Theodor Geisel (aka Dr. Seuss), *And to Think That I Saw It on Mulberry Street,* was rejected by publishers twenty-seven times. "Editors complained," reports pastoral theologian Herbert Anderson, "that the book had no moral or message." Outraged, Geisel asks, "What's wrong with kids having fun reading without being preached at?" Fifty-three years of publishing, forty-seven books, and one hundred million copies later, Dr. Seuss had his answer: not a thing.

"One of the gifts of being a grandfather," exclaims Anderson, "is having permission to read Dr. Seuss again. Because I was only read bible stories as a child, I was delighted to discover the whimsical world of Dr. Seuss when my children were young." The genius of Dr. Seuss lies in his ability to enter the playful world of children, a world valuable in itself with children's qualities of vulnerability, immediacy, openness, and neediness that adults forsake at their own expense. *And to Think That I Saw It on Mulberry Street* is perhaps his boldest statement about the problems of adult parochialism and narrowness. Asked to report on what he saw to and from school—a routine question posed by an adult to a child—Marco cannot convey what he has seen and imagined, and he isn't sure his father would be receptive to it anyway. He has seen an old red wagon and horse, but he imagines a zebra pulling the wagon and then, better yet, a zebra pulling a colorful chariot, or perhaps an elephant with a rajah, and so forth. So he gives a routine answer: " 'Nothing,' I said, growing red as a beet, 'But a plain horse and wagon on Mulberry Street.' "

For young children, a story is true not because it is factual, says theologian Anne Thurston, but because it "connects with their own experience." Children who recognize such imaginative truth are especially open to the "myth and poetry and truth of the biblical stories." She likens story to both play and liturgy. Story also has the capacity to alter time and space, create a hoped-for world, and empower us to live into its future. "The story told over and over again becomes a means for the child of interpreting her own experience. We remember, we imagine, we hope. This is precisely what we do in liturgical contexts." We need to remember and imagine to reconstitute our lives.

"I almost don't want to see the movie," asserts one son. "I've pictured Frodo and Gollum in a certain way. I don't want some other view to destroy that." The written word allows one's mind to wonder and hope in a way most media do not. Even book illustrations and books on tape do not impose themselves to the same intrusive extent as television and film. Words and pictures in books create a powerful visual world while one reads, without exhausting the potential of the imagination, producing in readers as many versions of Frodo and his battles with good and evil as there are readers.

I'm sorry my grandma didn't like Seuss and my mom Tolkien. They missed some great books, even though they likely found other books that offered them laughter and a degree of self-transcendence. The world of whimsy and rhyme where elephants hatch eggs, moose offer hospitality, grinches steal Christmas, turtles build kingdoms on the backs of other turtles, Zooks and Yooks battle over butter and bread, and Sam-I-Am suggests we all try green eggs is a world full of hope. It is world with a little less greed, a little more compassion, and a lot more humor. So also is Tolkien's world of hobbits, wizards, elves, and dwarves, all managing through the bonds of mere friendship to beat the insidious power of evil. When one of my sons tells me that I "should write books that people actually read," I think this is precisely the kind he has in mind.

INGESTING: READING AS FORMATIVE

I love books (I am surrounded by piles of them at the moment). Not too different from my Peter Rabbit son, I even love the feel of them. I doubt I'll ever enjoy reading a book on the Web. But it isn't just this tactile pleasure and connection that makes reading a potential act of faith. Reading shares with the focal practice of play (discussed in the preceding chapter) other qualities beyond sheer pleasure. Books bring us into deeper moral and intellectual relationship with ourselves, others, our world, and God.

We can explain the rather inexplicable staying power of books that otherwise seem without serious merit, theologian Rowan Williams suggests, by their ability to create a sphere of acceptable irresponsibility where children can try out adult choices without consequence and implication. "Perhaps the most liberating thing about such literature is the sense conveyed that the 'normal' world, the habitual ways in which life is structured and control exercised, is not so self-evident that we can't think ourselves around its edges." Such books offer "a space for seeing the self and its world afresh" in preparation for more mature adult agency. Drawing on Robert Coles's work on story and moral life, psychologist Paul Vitz agrees. "A very effective way to introduce children to the moral life, short of actually placing them in morally challenging situations," he says, "is to have them hear, read, and watch morally challenging narratives." Children need a sanctioned place for fantasy and imagination to acquire the ability to make moral and spiritual choices later in life.

This is really not a new idea. Several centuries ago the father of eastern orthodoxy, John Chrysostom, ranked storytelling high on his list of ways to nurture children in a Christian "pattern of life." He goes to great lengths to give parents hints on what kind of stories to tell, at what age to tell them, and even how to tell them so as to challenge a child's imagination and reflection. Compare the story of Cain and Abel with the story of Jacob and Esau, and talk about sibling rivalry and obedience to God. Tell these stories not just once, but over and over. Tell fearful stories only when children are old enough that the story will not "impose so great a burden on his understanding." Stories from scripture are best, he says, but he also encourages parents to use the heroes and marvels of pagan stories to stir a child's imagination and prepare them for stories of faith.

Although children's books need not be overtly religious to be valuable, reading as a practice of faith must include books that offer an alternative to some of the prominent stories of wider culture. These all-too-familiar scripts for life creep into almost all forms of popular media ("might makes right," "violence is redemptive," "God blesses America," "look after your own good," "you are what you own," "be a winner"). The gospel tells a radically different story about the power and risk of love of God and neighbor. This alternative story suggests the poverty and distortion of our cultural myths of violence, success, domination, and profit. Reading as a practice of faith looks and listens for this message of good news to help set us on a better course.

On a closer look, the colorful nonsense of Dr. Seuss is actually full of moral lessons, including urgent calls to care for the environment (*The Lorax*) and to stop the proliferation of nuclear weapons (*The Butter Battle Book*). Like many imaginative authors, Seuss creates what Anderson calls "a moral vision without moralism" that invites the reader to engage genuine dilemmas without hitting one over the head with a simple moral message. Anderson can't imagine a kid who has read *The Lorax* growing into an "entrepreneurial Once-ler" whose greed and neglect guts the environment. *I Had Trouble in Getting to Solla Sollew* (a land entirely without troubles) makes clear there is no perfect world without human brokenness. In turn, books where Horton the elephant "hatches an egg" (while the real mother bird vacations) and then "hears a Who" (crying for help from a speck of dust) encourage moral persistence and patience. "Without being a moralist," asserts Anderson, Seuss "managed to provoke the moral imagination of children 'who have ears to hear.'"

Even books that make little room for the imagination, like those in the Berenstain Bears series, can have an important moral role. Authors Jan and Stan Berenstain make no bones about their didactic purpose to help families live better lives in a consumerist, individualistic, fast-paced society. Supported by Dr. Seuss himself, they write books that grapple with all manner of ordinary problems straight out of their own lives: strangers, chores, manners, junk food, doctors, dentists, guns, homework, competitive sports, money, pets, camp, friends, fights, stage fright, drugs, clothes, bad habits, too much vacation, and the dark. In every case, Mama and Papa Bear possess an enviable and ingenious bag of tips and tricks that, the books imply, readers just might want to emulate. Although my kids found some of the books pedestrian, others such as *The Berenstain Bears and Too Much Pressure, Too Much Teasing,* and *Mama's New Job* served as welcome reminders about how to reorient our lives toward more faithful living.

In one of our library excursions, I stumbled on the book *Pink and Say* by an author, Patricia Polacco, with more nuance and depth than the Berenstains or Seuss. We'd already discovered the appeal of her other wonderfully illustrated, cleverly told books, which transport readers into numerous ethnic worlds, especially the Russian, Ukrainian, and Irish cultures of her own heritage. Her books are not primarily about the customs and dress of these cultures, vividly portrayed though they are, but rather about fundamental patterns of moral living. *Thundercake,* for example, deals with nebulous fear (of thunder) and the solace of love (baking a cake together with grandma). *The Graves Family* and *Just Plain Fancy* explore hostile reactions to people who are strange, poor, or just plain ordinary, insisting that we look below the surface.

I choked up no matter how many times I read *Pink and Say* aloud with my kids. It is a story from Polacco's own family history, passed down to her from her great-grandfather, about a lasting friendship between two young boys caught up in the Civil War. Pink, who is black, rescues Say, who is white (Polacco's great-grandfather). Say has been wounded and is fleeing his unit. Pink's mother, once a slave on a Georgia plantation, nurses Say back to health before marauders arrive to kill her. On their way back to fight, bound in a new way, Pink and Say are captured. In the end, Pink is hanged, but Say survives to pass on the story. Say had told Pink that he once shook hands with Abraham Lincoln, and so Pink yearns "just one last time" to "touch the hand that touched Mr. Lincoln." They clasp hands before soldiers wrench them apart in prison.

The book is a testimony to Pink's life, to the friendship of these young men, and to the hope that bonds of love—touching the hand that touched the hand down to today—can overcome racism, strife, bloodshed, and death. The last page invites the reader to grab on and say Pink's name, Pinkus Aylee, "out loud and vow to remember him always." In doing this, readers enter a kind of covenant of peace and justice created through the practice of reading.

Each time my kids and I said "Pinkus Aylee," we traversed imaginative space and time. We were not just reading to get beyond our own "not-very-satisfactory real world" to some alternative world, to borrow Thurston's characterization. We read to move "into the shoes of another, and thus ultimately to learn compassion."

Of course, in an even more obvious sense, reading is about expanding one's horizons. "Read," intones founder and president of the Children's Defense Fund Marion Wright Edelman. (Her recommendation to keep learning and reading is number fourteen in her twenty-five lessons she wants to pass on to her own children and children at large.) "Not just what you have to read for class or work, but to learn from the wisdom and joys and mistakes of others." "Read" is also a recommendation emerging from an empirical study by the Search Institute, a resource center promoting the welfare of children and youth. Reading "for pleasure three or more hours per week" is one of the "forty Developmental Assets" identified as helping young people "grow up healthy, caring, and responsible." Of course, many books are about plain, ordinary learning—how to speak, count, color, read, and think, including the Seuss classics *One Fish, Two Fish, Red Fish, Blue Fish; Ten Apples up on Top; I Can Read with My Eyes Shut; Oh, the Thinks You Can Think.*

Edelman was brought up in a household where reading offered even greater transcendence than just acquiring knowledge. Her own father valued reading "almost as much as prayer," she remembers, and made her read alongside him each night. When he caught her hiding a frivolous magazine behind the cover of more educational reading, he made her read the magazine aloud and comment on its value. They had "more books and magazines than clothes or luxuries," and it made all the difference. "All of this was, I think, the reason why I always thought the whole world was mine to explore and why I still resist anyone's efforts to relegate only a part of it to me— or to any child." Through reading, we transcend the "artificial boundaries of race, gender, class, and things."

That reading expands horizons is another reason religious traditions have sometimes suspected its place in the spiritual life. If we go back several centuries, suggests Steve Jones, a communications professor, we find that "people were enormously suspicious about the printed word. Somebody's words, written down and distributed on a mass scale, were thought to be dangerous." There must still be anxiety about the disruptive danger of reading, or books wouldn't continue to be banned from schools and burned by political regimes. Books arouse us, challenge accepted ideas, and stimulate new ones.

When it came time to choose a Bible for my middle-school-aged son, I did not select a traditional Sunday School Bible but rather one with historical and theological notes. The Bible is a book composed of many shorter books, of course, so this annotated Bible lends context and information about each one, much of it unfamiliar to many Christians far older than he. Explanatory notes offer a brief background on each book and describe the circumstances under which it was written and its primary message and components. At the bottom of each page, one finds commentary on individual verses, definitions of terms, cross-references, explanations, and citations for further understanding. I didn't even know annotated bibles existed until I took my first course on the New Testament in college. Why didn't I know about such a great resource earlier? Did someone think I would be too lazy or un-intelligent to desire more knowledge of the Bible? Or did someone fear that such knowledge might be a threat to faith rather than a means to deepen it? What about excellent theological books, which can be so helpful as we ponder important questions of faith? I hope the time will come when ministers share what they read and learned in their graduate training more fully with all members of the church.

DIGESTING: READING AS TRANSFORMATIVE

The practice of reading shapes us morally and intellectually. We master certain ideas, broach new values, and stretch our minds and hearts. I personally never do anything until I've read a book about it (well, almost anything). Yet reading has even greater implications. Philosopher and activist Simon Weil, who lived in France before the Second World War, argues that the practice of "school studies," regardless of what we learn, whether we like what we're learning, and even whether we are successful at it, is important to the spiritual life when done for the love of God.

How can this be so? "School studies" hone attention. As we saw in the practice of pondering, attention is the key to faith, and study (whether the struggle over a math problem or a line from a classic French tragedy) sharpens attention. In fact, contrary to popular pietistic opinion, "warmth of heart cannot make up" for attention. Weil doesn't mean forced concentration with furrowed brows and clenched muscles. Rather, attention springs forth from the work of close careful reading, like flow (discussed in the preceding chapter), when it is funded by desire, pleasure, and joy. The capacity to love our neighbor—to *read* his or her situation—comes from exactly the same cut of cloth.

The view that reading can be spiritually transformative has a long history, back to the Benedictine practice of prayer called *lectio divina,* or "divine reading," that many people continue today. Lectio divina's four steps—*lectio, meditatio, oratio,* and *contemplatio*—are intended to move the reader into deeper relationship with the text and through that with God and oneself. One listens, ruminates, engages, and rests in the Word. To read well requires a ritual process of connection and release that has a distant resemblance to lectio divina. To hear a story truly, as Sandy Sasso says, one must "quiet the self," "be fully present," and ultimately "relinquish control."

So we read for pleasure. We read to learn, grow, experience new worlds, and connect to others. Ultimately we also read out of a fundamental spiritual need. We seek meaning and answers to profound questions of existence.

Years ago, when I read Margaret Wise Brown's *The Runaway Bunny* to my young sons, I wasn't really thinking about our deep-seated anxiety over attachment and separation. But I knew my sons and I were all wondering, day to day and in the long run, who would leave who first and for how long. So it was some solace to share together a story about a baby bunny who keeps running away from his mother only to discover that mother bunny comes steadfastly after him. I could read along and indirectly at least tell my sons how much I love them despite the fact that I sometimes leave them to do other things I also love; they could acknowledge how much they want both to flee and stay immersed in that love. "If you run away," says the mother, "I will run after you. For you are my little bunny." Whether the bunny becomes a fish, mountain climber, or crocus, the mother will fish, climb, or garden and "find you."

Likewise, when we read Maurice Sendak's *Where the Wild Things Are,* I wasn't trying to tell my kids that they were wild or wicked (although they sometimes were). But the book still gave each of us time to think in another way about how to deal with our "mischief of one kind and another." Some authors take more profound issues head-on, like DePaola's *Nana Upstairs, Nana Downstairs,* a story of a boy's wonderful relationship with his grandma in the kitchen downstairs and his great-grandmother in the bed upstairs. Until Nana Upstairs dies.

Why is there evil? Why do people suffer? Why do people die? Who is God anyway? We didn't wait to read these books until our children could "handle" such questions. We dove right in. If people like Robert Coles, Jerome Berryman, and Bruno Bettelheim are right, children think about these questions from the get-go. They also have their own answers and "theologies," or theories about God's role in each case.

Sometimes the existential dilemmas of daily life itself, big and small, leave us speechless. At such times, a single recognized line from a book—a bit like a proof text from scripture—can paint a thousand words. Books give us something to say about life and its anger, frustration, terror, bereavement, and despair—commonly shared human sentiments—when we don't have anything else to say.

One morning, nothing was right for my son. He complained that the pancakes were "burnt." He couldn't find his favorite pencil. Then I had to go and say something "so obvious" like "Maybe it's in your backpack." He resisted his father's goodbye hug so fiercely that you would have thought Mark had a highly contagious disease. So, as he departed through the front door—cross as a cuss—instead of my usual litany of "Have a good day, learn a lot, have fun," I sent him off with the only words that came to mind, "Bye, Alexander. Have a terrible, horrible, no good, very bad day. Even in Australia. . . . See you this afternoon."

In my happily-ever-after version, my mention of Alexander finally makes him smile. Although no actual smile appeared that morning, I like to think that under the surface he was at least chuckling a little. It had been years since we read Judith Viorst's *Alexander and the Terrible, Horrible, No Good, Very Bad Day,* but he knew exactly what I meant. Some days are rotten, even in Australia. Sometimes we are just in a foul mood for no reason. Sometimes for good reason. Either way, it would have been pointless to say, "Have a good day."

The practice of reading allows children and adults alike to find relief from suffering alone and together. Reading is cathartic. It helps us introspect, express feelings about life's most troubling questions, and understand others as they encounter them. Reading also allows us to test the limits of life, shaking up our easy answers. Some children's books actually solicit philosophical thought on the part of the reader. Philosopher Gareth Matthews is "fond of telling anyone who will listen that, for example, Arnold Lobel's *Frog and Toad Together,* which is so simple in its vocabulary as to count as an 'I can read book,' is also a philosophical classic."

In one story, Frog and Toad wonder if they are brave, like those who fight giants and dragons in the stories they read. They decide to prove their bravery through a series of daring feats: climbing a mountain, escaping a hawk, avoiding an avalanche. Through these adventures, however, they seem panicky and nervous. In the end they run back to Toad's house, where one jumps under the covers and the other into the closet. They stay there a long time, "just feeling very brave together." This final line, like many others, reminds us of "our ignorance and uncertainty" (in this case, about what bravery really entails) and encourages us to wonder more about it.

Whereas Lobel focuses on logic, other books such as *Charlotte's Web* and *Tuck Everlasting* turn us to the illogic of death and how animals and people of good faith prevail over it. Reading also touches on what terrifies us. Stephen King, a best-selling author, once commented that "his mother told him, 'If something terrifies you, say it three times and you'll be OK.'" So, according to Sandy Sasso, King says, "That's why I write, I write about what's terrifying." Through reading, you get to "experience terror safely," as author Walter Wangerin claims, determining in the middle of terror whether to shut the book or keep reading, usually with greater control than one feels in a theater.

Alexander, the youngest of three brothers, like Viorst's own boys and the son I sent off to school that day, has a horrible day. No wonder this book, which has sold more than two million copies, is so well loved by kids and adults alike. This may also explain the popularity of Lemony Snicket's *A Series of Unfortunate Events.* Such books don't explain away injustice, disappointment, and plain old drudgery, but in their own meandering way they do help us live more deeply and faithfully when these things come to cloud our days. Viorst hoped that the notion of "a bad day" could serve for [her son], and for all kids, as it does for adults, a "container" function, suggesting that this day—this bad news—would (honest and truly!) come to an end. I was also tacitly suggesting in the book that everyone, just not our hapless hero, sometimes has bad days and that neither the fictional nor the real-life Alexander has been singled out for a unique fate. Furthermore, these bad days happen everywhere, even in Australia, and since we can't escape them we might as well muddle through them and maybe even try (at some point) to laugh about them.

Other Alexander books—*Alexander, Who Used to be Rich Last Sunday* and *Alexander, Who's Not (Do You Hear Me? I Mean It!) Going to Move*—that are less well known also deal with common human struggles.

Before I began this chapter, I took a trip up to our attic. There we have stored our most treasured children's books, from those with single words on each cardboard page to more advanced reading, such as *Charlotte's Web* and *My Brother's Dragon*. We recently retired these last two books to the save box while cleaning out my fourteen-year-old's room. I have had a twinge of regret with each such transfer and then a coinciding twinge of hope, as we store them temporarily, that I may once again read them to other children. How do we determine which books to save? Although we never speak or think explicitly about it, I think we save those that speak profoundly to us and will likely speak to others.

READING AS EVOLVING PROCESS AND PRACTICE

Pilgrimage to our favorite local library, organized around the ever-revolving three-week due date, was an integral part of our larger practice of family reading. We used to live within walking distance. A wonderful grandfatherly man in our church, someone who had rescued us when our car broke down and regularly bestowed vegetables from his garden, gave us an incredible tricycle after our first son was born. It was red, of course, and taller than typical trikes. Its most distinctive feature was a little wagon behind the black seat with its own trailer hitch, as if kids might want to tow a boat or trailer or something! Initially we put blocks on the pedals so our son could reach them. Eventually it became a favorite mode of transportation, perfect for hauling the fifteen or twenty picture books we'd checked out. I'd follow with the stroller or a second wagon, hauling kids or books, depending on preference, precedent, and who was peddling.

The library had the feel of sanctuary: a cool, quiet, welcomed respite on our way in and out of the sun and the rest of the world. In hushed voice (so nice to have an outside authority telling my kids to be quiet), we browsed. We sat on the floor, leafed through books, picked this one, put that one back, and then read a few together before final decisions on what to check out and load into the wagon for the trip home.

The books felt like gifts, much more precious than if we had gone to the store to buy them. I even liked explaining to our kids how a public library works—a community agreeing to pool resources and share the wealth so all, the haves and have-nots, can benefit. But this only works as long as borrowers abide by the covenant of care for the books, returning them as they received them. So people "hand on" what they "received," much like Paul passing on the tradition of the breaking of the bread (I Corinthians 11:23) or people handing on stories they have known and loved from one generation to the next.

Mark and I discovered a lot of books on these treks, some wonderful authors never heard of before, and others (like Virginia Lee Burton's *Mike Mulligan and His Steam Shovel*) evoking deep-seated memories from our own childhood. One has to develop a discerning eye. I cannot easily describe our criteria for selection. Our choices had something to do, once again, with sensual, aesthetic appeal: size, color, quality of picture, word spacing, feel of the book in our hands, and ultimately whether a word here, a sentence there, or a bit of a story captivated any one of us enough to keep reading. If so, we took it home.

We stretched our bedtime ritual about as long as age, growth, and adult fatigue would sustain it, reading longer books such as the *Lord of the Rings* (my oldest son can still do a fairly good imitation of me dozing off midsentence). It took us over two years to get through that trilogy, starting when he was in third grade before we moved and ending when he was a fifth grader (that's what happens while you're reading and sleeping). One of my friends told me that he still reads aloud with his teenage boys at night. But it doesn't happen in my house anymore. I miss it. I miss its joy, bonding, tangible intimacy, and hints of the divine.

It doesn't have to be this way. I know an older couple who read to each other on car trips. I remember my dad reading Henry van Dyke's *The Other Wise Man* with my mom and brothers on Christmas Eve (abridging, thank goodness, the belabored depictions of costume and context, following the pencil marks of his own mom, my grandmother). Robert Coles tells how he could barely squelch his teenage annoyance (and curiosity) at his parents reading George Eliot, Dickens, and Tolstoy to each other in the living room every evening, forcing his brother and him to listen to "Amos 'n Andy" on the smaller radio in the kitchen. Living with the sound of their reading voices in the background, trying to figure out why they did this, and listening to their various explanations (one was, "Your mother and I feel rescued by these books") became one of the most pivotal influences on his life.

Eventually my kids began picking out books themselves, and sometimes I follow their choices. They chose books through the elementary school's monthly Scholastic Book Club flyers, at middle school library fundraisers, and from lists assigned by high school teachers. I read books their English classes require or books they like (although I draw the line at the endless *Star Wars* series and Stephen King). Right now I'm reading one of my son's favorite novels, *Eragon,* about a teenager with hidden powers to use magic, ward off evil, and save the world. No wonder he likes it. But to reduce this novel's meaning for him to his own qualms and hopes as he grows into manhood, like Eragon, is unfair.

Instead, this practice of reading what they read stretches the range of my own reading in general, exposing me to their world and leaving me open, interested. I ask, "Did it seem to you like all the adults in Philip Pullman's *His Dark Materials* trilogy were awful?" Or, noticing how different a book seems when read twenty years after the

In the Midst of Chaos

first time, I say, "The *Lord of the Rings* was a lot darker when I read it as an adult. Does it seem so doomed and forbidding to you?" I was especially gratified the other night when I heard a character in *Eragon* proclaim, "These books are my friends, my companions. They make me laugh and cry and find meaning in life"—my conviction precisely! Nice to see a book pick up in my kids' eyes where I have left off.

The next book in the *Eragon* trilogy came out this past fall. "Will you take me to the bookstore to buy *Eldest*?" asked my son the day it debuted. I doubt I'd run too many errands at the drop of the hat and lay out $22.94, especially for someone who earlier that afternoon had called me "stupid." But I stopped what I was doing and headed off to the bookstore. A request to buy a book can almost always turn my heart.

Nurturing adult readers: maybe that's my contribution to the common good honed through the practice of caring for children. Or so I thought on the way home. I hope that once I finish making sure each son reads well and widely, I will, like my mom, tutor others less fortunate to love this practice and help them find the means to support it. Buying, borrowing, or otherwise finding some way to read a book should not be a privilege of class and social position. Just as we all need food, we need to read, and we need to "nourish a reading culture in our churches," as theologian Stephanie Paulsell says. Reading feeds the heart of the believer. It strengthens the backbone of congregational life. It also builds up the body of the community. None of this is restricted to the elite. All of this is a necessity for the sustenance of faith itself for everyone.

On a summer night this past August, my youngest son wonders if we can make popcorn. We do. I look around. My oldest son is out and about with friends, but the rest of us are curled up reading or— more accurately with teenage boys, sprawled out reading. No one is reading anything terribly profound. I'm indulging in the latest Harry Potter, my sons are rereading beloved books, and Mark has begun *Little House in the Big Woods,* on a banjo lover's pursuit of lyrics from old-time music songs. We are a family of readers. It's not always idyllic (on another night I will be yelling about too many video games). But tonight we read. My heart is glad.

Chapter 9

BLESSING AND LETTING GO

The dorm room smelled. That's what I remember about the day we dropped off our oldest for his first year of college. We had parked our loaded van nearby and joined a stream of parents and kids lugging boxes and pushing dollies into the dorm. Inside, we found a room that was barren and cell-like and forlorn, as if it had said good-bye to too many inmates over the years. A room that smelled. Of old furniture, rotting socks, and mold.

In a sense, I had been preparing for this late August day for many years. Indeed, a reminder of how many years I have spent taking leave of my sons still appears a few minutes after eight every morning, as a yellow school bus rolls by our house. I don't recollect much about the days each of my kids clambered on board for the first time, but they don't seem so long ago. The ache I have as I remember them is a lot like that dorm-room smell. It gets stuck in my throat. It feels like a punch to the stomach.

For many years, I posted on my office door a poem that announced to all who entered, "Hey, everyone, I'm in perpetual mourning." The short phrases of "Kindergarten Days" echo the tone and pattern of an adult speaking to a child. "You'll be the first one on the bus. . . . It goes to kindergarten, remember?" "Of course we'll wave." "No, Mrs. Klose won't squeeze you to death if you talk in kindergarten. I promise. Who told you that?" "Yes, the house will still be here after school. OK, it's not called school. It's kindergarten." The final lines of the poem get shorter and shorter, growing more desperate and earnest but at the same time more assuring and truer:

> Yes, Mom and I will be here.
> Go ahead now.
> Remember, wave until you pass the pines.
> We'll stand right here.
> Yes.
> Good-bye.
> Don't forget to keep waving.
> Yes, we'll still see you.
> The bus windows aren't that dirty.
> Yes.
> Have fun.
> Good-bye.
> Yes.

This poem still makes my eyes water and my side ache. I ache for the loss, but I am also moved by the intimacy of child and parent, the parent's love for the growing child, and the child's naïveté, wisdom, and trust. Why did I put the poem on my door? Perhaps I was trying to remind passersby of the grief of daily living, hoping they would also acknowledge its reality and experience it for themselves. Perhaps I was inviting them to share their grief so that I could give them a blessing. Perhaps I was asking those who passed by for a blessing, hoping to hear them say "Yes, go ahead now" to me.

"Yes." "Good-bye." "Have fun." "We'll see you." "Wave until you pass the pines." "Go ahead now." "Yes." A hug, a touch, a kiss, a tear. These are all blessings we give all the time, marking our gratitude and care and granting peace and goodwill as our loved ones come and go. Blessings are also gestures that speak when words don't, the same gestures that were just about all I could muster the day we took our eldest to college. These small words and movements can feel so inadequate, so utterly mundane that we don't even notice them. Yet they actually have great importance, and it can be helpful to recognize them for what they are. They are the blessings we bestow daily, coming and going, gracing others with our love, assuring them of our continued presence, and turning them over in trust to God and the wider world. Blessing is not an easy practice, nor is it one that calls attention to itself. But it is a trust-filled, hope-filled, love-filled practice at the core of Christian faith.

The word *bless* wraps up in one term a whole collection of powerful meanings: to hallow or consecrate by religious rite or word; to invoke divine care for and protection of; to confer prosperity. A blessing is also said over meals as an act of gratitude and praise, the food of the common meal a cousin to and a daily reminder of what Catholics call the "Blessed Sacrament" of the consecrated bread and wine of the Eucharist, Christ's body and blood. The benediction that ends a worship service and sends people forth with God's love for the sake of the world is also a blessing. For Christian communities, the practice of blessing stands at the center of worship and is essential to the common good.

This practice is also part of every family. Different from monastic life and the Christian mandate to love all humankind universally, we labor in families to love particular people. Then we must let them go. If that's not hard enough, we fail in our labor to love these particular people. We labor to practice our faith with them, and we fail again, probably more than we succeed. This hurts, in every sense of the word. One of the hardest challenges of family life is to move through and beyond the loss, the failure, the hurts of everyday life. But the most gracious aspect of family life also comes here, when we are able to move through failure and loss into the practice of blessing.

The whole subject of "mundane grief"—the daily nontragic grief so rooted in family life—is remarkably absent from most discussions of loss, as well as from discussions of the family. It is not a coincidence, then, that one of the most overlooked daily practices of faith in families is the practice of blessing and letting go of the other person and your own lament and sorrow. The problem is you can't just up and bless someone you love out of the blue. Blessing commits us to a way of being with one another and comes with some very sticky strings attached: the strings of attachment, separation, loss, and failure. To get to blessing, you have to go through (or maybe it's best to

Blessing and Letting Go

say "muck around in") its component parts. You have to acknowledge life's limits. You have to offer and receive forgiveness as a step toward receiving and bestowing blessing. Finally, you have to let go in trust. The practice of blessing, like a good benediction, declares our willingness to live joyously and gratefully within finite existence and to set our loved ones free to do the same.

Recognizing Limits

One big problem with any book on spirituality is that there is hardly any way to read along and not feel as if you were just assigned one more thing to do. Almost inevitably, we see the advice as a blueprint for what we must do to earn our way into the spiritual elite, the inner circle of spirituality of those who are calm and prayerful. In this chapter, I would like to make one more attempt to dispel that myth.

The phrase "in the midst of chaos" itself suggests that our efforts to practice our faith usually take place amid conditions we don't really control. Parenting constantly brings us to relinquishment, of self and ideals and dreams, of the other person, the infant, soon to be a child, soon to be an older child, soon to be a youth, soon to be a young adult. Just when I thought I had it down in those early weeks and months of parenting, my child would up and change. Damn. (A far cry from "God bless it," I'm afraid.) Of course, those early changes were just the beginning.

We parents are always coming up against our limits—limits that come in all shapes and sizes. The first and often hidden step in the practice of blessing and letting go is to recognize this.

Mundane Grief

How can a parent describe the chronic sense of loss that seeps into every nook and cranny of family life, no matter how much one ignores and refuses to look at it? For several months, as my son's senior year in high school wound down, I experienced what psychologists call "anticipatory grief." I imagined the absence of his light humor at our dinner table, the emptiness of his room, the house without his music. I rehearsed over and over the loss that lay ahead. Like a tongue searching the raw gum after a lost tooth, I'd stretch toward it, find the missing spot, and then shy away, but not before feeling a jab of pain.

None of us wants to spend much time exploring the edges of our loss. But truth be told, at midlife, as I gray and wrinkle, as my parents receive with gratitude their continuing days of good health, and as my three sons surpass me in height and life expectation, I spend more time grieving change than I ever anticipated. I have come to call this kind of grief—everyday, not tragic, a tug in the present, not only in the future—"mundane grief."

Compared to the death of a child, daily loss is nothing. "No parent should have to bury a child," exclaims King Theoden in the *Lord of the Rings* when he awakens from an evil spell to find his only son dead at the hands of the enemy. Nothing is more disturbing than the searching memoirs of parents who have lost children. "It's so wrong, so profoundly wrong," exclaims Nicholas Wolterstorff, who lost his twenty-five-year-old son in a disastrous mountain climbing accident, "for a child to die before its parents." The death of a child brings one to the nadir of hopelessness. This is an experience no one should have to endure.

Yet there is a connection between tragic and mundane loss. All parents stand on an evolving continuum as people vulnerable before the utter precariousness of the created lives dearest to them, whether they live with present loss or contemplate impending loss. In fact, those who have suffered the death of a child are precisely those who are in a good position to remind the rest of us, as pastoral theologian Bruce Vaughn does, that mourning is "an ongoing and fundamental dimension of what it means to be human." It is not a "discrete, diagnosable, and transient clinical entity" to be spotted and cured but a fundamental aspect of parenting and an unavoidable dimension of parental spirituality.

My thesaurus lists some interesting substitutes for *mundane*: earthly, secular, temporal, worldly. In all these supposedly nonspiritual words, we see the Western Christian tradition's tendency to segregate the sacred from the ordinary, the religious from the run of the mill. Just as I have argued against dividing things in this way throughout this book, I now want to emphasize that the sacred is present in mundane loss as well. If day-to-day parenting is a practice that is deeply spiritual, and if parenting is filled with loss, then learning to grieve within families is essential to our lives with God and one another.

Parents "inevitably begin losing their children as soon as they are born," remarks historian Anne Higonnet. In fact, the word *care,* according to poet Kathleen Norris, "derives from an Indo-European word meaning to 'cry out,' as in a lament." In her poem "Ascension," written as she thinks about her birthing sister bearing down in labor on the day commemorating Jesus' rising to heaven, she pictures the "new mother, that leaky vessel," nursing her child, "beginning the long good-bye." Beginning the long good-bye.

Most parents exaggerate when they attempt to capture the anguish of this extended good-bye. "Nothing makes up for the loss," declares Virginia Woolf, speaking through Mrs. Ramsay, the central character in her novel *To the Lighthouse* and mother of eight children. She "would have liked always to have a baby," for "she was happiest carrying one in her arms" and her child "will never be so happy again." Another mother warns her friend, "When they leave the adjustment is worse than when they first come." Yet another mother says, "Each new separation causes anguish in me, preventing my life . . . from going on as before. . . . Climbing rocks. Going to camp. Crossing streets. Growing up."

The deep irony here is that these moments of letting go are also, at the very same time, celebrated moments of blessing. I doubt there is one parent out there who isn't also exceedingly relieved *not* to always have a baby in his or her arms. We are glad the baby got out of diapers, climbed rocks, crossed the street, went to camp, and, yes, grew up. So the adjustment of parenting is marked and marred by this ambivalence and paradox.

The only account of Jesus' childhood that appears in any of the four canonical gospels is a story shaped by this very paradox. It begins when Jesus' parents, who are returning home to the small town of Nazareth after spending Passover in the crowded city of Jerusalem, discover that they have left their twelve-year-old son behind (Luke 2: 41–52). Hastening back into the city, they find him in the temple discussing religion with the teachers. The one they have been so worried about is actually not lost but perhaps precisely where he should be.

In her analysis of this story, biblical theologian Beverly Roberts Gaventa argues that the New Revised Standard Version ("your father and I have been searching for you *in great anxiety*") fails to "capture the poignancy of the word Luke selects (*odynoun*)." In a better translation, Mary, who speaks so few words in the scriptural canon, exclaims, "Behold, your father and I have been looking for you *in anguish,*" when she and Joseph find Jesus in the temple. The emotional claim that Mary makes here "is the real and present terror of parents who do not know where their child is." I once dropped off a twelve-year-old son at Starbucks to let him walk across the street with his drink to meet me in my office; he got lost on the university campus and did not show up until thirty minutes later. I was terrified after twenty. Mary and Joseph searched for three whole days—an almost unfathomable amount of time compared to parents nowadays who become hysterical when a child fails to show up at an appointed time and place. In essence we are not all that different from Mary, the mother of God, who, as Gaventa notes, contends with a child that is "profoundly hers and yet not hers at all."

None of us can vanquish life's sorrow—either our own or that of our children, whose sorrows magnify ours—by a wave of the hand, an effort of the will, or even an act of deep faith. When Martin Luther lost Magdalena, his thirteen-year-old daughter, he found that even his faith in the "death of Christ" was "unable to drive out sorrow from our inmost depths as it ought to do." Neither Luther nor the nineteenth-century theologian Friedrich Schleiermacher, who lost his nine-year-old son Nathanael, called their loss a blessing in disguise or expressed relief that the child would be spared from corruption as an adult in the world. Both knew that this way of thinking simply does not work.

Nor can we ultimately protect our children from suffering and death. The little one growing inside me must finally face death like the rest of us, I realized in a thought that came unbidden when I was

Blessing and Letting Go

first pregnant. "You shall go through it all," says Woolf's Mrs. Ramsay, as she regards her children, "love and ambition and being wretched alone in dreary places . . . the eternal problems: suffering; death; the poor." "Though theologians insist that grace is freely given," writes the usually humorous author Anne Lamott, "the truth is that sometimes you pay for it through the nose. And you can't pay for your child's way."

Mundane Failure

To make matters worse, most grief is mingled with regret. I have always loved the title of an essay by my friend Herbert Anderson, "Between Rhetoric and Reality." Popular rhetoric about equality between women and men in families simply does not match the reality in many women's lives, the essay argues. Despite dramatic changes in gender roles, many women find that their workload has simply doubled as they come home from work to begin the notorious second shift.

Beyond this issue, however, the phrase also captures precisely where we stand almost all the time in other areas of family life. Every single day, we live somewhere between rhetoric and reality. Perhaps this sense of being betwixt and between is just another way to describe our human condition, as Christianity has long understood it. We stand caught between the hope that is ours in creation and redemption and the actuality of our fallen existence.

Sometimes the graphic physicality and relentlessness of this "continuing dimension of failure" with children are almost indescribable. Although many other forms of human suffering are "self-evidently horrific," British Catholic theologian Margaret Hebblethwaite observes, the only way to convince those without children about the hardship entailed in parenting is by detailing it in its very minutiae:

> I run the bath, which is by now half an hour late. Dominic
> [four and a half] comes in the bathroom with his bouncy
> ball. A second later "Mummy, I've lost my bouncy ball." I

say I will look for it when I have finished running the bath. He accepts this. Success. I undress him. He goes to the loo to pee. As he lifts the seat it falls off and on to the floor with a crash. He cries. I am now a bit fed up, and I say "Don't cry, just pee." He stops crying. Success. He gets into the bath. I ask if he has had a pee. He does not answer. I ask again. He says "Yes." Cordelia [two and a half] comes in and announces she has shat in her tights. I look to see if it is true. It is very true. I am very irritated, for several reasons. Firstly, because I should not be irritated with Cordelia for shitting in her tights. Secondly, because I was already irritated before this happened. Thirdly, because we are half an hour late, and a late bed means I get no work done before dinner. Fourthly, because if I had not saved a couple of minutes before we went out by leaving her nappy off she would not have dirtied her tights. Fifthly, and most of all, because every time she wears these tights she seems to manage to get shit on them first day on. . . . I had moreover . . . bought her a second pair . . . only two days previously, and it is this new pair that is now so dramatically and rapidly shat upon. What is she to wear tomorrow?

So it goes. And continues to go (several pages worth). Success is hard-earned, failure pervasive, however one judges her parenting and the relative absence of her husband, the theologian Peter Hebblethwaite.

That's just the point: we are always standing in judgment of our own and other people's parenting and in judgment of our own and other people's faith. By most standards, most of us fall short. Even on a relatively uneventful, nontraumatic evening in a family where the kids sleep, one parent earns a living wage, and both parents are theologians. It's amazing we have so little patience with those who have far fewer means than Hebblethwaite and Hebblethwaite.

Does it seem overwrought to use words such as *failure* and *guilt* for how we parents fall short when we are rushed or cranky? I don't believe it is. Care of children asks much of us, and there is failure and guilt involved: dreams abandoned, conversations interrupted, projects forsaken, friendships neglected, practices failed. The small missteps of parenting lead right into some of the biggest questions theologians and philosophers ask about what it means to be human—finite, vulnerable, and mortal, yet also full of love and hope. We "lay down a piece of our lives," says a friend, "when caring for children." Children make readily apparent that we must choose among many possibilities and then live well enough within the fixed parameters of these choices. They teach us about the need to surrender before our limits and cut our losses. They are often the best reminder of our ultimate fallibility and vulnerability before life's whims and its ultimate end.

Over the years, human beings have pursued various ways of dealing with this unpleasant reality of finitude and failure. Christianity proposes a different response from the resigned acceptance of Stoicism and its contemporary variations. Common Stoic rhetoric today claims dying, for example, as a natural part of life, as much a part of life as birth. At a fundamental level, the Christian tradition does not agree.

The early tradition—Paul and then, most definitively, Augustine—declared death a punishment for sin. Seeing loss in this way sounds antiquated to us, but it captures an important facet of Christian faith. There is a decided relentlessness to time and finitude against which even faithful Christians fight. Not much can really be said in the face of this, as is clearest in dire situations. Wolterstorff implores, "Please: Don't say it's not really so bad. Because it is. Death is awful, demonic. . . . What I need to hear . . . is that you recognize how painful it is." The very goodness of creation "makes death all the more difficult to live with." Although Christians do not worship the world or the human body, doctrines of creation and salvation affirm the inherent worth of embodiment. We are more than our bodies, but "of nothing on earth do we have more intimate possession." Grief involves the real loss of the materiality of ordinary touch, nurture, and affection.

Guilt intensifies this loss because it adds to the anxiety of death, in Paul Tillich's words, "an anxiety which it would not have without guilt, namely, the feeling of standing under judgment." People are anxious about the future, not only because of its brevity but also because of "its impenetrable darkness and the threat that one's whole existence in time will be judged as a failure." Whereas Stoic rhetoric asserts, "Be calm and accept death as a part of life," Jesus says, "Blessed are you who weep" (Luke 6:21b). He himself wept with others before the grave of his good friend Lazarus (John 11:35). Lazarus was dead. His loved ones were deeply grieved.

OFFERING AND RECEIVING GRACE

One summer, I spent a week with teenagers yearning to embody the Christian faith in their daily lives. We had talked together about the weight of material possessions and the stuff that burdens us. Several teens were troubled in particular by the craze in the United States of wearing brand-name clothing. They turned their shirts inside out so that "Old Navy" and "Abercrombie and Fitch" wouldn't show. No longer would they give these and other merchants the benefit of free advertising by parading around with labels on their own bodies.

Before you knew it, however, a practice that had seemed hopeful turned into a new mandate and stigma. Those who didn't abide—the right-side-outers—were guilty by omission. One night, a wise youth sponsor stood up and nudged us back to the path of grace. He reminded us all: the intent is love and grace. Do not mistake the means for the end, the rhetoric for the reality. "It's not so much about practice. It's all about love, being in love. The practices alone will kill you. You are God's beloved," he declared, "and God's love will not fail. There's nothing you can do that will cause God to love you less." We adopt specific faith practices for God's sake and in response to God's love, and not for the "sake of a preferred way of life," as theologian Miroslav Volf puts it. We adopt them because they connect us, enliven us, and move us to experience God.

Ahh, so easy to mistake the practice for the real thing, maybe because turning our shirts inside out is, at least momentarily, doable. Living faith daily is less so.

We were helped immensely that week by music. The favorite by a long shot was a South African freedom song, "Bambelela." The repeated lyric urges "bambelela": "Never give up." In times of trouble, when times are hard, when in pain, we should never give up. The refrain, like good liturgy, allows the singer to moan in lament and then echo "Never, never, never give up." Bambelela. God triumphs.

Several years ago, when my son walked into our house after returning from his high school graduation, he said without recrimination, "Where were you after the ceremony?" He described how other families had come down to the floor of the cavernous agricultural center to take pictures. Where were we? We had proudly watched him and others march across the stage from our seats miles away. But then we made a beeline to our van, glad to beat the crowds and traffic, unaware that families and friends could greet graduates on the amphitheater floor. Now aware, we felt awful.

I spent a rare day the next day in regret and self-recrimination when an e-mail came asking if I would write an article about a huge oversight in Christian practice: self-forgiveness. Christianity speaks easily about forgiving others, it said, but "what seems to have been forgotten is how to forgive ourselves for mistakes brought on by our own poor choices." I'm not saying God sent this, but I got the message. I had some work to do.

Of course, in the greater scheme of life, my remorse was trivial. More serious failures arise in families. But still this smaller failure hurt precisely because it represented more than the actual incident itself. It reminded me of other times I'd missed the mark and fallen short of my son's hope, my hope, God's hope.

Fortunately, by the time I read the e-mail, I had taken steps toward reconciliation, although that's the first lesson: self-forgiveness, like forgiving others, is slow. One cannot simply dump feelings of guilt and remorse by telling oneself to get over them. I called my good friend. It helped to pour out my undoing to someone outside the situation who nonetheless understood it intimately. She reminded me that I'm generally a good parent. She pointed me toward a few other steps besides self-affirmation: reassessment of distorted standards of self-perfection, and asking my son directly to forgive me even if he didn't think I'd done anything wrong.

Sometimes, of course, we experience guilt when it is not warranted—for example, when we fail to devote ourselves to our children 24/7, an expectation that is absurd. (Self-love is absolutely necessary for love of others, as the commandment to "love others as one loves oneself" actually implies.) Some guilt, however, is real. After the graduation, I was grateful for my religion's long tradition of practices of confession and prayer supporting forgiveness. Psalms are loaded with self-confessions. The Lord's prayer itself puts forgiveness before God at its heart and links it with forgiveness of others ("forgive us our sins for we ourselves forgive everyone indebted to us"; Luke 11:4a). My friend told me about a Jewish practice of going to the person wronged to admit your mistakes. If you confess your sin once, twice, three times, the other person is obliged to grant absolution.

Living side by side, intimately, day in and day out with those you love (and sometimes hate) requires a huge amount of patience, forbearance, and forgiveness. Children forgive easily, youths less so; adults have almost permanent barriers in place—a mark of our "maturity." Yet we adults have to model forgiveness if we are going to expect it of our own kids.

After one episode when Lamott tangles with her son Sam—whom hormones have turned into tense, sullen, and contemptuous "Phil" while she has become in turn the midlife "Menopausal Death Crone"—they move to reconcile. It takes time, distance, prayer, and mutual understanding. Ultimately, she demonstrates, it takes mutual apology:

> He sighed and began to speak. "I'm sorry I was such an asshole," he said.
>
> I'd sort of been hoping he'd say something I could report back to my pastor, but I saw how bad he felt, how lonely.
>
> "OK?" he said.
>
> I shook my head and sighed. "I'm sorry I was such an asshole, too."

I bet Lamott's own mom never said this to her. Times have changed if parents now occasionally join their children in admitting fault. In

Blessing and Letting Go

such moments, "we let go of our self-serving expectations for one another and rejoice in a simply loving presence that flows freely between us"—a friend's definition of mutual forgiveness that you could report to the pastor. Forgiveness transforms the desire to curse into the gift of blessing.

BESTOWING BLESSING

Well, it took a while to get here. Long enough that after writing about loss and failure one day, I called Mark, distraught. I tried to explain to him why I thought I needed to lead readers of this chapter through grief and failure if I wanted to write truthfully about blessing and letting go. As is sometimes the case, I found myself saying out loud what I couldn't say on paper: "Ultimately blessing only comes when we have reached our limits. Only then does it become a truly spiritual practice—maybe even the only response we can offer and receive."

"I will not let you go, unless you bless me" (Genesis 32:26b). These are Jacob's words. The son of Isaac and the father of a large clan, Jacob was in big trouble with his older brother Esau, and he truly expected Esau to attack, take all his possessions, and destroy him. He probably deserved as much.

Years earlier, Jacob offended Esau in one of the most damaging ways possible: he stole his blessing. Hard to imagine now, but at that time this came about as close to stealing someone's life and welfare as you could get. One's inheritance, the land and the animals, determine whether one lived or died. But the father's blessing meant even more: according to one biblical commentary, people believed it "released a power that determined the destiny of the recipient and [once given] could not be retracted." Jacob has run away for a long time, but Esau is now on his doorstep. No wonder Jacob can't sleep. Most of us would toss and turn too. He wrestles "until daybreak" with a man who finally strikes and injures Jacob's hip, demanding that Jacob let him go. When Jacob refuses until blest, the man christens Jacob "Israel" and blesses him. In this fought-for blessing, he believes he has witnessed the "face" of God (v. 30).

The very next morning, Jacob shakes in fear as Esau and his four hundred men approach. But as they draw near Esau runs to meet him, embracing and kissing him. In Esau's forgiveness, Jacob is again blessed: "For truly to see your face is like seeing the face of God—since you have received me with such favor" (Genesis 33:10b).

In blessing, we find reprieve and release. We step under the wide umbrella of God's grace. We see, as Jacob did, the "face of God." Sometimes we have to wrestle fiercely for our blessings through dark nights. But ultimately our ability to bless each other rests in God's blessing.

The sheer number of places that blessing arises in the narrative, didactic, and homiletic material of the Jewish and Christian tradition is a bit overwhelming. God blesses creation (Genesis 1:22, 28; 2:3; 5:2). God blesses Abraham and Sarah and blesses posterity through them (Genesis 17:1–27; 18:18). God issues a blessing to the liberated people of Israel through Moses that assures them, once again, that God's "face" shines on them and God's "countenance"—God's face again—conveys peace (Numbers 6:22–27). Even before Jesus does much at all, a "voice from heaven" pronounces a blessing on his baptism: "You are my Son, the Beloved; with whom I am well pleased" (Mark 1:11; Matthew 3:17; Luke 3:22). The Lord's prayer is predicated on blessing God; "hallowed be thy name" (Matthew 6:9b; Luke 11:2b). Blessing stands at the center of the proclamation of those whom Jesus honors in the Beatitudes (Matthew 5:3–12; Luke 6:17, 20–23).

In one of the most powerful biblical moments of blessing, when Jesus blesses the children, the blessing is tactile. He lays hands on them. This is precisely what the people want: they bring children so he might "touch them" (Mark 10:13, 16; Matthew 19:13, 15; Luke 18:15).

The term *bless* and it variations (blessed, blessest, blesseth, blessing) take up over a full page in the tiny-print Concordance, including tongue-twisting extended blessings, like when Isaac blesses Jacob. Isaac says that his own blessing will reverberate because Jacob will be "blessed by everyone who blesses you!" (Genesis 27:29b). There is a striking relational richness in all this blessing, as British theologian David Ford observes: "God blesses creation and human beings within it, creation blesses God, human beings bless God and creation and each other."

There is both asymmetry and mutuality here, notes Ford. We are to offer God blessing regardless of our circumstances, as most powerfully portrayed in the biblical story of Job who, caught in a wager between God and Satan, loses everything he loves—family, home, flocks—and still proclaims his love of God (Job 1:21). This blessing or hallowing of God's name has been "practiced by Jews in every sort of setting, including many Job-like situations, down the centuries," Ford says. But the promise of blessing is the gift of its love shared more abundantly. So there is also an amazing mutuality, a non-coercive and noncompetitive giving of love, between God and each of us. In blessings bestowed, we are at once bestower and recipient.

"What have I done?" So pleads Reverend John Ames, the central character of Marilynne Robinson's novel *Gilead,* after baptizing the woman who will become his wife. He questions not because of any uncertainty, but because no matter how hard he tried, he felt "outside the mystery of it." At some point blessing is simply a mystery to which we can only witness.

This realization evokes a memory from Ames's own childhood, when he and his peers, being the "very pious" children they were raised to be, took to baptizing a litter of kittens. Gowned in a doll's dress, he himself "moistened their brows" and repeated the Trinity. Though the mother cat eventually put a stop to the whole affair and his own father later made clear the Sacraments are not intended for cats, he is still left with some questions: "For years we would wonder what, from a cosmic viewpoint, we had done to them." He understands baptism as a blessing that doesn't exactly "enhance sacredness" but primarily acknowledges it. "There is power in that," he says. "I have felt it pass through me. . . . The sensation is of really knowing a creature, I mean really feeling its mysterious life and your own mysterious life at the same time."

Touching someone with the intent of blessing holds power. "I don't know why there is so little about this aspect of the calling" in ministerial literature, Ames remarks. Neither do I.

Blessing may even be the "most essential thing in, for example, teaching and leadership," Ford suggests, because blessing has the capacity to be "prophetic, transformative and controversial." Just notice, he points out, "how many points of conflict in both the Bible and in church life are connected with acts of blessing—Isaac blessing Jacob and Esau, Jacob wrestling for a blessing at Jabbok Ford, the blessing of marriages and other partnerships, the blessing of the elements in the Lord's Supper or Eucharist, the granting of absolution for sins, the laying-on of hands in ordination." The history and power of blessing then calls for wise discernment in its practice: "who to bless, what to bless, and why, when, how, where."

One thing Reverend Ames of *Gilead* does know for sure: the practice of blessing is mediated through the gift and joy of our "physical particularity." This is something the seventy-year-old man, ailing from a serious heart condition and writing as a testament for his son, most acutely anticipates losing. He feels blessed in the midst of painful circumstances of material loss: a fire that destroys a church, a grave that marks his grandfather's demise, his namesake who tests him, and most poignantly his beloved wife, child, and vocation in ministry. As he ruminates on these things, he recognizes "how I have loved my physical life." His sense of blessing grows immediately out of this. He sees blessing in the most mundane moments, moments of daily life many of us often miss. He even wishes that he himself had paid more attention to it.

So I touch and embrace my sons as they come and go. My husband and I try to bless their leaving, sometimes more successfully than others, often with a simple "We love you" or litany of hopes: "Learn a lot, work hard, have fun." (Only occasionally do I send them forth by telling them to have a "terrible, horrible, no good, very bad day.") Maybe good-bye itself says more than we realize. It is, after all, a much diminished derivative of "God be with you."

I hadn't thought about this much until I spent nine months in Dakar, Senegal, in my junior year in college, where the blessing of God is more evident in the hellos and good-byes. We learned rudimentary Wolof, a national language. In Wolof, a proper greeting has serious consequence. *Asalaa-maalekum* (peace) and *malekum-salaam* (peace be with you) are only the beginning of a long string of patterned exchanges designed to recognize the other person fully in all their relationships. Ignore this in approaching someone, and they will ignore you.

We almost always tuck in our kids at night, although we certainly wouldn't call it that now or use the old prayer, slightly modified, "Now I lay you down to sleep, I pray the Lord your soul to keep. Keep you safe all through the night and wake you with the morning light." Now I roll all the ambiguity of separation, failure, and blessing into one pithy and powerful (even if I don't realize it) phrase and simply say, "God bless you."

When Herbert Anderson asked people what they remember about what was said when they or their children left for college, he discovered that most people recall very little. He suggests we consider our words of parting and expand our vocabulary. Indeed, "properly understood, a blessing is the essential condition for leaving home." At the actual moment of departure, a blessing "without strings" granting affirmation, support, and hope is best.

I first heard what is now my favorite blessing at a family retreat village. It was bestowed during evening worship to villagers who were departing the next day, and it captures what I might have said to my son as he departed for college, or to all of my children before they climbed on the bus: "Lord God, you have called your servants to ventures of which we cannot see the ending, by paths as yet untrodden, through perils unknown. Give us faith to go out with good courage, not knowing where we go, but only that your hand is leading us and your love supporting us. Through Jesus Christ our Lord, Amen."

I like the blessing because it asks for grace and courage amid "perils unknown." I know it has woven through the hearts of many who have come and gone to create a tapestry of God's beloved making their way in the midst of it all.

Our society may not accord blessing the same status and power it assumed in Jacob and Esau's time. But we underestimate its importance at our own risk and loss.

LETTING GO

Even once a blessing is said and benediction given, we are not quite done. The practice of blessing isn't finished yet. We must let go.

A first-time mother I admire greatly handed her newborn to me (without hesitation or anxiety, I thought) and did her presentation to all those gathered. Frankly, I didn't know how she could stand it. She seemed to have no trouble letting her infant go from arms to arms around the room. I had a terrible time letting any of my sons go to other people, most of all my first-born.

What was that all about, that obsessive possessiveness? Especially when passing him on might have given me a moment of relief? Surely I needed that. Why couldn't I relax? What was I protecting? What was this dire feeling of my child's complete vulnerability? Was it a hint of my own limitation and precariousness? Like the first scratch. That was painful too. Or the first tooth falling out. The body undoing itself. The presence of death within life. Maybe letting go is not my specialty or strength. But I'm not alone.

"When my last child was born," admits Jewish religious ethicist Laurie Zoloth, "it was weeks before I could comfortably bear to have another person hold her. It was, I explained to myself, as if they were holding a piece of my body, some internal organ, my heart, my liver, something that was flesh of my flesh, bone of my bone taken from my side, warm with my own heat, carried around outside my body." She reaches a stark conclusion: "*What is at stake is death,* and the urgency of this recognition is both made sharper by childbirth and made curiously more comforting. When I die, this next one will live after." So we cling to them.

The passage of time is not an abstraction with kids. It is, as they might say, "in your face." In my Christmas letter a year ago (notoriously sent in January), I noted that my youngest son "looks me in the eye" (I am five foot seven and shrinking). A few days after I posted the letters—I'm not kidding—he no longer was. He was looking *down*. By summer he neared five foot eleven.

If that isn't a message of one's own diminishing stature, I'm not sure what is. He lets me know it regularly, just as it should be.

Sometimes when I call attention to his growth—bless it, so to speak—he beams, or more accurately tries to suppress his pleasure. I grin too, with a hidden twinge of . . . what is it . . . regret? Sadness as I let go?

Letting go of children goes against the grain of human self-preservation. It is hard because we have to let go of part of ourselves—a very precious part of ourselves, at that—that we have incorporated into ourselves in loving the other. Letting go requires trust that we—and they—are preserved and upheld by a force greater than our own efforts.

The Christian tradition has long sought to sustain such trust. Children are gifts, given to us on loan by a gracious God as part of God's good creation. Perhaps the hardest spiritual lesson or the most difficult virtue to acquire in the care of children over the long run is returning oneself and those most loved to God's care and protection. As Robinson writes through the narrated voice of Reverend Ames: "It seems almost a cruelty for one generation to beget another when parents can secure so little for their children." Parents can do little else than relinquish their children to the wilderness, trusting that God will honor the parents' love "by assuring that there will indeed be angels" watching over them. It is only such trust that finally allows parents to stop short of using children to build up themselves, and love their children genuinely.

My kids help sometimes. They remind me that grasping after life, after them, only means I lose them. Letting go brings hope of eternal return. Over and over in many ways and in many publications, Anderson reiterates, a "family's capacity to be together depends on its ability to be separate and honor the autonomy of each member. . . . We leave our families of origin in order to go home again; if we can't go home again, we probably never left."

One hears in Anderson's words the echoes of the reverse psychology of family systems theory: the tighter held, the more the person flees; walk the other way, and the child will follow. Though this may appear to be manipulative, it is guided by deeper wisdom. Parents must find the balance of hopeful care somewhere between neglect and overbearing control, both of which interfere with a child's growth.

A friend told me that her mother had made a wonderful practice of giving each of her children a particular gift when they reached twenty-one. Hers arrived in the mail in a tie box, where she was living on her own trying to write the great American novel. She knew before opening it what was inside the package: a neatly ironed pair of apron strings, snipped with pinking shears from her mother's well-worn lavender gingham apron. "I love you enough to let you go," the card read. Her older brother had received his apron strings two years earlier on his twenty-first birthday. Her younger sister received her set at her bridal shower when she was twenty, and her younger brother handed his pair back, saying simply, "I'm not ready." It was nearly two years before he asked her to give them to him. My friend concludes, "Sometimes as parents we do not cut the apron strings at the time we would choose, because the child needs the blessing of being held on to, rather than let go. Paradoxically, this too needs to be done with 'no strings attached.' "

The parental role must be, as Catholic ethicist Christine Gudorf remarks, "a constantly diminishing one in the life of a child." Her claim is accurate in one sense, but it also exaggerates or simplifies a complex process that involves something a bit different than mere diminishment. Instead, letting go requires seeking new and creative ways to sustain and deepen intimacy under increasingly distant and more limited circumstances. In the best of all possible worlds, a decreasing role in one sense is balanced by a new, possibly richer kind of connectivity in another sense.

Poetry once again captures the complexity of this practice. A wonderful final section of Mary Oliver's poem "In Blackwater Woods" conveys powerfully the flux and flow of this process of loving and leave taking, whose meaning we can never fully know. "To live in this world," she says, "you must be able to do three things: to love what is mortal; to hold it against your bones knowing your own life depends on it; and when time comes to let it go, to let it go":

In Blackwater Woods

Look, the trees
are turning
their own bodies
into pillars

Blessing and Letting Go

of light,
are giving off the rich
fragrance of cinnamon
and fulfillment,

the long tapers
of cattails
are bursting and floating away over
the blue shoulders

of the ponds,
and every pond,
no matter what its
name is, is

nameless now.
Every year
everything
I have ever learned

in my lifetime
leads back to this: the fires
and the black river of loss
whose other side

is salvation,
whose meaning
none of us will ever know.
To live in this world

you must be able
to do three things:
to love what is mortal;
to hold it

against your bones knowing
your own life depends on it;
and, when the time comes to let it go,
to let it go.

Hearing the last step twice, the final sentence of the poem, reminds us that it is not easy to let go but, with practice and coaching and maybe a little grace and repetition, it is doable.

When we hear and retell Jesus' parable of the prodigal son from Luke 15, we usually focus on the younger brother, who takes and squanders his inheritance, or the older brother, who gets angry when his father celebrates his brother's return. But the father is quite remarkable. He loves his sons but does not romanticize or micromanage their lives. He gives them all he has ("All that is mine is yours") yet is separate enough to give them room to ask questions, explore, test their freedom, and fail. They can refuse or receive what he has to offer. He is generous but not manipulative, compassionate but not overprotective. He takes both of his children seriously enough to honor the contrasting ways to bless them and let them go.

ON EAGLE'S WINGS

The day had come. I wasn't sure what I would say. I didn't know what Mark would say. I did know that we could never say all that was in our hearts. It was the day of blessing the graduating seniors in our congregation, and my son was among them. Our minister who works closely with the youths had asked us each to take a moment following a community meal to say a few words to our children. She created the space in which Mark and I, in turn, could offer our child a blessing—out loud and in the presence of others.

All the parents, in their individual ways, took the chance to say publicly and personally how much they loved their child, as well as how much they and the church would continue to hold the child/youth/adult in their heart and in the palm of their hand. Some were more eloquent than others, but each spoke from the heart. Lest words not be enough, each family had also compiled a notebook to give to the child, a notebook filled with pictures and letters from friends, relatives, adults in the congregation, other adults in the child's life, ministers, and the parents and immediate family. We watched a slide show with two or three pictures of each child, a cute kid hugging a stuffed animal or wearing oversized cowboy boots in one shot transformed into a handsome young woman or man donning a graduation cap in the next. Prior to the meal, we worshiped together, led in prayer and song by our own tall children. They prayed, preached, offered communion, and sang. We admired, listened, partook, applauded, and cried.

There is the dear, nagging paradox again. I simply can't believe I have to go through this two more times with my other kids. I would be stricken if I didn't get to do so for any reason.

Soon after I first recognized anticipatory grief in myself a few years ago, I drove to pick up my oldest son at the airport. I waited, as person after person filed past, for him to appear around the corner. When he did, I found myself surprised by tears, tears that mixed love and loss in equal portions. The more I tried not to cry, the more I did, and the more my son looked at me strangely. I really couldn't explain it to him easily. To stare finitude straight in the face when the face is so beloved . . . how could you *not* cry?

Even though I can't fully explain all this to my kids, I do know that I have learned a few things during twenty years as a parent. I know that I will never leave mundane loss or failure behind. But I also know that with years and practice I may get better at blessing and letting go, as I see often happens with grandparents. I also have realized that children and those who care for them receive blessings that far outweigh all the loss and failure.

Ultimately God has promised more abundant life than sorrow. Jesus raised a stinking, grave-bound Lazarus. When he blessed the weeping, he promised them laughter. "Blessed are you who weep now, for you will laugh."

Our congregation often sings a refrain from a hymn, "On Eagle's Wings," as our benediction: "And I will raise you up on eagle's wings, bear you on the breath of dawn, make you to shine like the sun, and hold you in the palm of my hand." Before we moved here ten years ago, the choir in our previous congregation

sang this same hymn in full the Sunday morning our family celebrated our last day with them. I felt powerfully embraced by their
words. The hymn beautifully captures the blessing of Psalm 91. We
are reminded that we abide in God's shelter and shadow, that we
need not fear the "terror of the night, nor the arrow that flies by
day" nor the "snare of the fowler," and that God's angels bear us
up. Resting in the palm of God's hand, I can let go. Shining together in the sun, we can laugh and love anew. Together we can
await the day when we shall all—adults and children alike—be
born up on eagle's wings.

References

PREFACE

Katherine Paterson's comment on children's nature appears in *The Invisible Child: On Reading and Writing for Children* (New York: Dutton Children's Books, 2001), p. 67. Parker Palmer names Merton's genius in his entry on "Thomas Merton" in Gordon S. Wakefield, ed., *The Westminster Dictionary of Christian Spirituality* (Philadelphia: Westminster, 1983), p. 265. Patricia Hill Collins talks about "othermothering" on pp. 119–120 in *Black Feminist Thought: Knowledge, Consciousness, and the Politics of Empowerment* (New York: Routledge, 1991). I have discussed the importance of shared responsibility for care of children in both *Also a Mother: Work and Family as Theological Dilemma* (Nashville, Tenn.: Abingdon, 1994), pp. 167–172; and *Let the Children Come: Reimagining Childhood from a Christian Perspective* (San Francisco: Jossey-Bass, 2003), pp. 165–167.

CHAPTER ONE

Some of these thoughts appear in my book *Also a Mother* and an article, "Contemplation in the Midst of Chaos," in *The Vocation of the Theological Teacher,* Gregory Jones and Stephanie Paulsell, eds. (Grand Rapids, Mich.: Eerdmans, 2002). I have since discovered two excellent articles contesting the traditional definition of spirituality:

Owen C. Thomas, "Interiority and Christian Spirituality," *Journal of Religion,* Jan. 2000, *80*(1), 41–60; and Janet Martin Soskice, "Love and Attention" in *Philosophy, Religion and the Spiritual Life,* Michael McGhee, ed. (Cambridge: Cambridge University Press, 1992), pp. 59–72, with a quote from p. 62.

For a portrait of early Christian thought on families and parenthood, see Carol Harrison, "The Silent Majority: The Family in Patristic Thought," in Stephen C. Barton, ed., *The Family in Theological Perspective* (Edinburgh: T&T Clark, 1996), pp. 87–105. The quote from Gregory of Nyssa's *On Virginity* is cited by Harrison on p. 93. Quotations from Thomas Merton are from *New Seeds of Contemplation* (New York: New Directions, 1972), pp. 7, 10. Wendy M. Wright's account of monastic life appears on pp. 2–3 of "Living the Already But Not Yet: The Spiritual life of the American Catholic Family," *Warren Lecture Series in Catholic Studies,* no. 25, University of Tulsa, Mar. 21, 1993. Quotations from Henri Nouwen are from pp. 4, 35, 37, 47, and 63 of *The Way of the Heart* (New York: Ballantine, 1981). He refers to *The Sayings of the Desert Fathers,* Benedicta Ward, trans. (London and Oxford: Mowbrays, 1975), p. 8.

Ernest Boyer's question about child care in the desert and his comments on the Catholic tradition appear in *A Way in the World: Family Life as Spiritual Discipline* (San Francisco: HarperSanFrancisco, 1984), pp. xi, 34–35. Thoughts on women and sainthood appear in Elizabeth A. Johnson, *Friends of God and Prophets: A Feminist Theological Reading of the Communion of Saints* (New York: Continuum, 1999), p. 28.

Scholars who have recently enriched Catholic understanding of family as "domestic church" include Lisa Sowle Cahill, *Family: A Christian Social Perspective* (Minneapolis: Fortress, 2000); Julie Hanlon Rubio, *A Christian Theology of Marriage and Family* (Mahwah, N.J.: Paulist Press, 2003); and Florence Caffrey Bourg, *Where Two or Three Are Gathered: Christian Families as Domestic Church* (Notre Dame, Ind.: University of Notre Dame, 2004). Tom Montgomery-Fate is the friend I mention who offers beautifully written thoughts on faith, fiction, and family from the henhouse in *Steady and Trembling: Art, Faith, and Family in an Uncertain World* (St. Louis: Chalice, 2005).

To explore alternative ways to think about chaos, anxiety, and peace, I refer to Catherine Keller, *Face of the Deep: A Theology of Becoming* (New York: Routledge, 2003); and "The Lost Chaos of Creation," *Living Pulpit,* Apr.–June 2000, *9*(2), 4–5; Ian G. Barbour, *Religion and Science: Historical and Contemporary Issues* (San Francisco: HarperSanFrancisco, 1997), pp. 183–184; Gabriel Fackre, *The Purpose and Work of Ministry: A Mission Pastor's Point of View* (Philadelphia: Christian Education Press, 1959), pp. ix-xi, 20–27; Paul Tillich, *Systematic Theology* (Chicago: University of Chicago Press, 1951, 1957), Vol. 1, *Being and God,* pp. 191–192 and Vol. 2, *Existence and the Christ,* pp. 67–68; Meister Eckhart, Sermon 86, Frank Tobin trans., in *Meister Eckhart: Teacher and Preacher,* Bernard McGinn, ed. (Mahwah, N.J.: Paulist Press, 1986), pp. 338–345, with thanks to Stephanie Paulsell for recommending this (see her own comments in " 'The Inscribed Heart: A Spirituality of Intellectual Work': Reading as a Spiritual Practice," *Lexington Theological Quarterly,* Fall 2001, *36*(3), 144); and Dorothy Bass, "The Peace of the Lord," *Cresset,* Reformation Issue (1998), pp. 28–29.

For other efforts in the Christian tradition to bridge contemplation and action, see Ignatius of Loyola, *The Spiritual Exercises of St. Ignatius,* Louis J. Puhl, S. J., trans. (Chicago: Loyola University Press, 1951); Timothy Fry, ed., *The Rule of Saint Benedict in English* (Collegeville, Minn.: Liturgical Press, 1982); Marilyn Schauble and Barbara Wojciak, eds., *A Reader's Version of the Rule of Saint Benedict in Inclusive Language* (Erie, Pa.: Benet Press, 1989); Delores R. Leckey, *The Ordinary Way: A Family Spirituality* (New York: Crossroad, 1982); Esther de Waal, *Seeking God: The Way of St. Benedict* (Collegeville, Minn.: Liturgical Press, 1984) and *Living with Contradiction: An Introduction to Benedictine Spirituality* (Harrisburg, Pa.: Morehouse, 1989); Joan Chittister, OSB, *Wisdom Distilled from the Daily: Living the Rule of St. Benedict Today* (San Francisco: HarperSanFrancisco, 1990).

In talking about prayer in families, both Wendy M. Wright (*Seasons of a Family's Life: Cultivating Contemplative Spirit at Home,* San Francisco: Jossey-Bass, 2003) and Marjorie J. Thompson (*Family: The Forming Center,* Nashville, Tenn.: Upper Room Books, 1996) cite

Brother Lawrence of the Resurrection, *The Practice of the Presence of God,* a critical edition by Conrad De Meester, Salvatore Scriurba, trans. (Washington, D.C.: ICS, Institutes of Carmelite Studies, 1994). The quote from Brother Lawrence cited by Thompson on pp. 81–82 comes from an earlier 1985 edition, p. 93. Howard Thurman's writing on prayer is voluminous, but a good place to start is *For the Inward Journey: The Writings of Howard Thurman* (Orlando: Harcourt Brace, 1984).

CHAPTER TWO

In rethinking faith in ordinary life, I cite Kathleen Norris, *The Quotidian Mysteries: Laundry, Liturgy, and "Women's Work"* (Mahwah, N.J.: Paulist Press, 1998), with quotes from pp. 15 and 76. Later in the chapter, I turn to Elizabeth Ann Dreyer, "Asceticism Reconsidered," *Weavings: A Journal of the Christian Spiritual Life,* 1988, *3*(6), 6–15, with a quote from p. 14, and *Earth Crammed with Heaven: A Spirituality of Everyday* (Mahwah, N.J.: Paulist Press, 1994), pp. 146–147; and Martin Luther, "The Estate of Marriage," in *Luther's Works,* Walther I. Brandt, ed., and Helmut T. Lehmann, gen. ed. (Philadelphia: Muhlenberg Press, 1962), with quotes from pp. 39–41.

To understand developments in mainstream religious practice and Protestant amnesia about our spiritual history, see Dean R. Hoge, Benton Johnson, and Donald A. Luidens, *Vanishing Boundaries: The Religion of Protestant Mainline Baby Boomers* (Louisville, Ky.: Westminster John Knox, 1994), with quotes from pp. 70–73; Margaret Lamberts Bendroth, *Growing Up Protestant: Parents, Children, and Mainline Churches* (New Brunswick, N.J.: Rutgers University Press, 2002), with her comment on the range of material on p. 3 and on Presbyterian family polity on pp. 125–129; a chapter by William R. Garrett, one by Jean Miller Schmidt and Gail E. Murphy-Geiss, and a third by Christine Firer Hinze in *Faith Traditions and the Family,* Phyllis Airhart and Margaret Lamberts Bendroth, eds. (Louisville, Ky.: Westminster John Knox, 1996). Observations about the place of the hearth in Martin Luther's household appear in William H. Lazareth, *Luther on the Christian Home: An Application of the Social Ethics of the Reformation* (Philadelphia, Muhlenberg Press, 1960), p. 29.

Reflections on Protestant faith come from Clark M. Williamson, "Theology and the Forms of Confession in the Disciples of Christ," *Encounter*, Winter 1980, *41*, 53–71, with quotes from pp. 53, 56, 61, and 69; Norman Maclean, *A River Runs Through It and Other Stories* (Chicago: University of Chicago Press, 1976); Nancy T. Ammerman, "Golden Rule Christianity: Lived Religion in the American Mainstream," in *Lived Religion in America: Toward a History of Practice,* David Hall, ed. (Princeton, N.J.: Princeton University Press, 1997), pp. 196–216, with quotes from pp. 196, 197, and 203; and Joseph D. Driskill, *Protestant Spiritual Exercises: Theology, History, and Practice* (Harrisburg, Pa.: Morehouse, 1999), with a quote from p. 7. The title of my chapter was suggested in part by the chapter title "The Sanctification of the Ordinary" in Douglas F. Ottati's *Reforming Protestantism: Christian Commitment in Today's World* (Louisville, Ky.: Westminster John Knox, 1995).

My understanding of parenting as a religious practice builds on the work of Dorothy Bass and Craig Dykstra in Dorothy C. Bass, ed., *Practicing Our Faith: A Way of Life for a Searching People* (San Francisco: Jossey-Bass, 1997) with quotes from pp. 8 (emphasis in text), 9, and 11; Craig Dykstra, "Reconceiving Practice," in *Shifting Boundaries: Contextual Approaches to the Structure of Theological Education,* Barbara Wheeler and Edward Farley, eds. (Louisville, Ky.: Westminster John Knox, 1991); and Dorothy C. Bass and Don C. Richter, eds., *Way to Live: Christian Practices for Teens* (Nashville, Tenn.: Upper Room Books, 2002). Robert Wuthnow's observations on "growing up religious" are found on p. xxxvii in *Growing Up Religious: Christians and Jews and Their Journeys of Faith* (Boston: Beacon, 1991).

For helpful understandings of vocation, I cite William C. Placher, "What Does My Faith Have to Do with My Job?" in *Why Are We Here? Everyday Questions and the Christian Life,* Ronald F. Thiemann and William C. Placher, eds. (Harrisburg, Pa.: Trinity Press International, 1998), pp. 130–142; and Frederick Buechner's familiar quote in *Wishful Thinking: A Theological ABC* (San Francisco: HarperSanFrancisco, 1993), p. 119. For other helpful works, see

Douglas J. Schuurman, *Vocation: Discerning Our Callings in Life* (Grand Rapids, Mich.: Eerdmans, 2004); Nancy J. Duff, "Vocation, Motherhood, and Marriage," in Jane Dempsey Douglass and James F. Kay, eds., *Women, Gender, and Christian Community* (Louisville, Ky.: Westminster John Knox, 1997); Claire E. Wolfteich, *Navigating New Terrain: Work and Women's Lives* (Mahwah, N.J.: Paulist Press, 2002), esp. chapter 3; and Julie Hanlon Rubio, *A Christian Theology of Marriage and Family*, chapter 5.

Quotes on the formative dimension of parenting come from my own book, *Also a Mother,* pp. 154–155; Luther, cited by Roland Bainton, *Here I Stand: A Life of Martin Luther* (Nashville: Abingdon, 1950), p. 302; and Wendy M. Wright, *Seasons of a Family's Life*, p. 3.

CHAPTER THREE

For a number of views of time and its use, see Juliet B. Schor, *The Overworked American: The Unexpected Decline of Leisure* (New York: Basic Books, 1991); Arlie Hochschild with Anne Machung, *The Second Shift: Working Parents and the Revolution at Home* (New York: Viking Penguin, 1989); Elaine St. James, *Simplify Your Life: 100 Ways to Slow Down and Enjoy the Things That Really Matter* (New York: Hyperion, 1994); Dorothy Bass, *Receiving the Day: Christian Practices for Opening the Gift of Time* (San Francisco: Jossey-Bass, 2000).

In addition to my own essay " 'Pondering All These Things': Mary and Motherhood," in *Blessed One: Protestant Perceptions of Mary,* Cynthia L. Rigby and Beverly Roberts Gaventa, eds. (Louisville, Ky.: Westminster John Knox, 2002), pp. 97–114, other commentary on Mary comes from Kathleen Hansley, "Supernatural Beings," *Christian Century,* Apr. 5, 2000, pp. 392–393 (her thought about the tone of the word *ponder* appears on p. 393); Sarah Coakley, "Mariology and 'Romantic Feminism': A Critique," in *Women's Voices: Essays in Contemporary Feminist Theory,* Teresa Elwes, ed. (London: Marshall Pickering, 1992), pp. 97–110, with her observation about Ruddick's "Mariology" on p. 171; Patrick D. Miller, "The Church's First Theologian," *Theology Today,* Oct. 1999, 56(3), 293–294; and Elizabeth A.

Johnson, *Truly Our Sister: A Theology of Mary in the Communion of Saints* (New York: Continuum, 2003). The quote by the mother of four who cannot identify with Mary comes from an interview in Claire E. Wolfteich's *Navigating New Terrain*, p. 147.

There are lots of resources for reclaiming the practice of pondering. Those to which I make explicit reference are Sara Ruddick, "Maternal Thinking," in *Mothering: Essays in Feminist Theory,* Joyce Treblicot, ed. (Totowa, N.J.: Rowman and Allanheld, 1983), with quotes from pp. 214, 217, and 222–223, and *Maternal Thinking: Toward a Politics of Peace* (Boston: Beacon, 1989), with quotes from pp. 24 and 121; Simone Weil, "Reflections on the Right Use of School Studies with a View to the Love of God," in *Waiting on God,* Emma Craufurd, trans. (New York: HarperCollins, 1951), with quotes from pp. 105, 113–115; Janet Martin Soskice, "Love and Attention," with quote from p. 70; Iris Murdoch, *The Sovereignty of Good* (London: Routledge and Kegan Paul, 1970), with quote from p. 43, cited by Soskice, p. 71; Herbert Anderson, "Practicing Theology in the Christian Life: Ordinary Awe," lecture manuscript (he cites Bainton as the source of Luther's remark on wonder leading to faith); Tom Montgomery-Fate, *Steady and Trembling*, pp. 47 and 100; and my own prior work on mothering, *Also a Mother*, where I talk about the pattern of body-mediated knowledge on pp. 147–148.

Other sources that indirectly influenced my thinking on this practice are Anne Thurston, *Because of Her Testimony: The Word in Female Experience* (New York: Crossroad, 1995); J. Bradley Wigger, *The Power of God at Home: Nurturing Our Children in Love of Grace* (San Francisco: Jossey-Bass, 2003); and Wendy M. Wright, *Seasons of a Family's Life*.

Garrison Keillor quoted Judith Viorst on his radio "Writer's Almanac" on her birthday, Feb. 2, 2000.

CHAPTER FOUR

To explore major changes in children's place in society, I draw on and use material from chapter 2 of my book *Let the Children Come*. Anne Higonnet's portrayal of new ways of seeing children in *Pictures of Innocence: The History and Crisis of Ideal Childhood* (New York: Thames and Hudson, 1998) proved pivotal for my thinking; direct quotes come from pp. 12, 209, and 224. Other histories that had a significant role in shaping my thought are Steven Mintz and Susan Kellogg, *Domestic Revolutions: A Social History of American Family Life* (New York: Free Press, 1988); John Demos, *Past, Present, and Personal: The Family and the Life Course in American History* (New York: Oxford University Press, 1985); Viviana A. Zelizer, *Pricing the Priceless Child: The Changing Social Value of Children* (Princeton, N.J.: Princeton University Press, 1994); Karin Calvert, *Children in the House: The Material Culture of Early Childhood, 1600–1900* (Boston: Northeastern University Press, 1992); and N. Ray Hiner and Joseph M. Hawes, eds. *Growing Up in America: Children in Historical Perspective* (Urbana and Chicago: University of Illinois Press, 1985).

The idea of "knowing children" resonates in the history of Christian thought. One can find rudimentary precedent for taking children's moral and spiritual lives more seriously, often submerged or distorted, in Christian scripture and tradition. Early Christian theologians, such as Augustine; later Reformation theologians, such as John Calvin; and even the notorious hell, fire, and damnation preacher Jonathan Edwards understood children as a complex mixture of *God's blessed creation* and *fallen creature*. Each theologian tried to define the intermediary position between innocence and guilt where children join adults in the struggle with faith. For further exploration, see Marcia J. Bunge, ed., *The Children in Christian Thought* (Grand Rapids, Mich.: Eerdmans, 2001).

To understand major demographic changes, I found useful Ron Lesthaeghe, "A Century of Demographic and Cultural Change in Western Europe: An Exploration of Underlying Dimensions," *Population and Development Review,* Sept. 1983, *9*(3), 411–435; two chapters in Arlene S. Skolnick and Jerome H. Skolnick's collection *Family in Transition,* 9th ed. (New York: Addison-Wesley, 1997), by Dennis A. Ahlburg and Carol J. De Vita, "New Realities of the American Family," pp. 21–29, with the statistic about the percentage of families including children on p. 24, and Donald Hernandez, with David E. Myers, "Revolutions in Children's Lives," pp. 256–266; and Tom W. Smith's

"The Emerging 21st-Century American Family," a report from the National Opinion Research Center (www.norc.uchicago.edu).

Comments about children's philosophy and the stories about children's profound remarks appear in Gareth B. Matthews, *The Philosophy of Childhood* (Cambridge: Harvard University Press, 1994), pp. 2, 4–6 (see also his *Philosophy and the Young Child* and *Dialogues with Children,* both published by Harvard University Press, 1980 and 1984 respectively); and Marjorie Thompson, *Family*, p. 82.

I appreciate those who have explored children's spirituality more methodically, such as Matthews, Robert Coles, Tobin Hart, and Jonathon Kozol. Coles's account of his interview with Connie and the girl facing desegregation appears on pp. 10–12 and 19–20 in *The Spiritual Life of Children* (Boston: Houghton Mifflin, 1990). Other quotations come from pp. 12, 19–21, 27, 39, and 340, footnote no. 7. Quotations from Hart appear in "The Mystical Child: Glimpsing the Spiritual World of Children," *Encounter: Education for Meaning and Social Justice,* Summer 2004, *17*(2), 3, 5, 7. Kozol, like Coles, has many books on children, among them the best sellers *Amazing Grace: The Lives of Children and the Conscience of a Nation* (New York: Harper-Collins, 1995) and *Ordinary Resurrections: Children in the Years of Hope* (New York: HarperCollins, 2000). Wendy Wright's comment about the changing aptitude for faith conversation with her teen daughter appears on p. 120 of *Seasons of a Family's Life*.

Matthews challenges developmental models of philosophy on pp. 16–18 of *The Philosophy of Childhood*. I draw parallels between this and Karl Rahner's essay "Ideas for a Theology of Childhood," from *Theological Investigations,* vol. 8 (London: Draton, Longman & Todd, 1971), with direct quotes found on pp. 33, 36, 40, 48, and 50. For a careful explication of this essay and more general background on Rahner, see Mary Ann Hinsdale, " 'Infinite Openness to the Infinite': Karl Rahner's Contribution to Modern Catholic Thought on the Child," in Marcia J. Bunge, ed., *The Children in Christian Thought*, pp. 406–445. She notes Rahner's everyday mysticism on pp. 418, 419–420.

The story of a father's reminiscence about the beauty and wonder of children appears in Marilynne Robinson, *Gilead* (New York: Farrar, Straus and Giroux, 2004), pp. 52, 65–66.

CHAPTER FIVE

I have been thinking about this topic for a long time. So I have many citations for this chapter, and they still do not properly represent the influences on my thought.

The quotes from Henri Nouwen come from *The Way of the Heart*, p. 47. To capture the weight and complexity of care giving, I refer to two Shel Silverstein books, *The Giving Tree* (New York: HarperCollins, 1964) and *Where the Sidewalk Ends* (New York: Harper-Collins, 1974), with named poems on pp. 35, 70–71. I also draw on comments from Elizabeth Green in "The Power of Attending: Family Life as Spiritual Practice," *Weavings: A Journal of the Christian Spiritual Life,* Sept.–Oct. 2005, *20*(5), 7–11 (quote from p. 10); and Tom Montgomery-Fate in *Steady and Trembling*, p. 47.

My historical portrait of mothering builds on material from Margaret Lamberts Bendroth, *Growing Up Protestant*, pp. 16 and 27; Elizabeth H. Pleck, *Celebrating the Family: Ethnicity, Consumer Culture, and Family Ritual* (Cambridge: Harvard University Press, 2000), pp. 8 and 15; Ann Taves, "Mothers and Children and the Legacy of Mid-19th-Century American Christianity," *Journal of Religion,* Apr. 1987, *67*(2), 203–219; Horace Bushnell, *Christian Nurture* (New York: Scribner, 1861; reprint, Eugene, Oreg.: Wipf and Stock, 2000), with quote from p. 237; and Anthony Fletcher, "The Family, Marriage and the Upbringing of Children in Protestant England," in *The Family in Theological Perspective,* Stephen C. Barton, ed., with quote from p. 128. On pp. 206–207, Taves cites Henry Ward Beecher, *Royal Truth* (Boston, 1866), and Bushnell, *The Vicarious Sacrifice, Grounded in Principles of Universal Obligation* (New York, 1866), in *Horace Bushnell,* H. Shelton Smith, ed. (New York: Oxford University Press, 1965), p. 282.

For illustration of diametrically opposed reactions to reclaiming the family as spiritually formative, I use Janet Fishburn, *Confronting the Idolatry of Family: A New Vision for the Household of God* (Nashville, Tenn.: Abingdon, 1991), with the quote from p. 86 on the one hand, and James Dobson, *Straight Talk: What Men Need to Know, What Women Should Understand* (Dallas: Word, 1991), p. 93 on the other hand, cited by Nancy J. Duff, "Vocation, Motherhood, and Marriage," p. 76.

To rethink mutuality and sacrifice, I turn to my own work *Also a Mother,* pp. 13–14; Beverly Wildung Harrison, "The Power of Anger in the Work of Love: Christian Ethics for Women and Other Strangers," in *Making the Connections: Essays in Feminist Social Ethics,* Carol S. Robb, ed. (Boston: Beacon, 1985), with quote from p. 18; Daniel M. Bell, Jr., "Sacrifice," in Donald W. Musser and Joseph L. Price, eds., *New and Enlarged Handbook of Christian Theology* (Nashville. Tenn.: Abingdon, 2003), with quote from p. 448; Brita L. Gill-Austern, "Love Understood as Self-Sacrifice and Self-Denial: What Does It Do to Women?" in *Through the Eyes of Women: Insights for Pastoral Care,* Jeanne Stevenson Moessner, ed. (Philadelphia: Westminster John Knox, 1996), with quote from p. 315; Barbara Hilkert Andolsen, "Agape in Feminist Ethics," *Journal of Religious Ethics,* 1981, *9*(1), with quote from p. 80; and Barbara Kingsolver, *High Tide in Tucson: Essays from Now or Never* (New York: HarperCollins, 1995), with quote from p. 90.

Other resources have had an important influence, even though not explicitly cited: my articles, "Sloppy Mutuality: Love and Justice for Children and Adults," in *Mutuality Matters: Faith, Family, and Just Love,* Edward Foley, Bonnie Miller-McLemore, Robert Schreiter, and Herbert Anderson, eds. (Lanham, Md.: Sheed and Ward, 2004), pp. 121–135; and "Practicing Theology in the Christian Life: Salvaging Sacrifice," unpublished Hein-Fry lecture, 2005; Valerie Saiving Goldstein, "The Human Situation: A Feminine View," *Journal of Religion,* Apr. 1960, *40*(2), 100–112; Christine E. Gudorf, "Parenting, Mutual Love, and Sacrifice," in Barbara Hilkert Andolsen, Christine E. Gudorf, and Mary D. Pellauer, eds., *Women's Consciousness and Women's Conscience: A Reader in Feminist Ethics* (San Francisco: HarperSanFrancisco, 1985), pp. 175–191; Susan Nelson Dunfee, *Beyond Servanthood: Christianity and the Liberation of Women* (Lanham, Md.: University Press of America, 1989); Pamela Cooper-White, *The Cry of Tamar: Violence Against Women and the Church's Response* (Minneapolis: Augsburg Fortress, 1995), esp. pp. 93–95; and Don S. Browning, Bonnie J. Miller-McLemore, Pamela D. Couture, K. Brynoff Lyon, and Robert M. Franklin, *From Culture Wars to Common Ground: Religion and the American Family Debate* (Louisville, Ky.: Westminster John Knox, 1997).

To consider the challenge of multiple vocations, I draw on Jane Lazarre, "The Mother-Artist: Woman as Trickster," in *Career and Motherhood: Struggles for a New Identity,* Alan Roland and Barbara Harris, eds. (New York: Human Sciences Press, 1979), pp. 162–176, with quotes from pp. 163, 174–175; Wendell Berry, "The Specialization of Poetry," in *Standing by Words* (New York: Shoemaker and Hoard, 1983), pp. 21–22; Cynthia L. Rigby, "Exploring Our Hesitation: Feminist Theologies and the Nurture of Children," *Theology Today,* Jan. 2000, *56*(4), 540–554, with quote from p. 540; Duff, "Vocation, Motherhood, and Marriage," pp. 79–80; Kingsolver, *High Tide in Tucson,* pp. 96, 131, 132; Julie Hanlon Rubio, *A Christian Theology of Marriage and Family*, p. 99; Ursula K. Le Guin, *Dancing at the Edge of the World: Thoughts on Words, Women, Places* (New York: Grove Press, 1989), pp. 212–237, with quotes from pp. 220, 221, 222, 226 (emphasis in text); Ernest Boyer, pp. 21–22, 31–32; Janet Martin Soskice, "Love and Attention," with a quote from p. 61; and Laurie Zoloth-Dorfman, "Traveling with Children: Mothering and the Ethics of the Ordinary World," *Tikkun,* July–Aug. 1995, 25–29.

CHAPTER SIX

The reference to Selya Benahib's characterization of ethics as ordinary conversation with a six-year-old appears in Laurie Zoloth-Dorfman's "Traveling with Children," p. 29.

To capture the contemporary neglect of justice in the craze over spirituality, I refer to Wade Clark Roof's comment about bricoleurs in *A Generation of Seekers: The Spiritual Journeys of the Baby Boom Generation* (New York: HarperCollins, 1993), p. 88, using Claude Levi-Strauss, *The Savage Mind* (Chicago: University of Chicago, 1966); Christian Smith with Melinda Lundquist Denton, *Soul Searching: The Religious and Spiritual Lives of American Teenagers* (New York: Oxford University Press, 2005); Phil Catalfo, *Raising Spiritual Children in a Material World: Introducing Spirituality into Family Life* (New York: Berkley Books, 1997) with quotations from pp. xiii, 7, 17 (emphasis in the text), 182, and 238. Other books, such as Tom McGrath's *Raising Faith-Filled Kids: Ordinary Opportunities to Nurture Spirituality at Home* (Chicago: Loyola Press, 2000), do a better job of acknowledging a debt to religious tradition and justice, although McGrath still advises, "Take what you like, and leave the rest" (p. 14).

I describe the tensions of negotiating justice within the family with reference to Mary Guerrera Congo, "The Truth Will Set You Free, But First It Will Make You Crazy," *Sacred Dimensions of Women's Experience,* Elizabeth Dodson Gray, ed. (Wellesley, Mass.: Roundtable, 1988), pp. 76–84, quoted from pp. 78–79; Bill Wylie-Kellermann, "Lives That Become the Gospel," *Christian Ministry,* Mar.–Apr. 1998, with quotations from pp. 16, 17, and 24; Audre Lorde's essay "Man Child: A Black Lesbian Feminist's Response," in *Sister Outsider: Essays and Speeches* (Freedom, Calif.: Crossing Press), pp. 72–80; and Kathleen and James McGinnis, *Parenting for Peace and Justice* (Maryknoll, N.Y.: Orbis Books, 1981, 1995), pp. ix, 1–2. Later quotations about living with teens come from chapter 8, "Ten Years Later," pp. 129–143.

My thoughts on the care of one's own children as itself a source of service draw on John Chrysostom, *On Marriage and Family Life,* Catherine P. Roth and David Anderson, trans. (Crestwood, N.Y.: St. Vladimir's Seminary Press, 1986), pp. 44, 57; and *Comparison Between a King and Monk/Against the Opponents of the Monastic Life,* translated and with an introduction by David G. Hunter (Lewiston, N.Y.: Edward Mellen Press, 1988), pp. 132–133, cited by Vigen Guroian, "The Ecclesial Family: John Chrysostom on Parenthood and Children," in Marcia J. Bunge, ed., *The Children in Christian Thought,* pp. 64, 66, 73; Martin Luther, *Luther's Works,* Jaroslav Pelikan and Helmut Lehmann, eds., 55 vols. (St. Louis: Concordia, 1955–86), vol. 44, p. 85, and "The Estate of Marriage," in *Luther's Works,* Walther I. Brandt, ed., and Helmut T. Lehmann, gen. ed. (Philadelphia: Muhlenberg Press, 1962), p. 46; William H. Lazareth, *Luther on the Christian Home*, pp. 133 and 183; and Marjorie Thompson, *Family*, p. 129.

The first-person testimony about how having children opened her eyes to other children comes from poet Camille S. Williams, "Sparrows and Lilies," *First Things,* Aug.–Sept. 1993, p. 12. The quote from Simone Weil is found in "Reflections on the Right Use of School Studies with a View to the Love of God," in *Waiting on God,* Emma Craufurd, ed., p. 111.

Sigmund Freud's comment about parental narcissism appears in "On Narcissism: An Introduction (1914)," in *General Psychological Theory: Papers on Metapsychology,* edited and with an introduction by Philip Rieff (New York: Collier Books, 1963), p. 72.

For exploration of the social ministry of the family, see Lisa Sowle Cahill, *Family,* p. 48; and *Sex, Gender, and Christian Ethics* (New York and Cambridge: Cambridge University Press, 1996), p. 207; Rodney Clapp, *Families at the Crossroads: Beyond Traditional and Modern Options* (Downers Grove, Ill.: Intervarsity, 1993), p. 155; Cheryl J. Sanders, *Ministry at the Margins: The Prophetic Mission of Women, Youth, and the Poor* (Downers Grove, Ill.: Intervarsity, 1997), p. 72. The observation about the parent's place in the fifth commandment is from Elliot N. Dorff, *Love Your Neighbor and Yourself: A Jewish Approach to Modern Personal Ethics* (Philadelphia: Jewish Publication Society, 2003), p. 129. McGinnis and McGinnis offer a rich range of concrete practices. See also Anne Meyer Byler, *How to Teach Peace to Children* (Scottdale, Pa.: Herald Press, 1981, 2003); Roland D. Martinson, "The Role of Family in the Faith and Value Formation of Children," *Word & World,* Fall 1997, *17*(4), 396–404; Merton P. Strommen, "A Family's Faith, A Child's Faith," *Dialog,* Summer 1998, *37,* 177–184; and Peter L. Benson and Eugene C. Roehlkepartain, *Beyond Leaf Raking: Learning to Serve/Serving to Learn* (Nashville, Tenn.: Abingdon, 1993).

In exploring justice in the home, I refer to Susan Moller Okin, *Justice, Gender, and the Family* (New York: Basic Books, 1989), with citations from pp. 14 and 22, and two essays from *Mutuality Matters*, Foley, Miller-McLemore, Scheiter, and Anderson, eds.: my own "Sloppy Mutuality: Love and Justice for Children and Adults" and one by Pauline Kleingeld, "Just Love? Marriage and the Question of Justice," with quotes from pp. 23 and 31. My earlier thoughts on the pitch-in family appear on p. 126 of *Also a Mother* and p. 133 of *Let the Children Come*. I also turn to work done with Don S. Browning, Pamela D. Couture, K. Brynoff Lyon, and Robert M. Franklin on *From Culture Wars to Common Ground*, pp. 287–288. I cite Christine E. Gudorf, "Parenting, Mutual Love, and Sacrifice," pp. 177–178, 181; and Erik H. Erikson, *Childhood and Society,* 35th Anniv. Ed. (New York: Norton, 1950), p. 69. The comment on children's duties within the home comes from Julie Hanlon Rubio, *A Christian Theology of Marriage and Family*, p. 163. Rubio also has a helpful chapter on the "dual vocation" of loving one's children and caring for the world, pp. 89–110, from which her observation on Jesus' view of the family appears on p. 97.

CHAPTER SEVEN

The framework of this chapter builds on Richard R. Gaillardetz's work in *Transforming Our Days: Spirituality, Community and Liturgy in a Technological Culture* (New York: Crossroad, 2000). I have referred in particular to pp. 9–12, 18–26, and 138. I use H. Richard Niebuhr's *Christ and Culture* (New York: HarperCollins, 1951) to suggest an alternative approach to play. I also found helpful a chapter by Don Richter with Jack DePaolo on "Play," in Dorothy C. Bass and Don C. Richter, eds., *Way to Live: Christian Practices for Teens*, pp. 125–138.

Sources for understanding the problems of raising children and play include Margaret Lamberts Bendroth, *Growing Up Protestant*, with a quote from p. 6; and Vincent J. Miller, *Consuming Religion: Christian Faith and Practice in a Consumer Culture* (New York: Continuum International, 2005), with a quote from p. 3. For an example of the language of toxicity, war, and assault, see James Garbarino, *Raising Children in a Socially Toxic Environment* (San Francisco: Jossey-Bass, 1995); Dana Mack, *The Assault on Parenthood: How Our Culture Undermines the Family* (New York: Simon and Schuster, 1997); and Sylvia Ann Hewlett and Cornel West, *The War Against Parents: What We Can Do for America's Beleaguered Moms and Dads*

(New York: Houghton Mifflin, 1998). I also make passing reference to problematic assumptions about play in David Elkind's *The Hurried Child: Growing Up Too Fast Too Soon* (Reading, Mass.: Perseus Books, 1988), using a quote from p. 198. The study on recreational sports is Rhonda Singer, "Are We Having Fun Yet?" in *Rethinking Childhood,* Peter B. Pufall and Richard P. Unsworth, eds. (New Brunswick, N.J.: Rutgers University Press, 2004), with quotes from pp. 207, 210, and 223.

Several sources furnish ideas for resituating play within the family as a religious practice. Both Erik H. Erikson and D. W. Winnicott talk extensively about play. I quote from Erikson's *Childhood and Society*, pp. 209, 212, and 221; and *Toys and Reasons: Stages in the Ritualization of Experience* (New York: Norton, 1977), pp. 30, 43, and 70; and from Winnicott's *Playing and Reality* (London: Tavistock, 1971), pp. 38, 40–41, and 50–55. Jerome W. Berryman builds on the work of these and other psychologists, extending their ideas to religious education in *Godly Play: An Imaginative Approach to Religious Education* (Minneapolis: Augsburg, 1991). His comment on play's benefits for young and old is found on p. 1.

Additional comment about play and language comes from Rowan Williams, *Lost Icons: Reflections on Cultural Bereavement* (Edinburgh: T&T Clark, 2000), pp. 12–13. For a similar way to understand play's "protective frame," see Pamela D. Couture, "Ritualized Play: Using Role Play to Teach Pastoral Care and Counseling," *Teaching Theology and Religion,* 1999, 2(2), 97. She cites Michael Apter, "Danger and the Protective Frame," in *Adult Play: A Reversal Theory Approach,* John H. Kerr and Michael J. Apter, eds. (Amsterdam and Berwyn, Pa.: Swets and Zeitlinger, 1991).

I also found especially useful Victor Turner's chapter "Variations on a Theme of Liminality," in *Secular Ritual,* Sally F. Moore and Barbara G. Myerhoff, eds. (Assen, Neth.: Van Gorcum, 1977). Both Erikson and Turner cite Johan Huizinga, *Homo Ludens: The Play Element in Culture* (Boston: Beacon, 1955). On pp. 48–52, Turner also cites and discusses Mihali Csikszentmihalyi, "Flowing: A General Model of Intrinsically Rewarding Experiences," *Journal of Humanist Psychology* (see also Csikszentmihalyi's "Play and Intrinsic Rewards" in the same journal), Summer 1975, *15*(3), 41–63. David Tracy compares revelation and game playing on pp. 113–114 of *The Analogical Imagination: Christian Theology and the Culture of Pluralism* (New York: Crossroad, 1981), and cites Hans-Georg Gadamer, *Truth and Method* (New York: Seabury, 1975), pp. 91–119. I explored some of these ideas in an earlier essay, "Through the Eyes of Mircea Eliade: United States Football as Religious *Rite de Passage,*" in *From Season to Season: Sports as American Religion,* Joseph L. Price, ed. (Mercer University Press, 2001), pp. 115–135. Anne Thurston connects play and liturgy on p. 45 in *Because of Her Testimony*.

I came across the citation from Sirach in Stephen C. Barton's article, "Jesus—Friend of Little Children?" in *The Contours of Christian Education,* Jeff Astley and David Day, eds. (Great Wakering, Essex: McCrimmons, 1992), p. 39, footnote no. 5. Richard P. Heitzenrater quotes John Wesley, Minutes of the Methodist Conferences (London: John Mason, 1862), 1:164 in "John Wesley and Children" in *The Children in Christian Thought,* Marcia J. Bunge, ed., p. 289. I am grateful to several biblical scholars working on children in scripture as part of a Lilly Endowment project on "Biblical Perspectives on the Child" for suggestive ideas about play and children in early Jewish and Christian texts.

CHAPTER EIGHT

I found Margaret R. Miles's essay "On Reading Augustine and on Augustine's Reading," in *The Christian Century,* May 21–28, 1997, especially helpful in grounding this chapter in Augustine's life. I have used her words from pp. 510, 511, and 514, emphasis in text. Augustine's account of his conversion appears in book VIII, chapter 12 of *The Confessions,* translated by Maria Boulding (New York: New City Press, 1997).

Important for my reflection on Jewish tradition is Sandy Sasso's "The Role of Narrative in the Spiritual Formation of Children," a paper presented at the American Academy of Religion on Nov. 22, 2004, in Atlanta, with quotes from pp. 4, 8, 17, and 18. Her references to Susan Handleman (*The Slayers of Moses,* Albany: State University of New York, 1982) and Stephen King appear on pp. 6 and 13 respectively. She cites Vitz's essay "The Use of Stories in Moral Development" (*American Psychology,* June 1990, p. 716) on p. 19. Major portions of this paper were published in "The Role of Narrative in the Spiritual Formation of Children: Walking in Cain's Shoes: Sacred Narrative with Question Marks," *Family Ministry,* Summer 2005, *19*(2), 13–26.

I love my friend Herbert Anderson's article "Sense and Nonsense in the Wisdom of Dr. Seuss," *New Theology Review* (Aug. 2001), pp. 37–50, and quote from it (pp. 38–39 and 48). His typology of children's qualities is laid out more fully in *Regarding Children* (Louisville, Ky.: Westminster John Knox, 1994), coauthored with Susan B. Johnson.

Anne Thurston helps me connect pleasure, play, reading, and liturgy on pp. 46–47 in *Because of Her Testimony.* Susan Stan comments on scriptural teaching as the sole purpose of children's reading in "Religious Topics in Children's Literature," *Word & World,* Winter 1995, *15*(1), 91–92. Thoughts on the sensual nature of reading as a child come from Michael Dirda, *An Open Book: Coming of Age in the Heartland* (New York: Norton, 2004) cited by Trudy Bush, "Bookish Lives," *Christian Century,* May 18, 2004, p. 32; Stephanie Paulsell, "The Inscribed Heart: A Spirituality of Intellectual Work," p. 143; and Rachel Hadas, "The Double Legacy," in *The Empty Bed* (Hanover, N.H.: Wesan University Press, 1995), pp. 48–49.

On the moral and intellectual dimensions of reading, I cite Rowan Williams on fantasy from pp. 14–15, 18, 19 in *Lost Icons.* Vigen Guroian describes Chrysostom's use of stories with children in "The Ecclesial Family," pp. 75–76. He refers to Chrysostom's *Address on Vainglory and the Right Way for Parents to Bring Up Their Children* in M.L.W. Laistner, *Christianity and Pagan Culture in the Later Roman Empire* (Ithaca, N.Y.: Cornell University Press, 1967). Marion Wright Edelman discusses reading on pp. 60–62 of *The Measure of Our Success: A Letter to My Children and Yours* (Boston: Beacon, 1992). For more information on the Search Institute and the forty Developmental Assets, see http://www.search-institute.org/assets/.

Tracy Major quotes Steve Jones's comment on the suspicion surrounding reading a few centuries ago in "What Are Video Games Turning Us Into?" *Boston Globe,* Feb. 20, 2005, p. 18. Paul J. Griffiths offers an extensive analysis of "consumerist" and "religious reading" in *Religious Reading: The Place of Reading in the Practice of Religion* (New York: Oxford University Press, 1999).

To explore transformative dimensions of reading, the deeper questions it raises, and its history as a meditative practice, I turn to Simone Weil, "Reflections on the Right Use of School Studies with a View to the Love of God," in *Waiting on God,* Emma Craufurd, trans., with quotes from pp. 105 and 115. Jean Leclercq discusses "active" reading in monastic history on pp. 72–73 of *The Love of Learning and the Desire of God: A Study of Monastic Culture* (New York: Fordham University Press, 1982). Reference to Mary Carruthers and her book *The Book of Memory: A Study of Memory in Medieval Culture* (Cambridge, Mass.: Cambridge University Press, 1992) appears in Milton J. Colater, "Am I My Patrons' Mentor? Theological Librarians and the Spiritual Discipline of Religious Reading," roundtable discussion presented at the annual conference of the American Theological Library Association, Durham, N.C., June 2001), *American Theological Library Association: Summary of Proceedings,* 2001, 55(1), 270–271.

I found Judith Viorst's comment on her book *Alexander and the Terrible, Horrible, No Good, Very Bad Day* on http://www.kennedy-center.org/programs/family/alexander/author.html. Gareth Matthews's thoughts about philosophical aspects of children's books are from pp. 4 and 106 of *The Philosophy of Childhood*. Walter Wangrin talked about the place of "safe terror" in children's literature in a paper presented at the American Academy of Religion on Nov. 22, 2004, in Atlanta, "But the Child *Is* the Hyena: Narrative, Identification, and Faith Formation." He cites Bruno Bettelheim's *The Uses of Enchantment: The Meaning and Importance of Fairy Tales* (New York: Vintage Books, 1977). Robert Coles shares memories from his own childhood and youth in *The Call of Stories: Teaching and the Moral Imagination* (Boston: Houghton Mifflin, 1989), pp. xi-xiii, and quotes his father on p. xii.

CHAPTER NINE

I have drawn extensively in this chapter on an initial reflection on mundane grief that appears in "Mundane Grief," in *Reflections on Grief and Spiritual Development,* Andrew J. Weaver and Howard W. Stone, eds. (Nashville, Tenn.: Abingdon, 2005), pp. 96–104. The poem "Kindergarten Days," with all its lament and blessing, by William Patrick is from *These Upraised Hands* (Rochester, N.Y.: BOA, 1995).

For reflection on the loss and recovery of the practice of lament, see Kathleen D. Billman and Daniel L. Migliore, *Rachel's Cry: Prayer of Lament and Rebirth of Hope* (Cleveland: United Church Press, 1999). Nicholas Wolterstorff speaks powerfully about lament from his own experience in *Lament for a Son* (Grand Rapids, Mich.: Eerdmans, 1987, reprinted, 2002), and I have used quotes from pp. 16, 31, 34, 36, and 86. So does Bruce Vaughn in "Recovering Grief in the Age of Grief Recovery," *Journal of Pastoral Theology,* Spring 2003, *13*(1), 36–38. Discussion of Luther and Schleiermacher's grief over their children appears in Jane E. Strohl, "The Child in Luther's Theology: 'For What Purpose Do We Older Folks Exist, Other Than to Care for . . . the Young,' " in Marcia J. Bunge, ed., *The Children in Christian Thought*, pp. 157–158; and Dawn DeVries, " 'Be Converted and Become as Little Children': Friedrich Schleiermacher on the Religious Significance of Childhood," in *The Children in Christian Thought,* p. 347. Strohl cites Luther, *Briefwechsel,* Kritische Gesamtausgabe, Series 4 (18 vols.; Weimar: H. Boehlau, 1883-), vol. 10, p. 3794, lines 20–29. DeVries cites Schleiermacher, *Servant of the Word: Selected Sermons of Friedrich Schleiermacher,* translated with an introduction by Dawn DeVries (Philadelphia: Fortress, 1987), pp. 211, 213.

In exploring mundane grief, I also quote Anne Higonnet, *Pictures of Innocence*, p. 200; Kathleen Norris, *The Quotidian Mysteries: Laundry, Liturgy, and "Women's Work,"* pp. 40–41, 87; Virginia Woolf, *To the Lighthouse* (Orlando: Harcourt Brace, 1927), pp. 58 and 60; Jane Lazarre, "The Mother-Artist," pp. 175–176; and Anne Lamott, *Plan B: Further Thoughts on Faith* (New York: Riverhead Books, 2005), pp. 81–82. I return to Lamott on forgiveness, her pp. 101–102.

For comments on Mary's anguish, see Beverly Roberts Gaventa, *Mary: Glimpses of the Mother of Jesus* (Columbia: University of South Carolina, 1995), p. 68; and "The Challenge of Christmas," *Christian Century,* Dec. 15, 1993, p. 1273, as well as my essay "Pondering All These Things," pp. 108–109.

Herbert Anderson's essay "Between Rhetoric and Reality: Women and Men as Equal Partners in Home, Church, and the Marketplace" appears in *Mutuality Matters,* Foley, Miller-McLemore, Schreiter, and Anderson, eds., pp. 67–82. Margaret Hebblethwaite describes the hardships of parenting on pp. 57 and 60–61 of *Motherhood and God* (London: Cassell, 1984). I talk about children and finitude on pp. 159–161 of *Also a Mother*. Quotes on Christian views of death and finitude by Paul Tillich are from *The Meaning of Health: Essays in Existentialism, Psychoanalysis, and Religion,* Perry Lefevre, ed. (Chicago: Exploration Press, 1984), p. 190; and *The Courage to Be* (New Haven: Yale University Press, 1952), p. 17.

In turning to grace and blessing, the African song I describe, "Bambelela," is adapted and recorded by Marty Haugen on "Turn My Heart: A Sacred Journey from Brokenness to Healing," GIA Publications (http://www.giamusic.com/scstore/P-547.html). Miroslav Volf's comment is from "Theology for a Way of Life," in *Practicing Theology: Beliefs and Practices in Christian Life* (Grand Rapids, Mich.: Eerdmans, 2002), p. 260. My reflections on forgiveness appear in "Christianity Teaches Forgiveness—and That Includes You" on the United Methodist Church Website (http://www.umc.org/interior. asp?mid=5378). David F. Ford's comments on blessing come from a lecture presented at a Practicing Theology Conference at Yale Divinity School, Apr. 3, 2005, "The Blessing of Theology: God, Wisdom, and the Shaping of Christian Thought and Teaching in the Twenty-First Century," pp. 21–23. Marilynne Robinson's novel *Gilead* makes blessing a primary theme; I have quoted from pp. 21–23, 27–28, 69, and 129.

For comments on letting go, see Laurie Zoloth-Dorfman's "Traveling with Children," p. 29, emphasis added; Herbert Anderson, "Faithful Becoming: Forming Families in the Art of Paradoxical Living in a Fragmented and Pluralistic World," *New Theology*

Review, Aug. 2005, *18*(3), 5–14; and Christine Gudorf, "Dissecting Parenthood: Infertility, in Vitro, and Other Lessons in Why and How We Parent," *Conscience,* Autumn 1994, *15*(3), 22. Anderson devotes an entire book to the "long and sometimes complicated process" of leaving in *Leaving Home* (Louisville, Ky.: Westminster John Knox, 1993). My special thanks to Susan Briehl for sharing the wonderful story of the apron strings and for her insights on the father in the parable of the prodigal son.

Michael Joncas put Psalm 91 to music in "On Eagle's Wings," New Dawn Music, 1979.

The Author

Bonnie J. Miller-McLemore is the E. Rhodes and Leona B. Carpenter Professor of Pastoral Theology at Vanderbilt University Divinity School, author of a previous book on children from Jossey-Bass (*Let the Children Come,* 2003), and a respected scholar in theology.

Index

Hippo, bishop of, 152
His Dark Materials (Pullman), 172
Historical amnesia, Protestant, 23–26
Hobbit, The (Tolkein), 157
Hochschild, A. R., 44
Hoge, D., 25
Home: doing justice at, 121–125; as mission field, 117; to world, doing justice from, 118–121
Hope: and anxiety, 15; in creation and redemption, 182; divine, dependence on, avoiding thinking about, 44; falling short of, 186; reading allowing for, 160; words falling short of our, 75
Hope-filled practice, 177, 192, 194
Hopelessness, 179
Horton Hears a Who! (Seuss), 163
Hosea, 110
Household economics: children contributing and participating in, 61, 74, 123–124; underestimating children's role in, 122; as a way of life, 32
Household income, 63
Huizinga, J., 143, 148
Human condition, describing the, 182
"Hurried" child, the, 146–147

I

I Can Read with My Eyes Shut (Seuss), 165
I Had Trouble in Getting to Solla Sollew (Seuss), 163
Ignatian convictions, 70
Ignatian spirituality, growing interest in, 7
Ignatius of Loyola, 7, 10
Illiteracy, 153, 154
Illness and health, 144
Imagination: in attending, 51; lack of, 119; in play, 130, 141, 144–145, 146; in reading, 160, 162, 163, 164; sanctioned place for, children needing, 162
Imaginative truth, 160

"In Blackwater Woods" (Oliver), 195–197
Income, household, 63
Industrialization, 61, 63
Ingesting, 156, 161–166
Injustice: heightened awareness of, 106; pattern of, 101; in the world at large, 102
Innocence, 63, 64, 65, 69
Inside creative play, 134, 139, 140
Instruments, playing, 128, 129–130, 139
Internet, the, time spent on, 131
Interruptions, issue of, 98–100
Inviting play, 149
Iraq, 48
Irish culture, 163
Irresponsibility, legitimate, 144, 161
Isaac, 101, 111, 188, 189, 191
Isaiah, 110, 150; 11:8, 150
Israel, the people of: blessing to, 189; leader of, 39

J

Jacob, 101, 162, 188–189, 191
James, W., 14, 73
Jeremiah: 5:14, 153; 23:29, 153
Jerome, 2, 3
Jerusalem, 46, 180
Jesuits, the, 7, 70
Jesus: on anxiety, 14, 15; ascension of, 180; baptism of, 189; birth of, 45, 46, 48; blessing by, 189, 197; books about, 159; as a child getting lost in Jerusalem, 46, 180–181; on the commandments, 113–114; confession of, 24; and culture, issue of, 135–136; on death and grief, 185, 197; discipleship to, demands of, ability to fully realize the, 97; as the embodiment of love, 123; on family life, 6, 116; growth of, 56; last supper of, 155, 156; a life of commitment to, reading about a, 152, 153; and Martha, 14, 15, 16; parable by, 196; prediction of, 7; raising, Mary's other tasks in addition to, 48; sum-

ming up the major notes of, 110;
truth of, and systems of theology,
27; welcoming children, 150
Jews/Jewish tradition. *See* Judaism
Job 1:21, 190
John: 1:1, 9, 153; 1:14a, 40; 11:35, 185
Johnson, B., 25
Johnson, E., 10, 46, 48
Jones, S., 165
Joseph, 181
Joy: and attention, 54; capacity for, aspect that destroys, 44; of children,
matching the, 21; embodiment of,
141; glimpsing, hope of, 140; potential for, 56–57; reading as pleasure and, 157–161
Judaism: and blessing, 189, 190; conveying the traditions of, amid the
Christmas season, 134–135; on forgiveness, 187; formation of, 113;
and the gift of children, 76; on the
goodness of all creation, 40; heroes
and heroines of, 159; influence of,
109; and interruption, 99; mandate
of, 85, 110, 113–114, 117–118; parasitical relationship to, 110; and
people of the Book, 154–155; practice rejected out of hostility to, 27;
and spirituality in family life, 23;
and tension between faith and
family life, 11; and a yearning for
fairness, 102–103
Judgment, 183, 184
Jung, C., 5
Just love, 122, 123, 124, 125
Just Plain Fancy (Polacco), 163–164
Justice: consuming spirituality while
leaving, 108–110; covenant of
peace and, readers entering a kind
of, example of, 164; doing, 110,
111, 118, 118–121, 121–125; negotiating, 103–108; spiritual mandate for, 110–111; spirituality in
family life ignoring, 103. *See also*
Fairness, issue of
Justin, J., 34

K

Kairos and chronos, 43, 47, 57
Keating, T., 4
Keller, C., 18
Kids, defining, xv, 68. *See also* Adoles-
cence; Children
Kierkegaard, S., 15
"Kindergarten Days" poem, 175–176
Kindness, loving, 110, 111, 118, 125
King, M. L., Jr., 111
King, S., 169, 172
King Theoden (character), 179
Kingsolver, B., 89, 96, 100
Kleingeld, P., 122
Knowing children, 64–65, 66, 67,
74–76
Knowledge: activity in the presence of,
71; traditional view defining, 50
Kozol, J., 66

L

Lactation, 49
Lamott, A., 182, 187
Language: learning, 144, 191–192;
power of, grasping the, 8. *See also*
Words/conversation
Laser tag, playing, 127, 133, 145
Laundry, doing, 21–22
Laundry, Liturgy, and "Women's Work"
(Norris), 22
Lawrence, 19, 20
Laying-on of hands, 189, 191
Lazareth, W. H., 115
Lazarre, J., 91
Lazarus, 185, 198
Le Guin, U., 97, 100
Learning: a language, 144, 191–192;
play as, 142–143, 144; reading as,
164–165
LeClercq, J., 156
Lectio divina, steps of, 167
Lectio, meaning of, 156
Legitimate irresponsibility, 144, 161
Lego sets, 134
Less-privileged class, the, 62. *See also*
Poor, the

Public library system, 171
Public schools, allegiance to, 105
Public vocation, needing, 97
Pullman, P., 172
Punishment, 64, 184
Puritans, 24, 27, 83, 128

R

Racism: addressing, in daily life, 120;
facing, 105; history of, attention
to, 119; reading about, 164
Radical mutuality, 86, 88, 91
Rahner, K., 24, 69, 70
*Raising Spiritual Children in a Material
World* (Catalfo), 108–109
Reading: consumerist, 153–154; as
evolving process and practice,
170–173; factors disrupting the
practice of, 151, 153; as a focal
practice, 161; as formative, 152,
156, 161–166; importance of, 152;
likening eating to, 156; listening
for the Word in, 153; as pleasure
and joy, 157–161; practice of, 154;
reasons for, 167; spending time involved in, 138; as transformative,
166–170. *See also* Bible reading
Reading aloud, 154, 172. *See also* Bedtime reading
Reading culture, nourishing a, 173
Reality: and fantasy, space and time between, 144, 145; of finitude and
failure, dealing with the, 184; living between rhetoric and, 182;
mistaking rhetoric for, 185
Rebekah, 101
Reconciliation, taking steps toward,
186
Re-creation: places of, 140; play as,
146–150
Recycling, 119
Redemption, hope in, 182
Reflective time: finding, 13; reading
as, 154
Reformation movement, 27, 29, 34,
46, 47

Regret, 186
Religion, requirements of, summing up
the major, 110
Religious and spiritual practices: cul-
tivating, 35–37; embedded, 32;
separating, along gender lines,
10, 11; types of, 31. *See also specific
practices*
Religious education, creative role of
play in, 145–146
Religious institutions, view of, 26
Remorse, 186
Renewal, quality of, play affording a,
147, 148, 149
Repentance, 137
Repetitious ritual, issue of, 133
Reprimand, 64
Rereading books, 173
Resigned acceptance, 184
Responsibility: for forming children in
faith, 26; meaning of, 109; shared,
xv, 11, 87, 91; transfer of, for fam-
ily welfare, 124
Resurrection, 110, 140, 146–150
Revelation, religious, 148, 155
Reverend John Ames (character), 190,
191, 194
Reverse psychology, 194
Rhetoric: mistaking, for reality, 185;
and reality, living between, 182
Rigby, C., 95
Rites of passage, 148
Robinson, M., 190, 194
Rogers, C., 5
Roman Catholic Church, 10–11.
See also Catholicism
Roman Empire, 116
Romans 13:13–14, 152
Romans, the, on child rearing, 2
Romanticization, of children, xii, 60,
64, 65, 147
Roof, W. C., 109
Rosary, the, 25
Rousseau, J., 64
Rubio, J., 97, 124
Rubio, J. H., 116

Ruddick, S., 49–50, 51, 52, 53
Runaway Bunny, The (Brown), 167
Russian culture, 163

S

Sabbath, the, 27, 32, 35
Sacrifice: salvaging, 90–93; transitional, 88
Sacrificial love, issue of, 82, 83, 85–86, 123
Saints, canonized, married women as, 10. *See also names of saints*
Salvage, defined, 90
Salvaging sacrifice, 90–93
Salvation: doctrines of, 184; of material things, 55
Sanctification, concentric circles of, 32
Sanctuary, feeling of, library having a, 171
Sanders, C., 117
Sarah, 189
Sasso, S., 155, 167, 169
Satan, wager between God and, 190
Sayings of the Desert Fathers, 8
Scary movies, 134
Schleiermacher, F., 181
Scholastic Book Club, 172
School bus, child's first day getting on the, recollection of our, 175–176
School shootings, 133
School studies, 166
Schools: private vs. public, attending, issue of, 105; as sources of books, 172
Schoolwork, reading as part of, 153–154
Schor, J., 44
Scripture reading. *See* Bible reading
Search Institute, the, 164–165
Second Vatican Council, 34
Second-wave feminism, 122
Segregation, 66
Self-forgiveness, 186
Self-help theories, 152
Selfishness, 82
Self-love, 92, 187

Self-reflection, deeper, reading cultivating, 154
Self-sacrifice: ideal of, 83, 90; necessity of, recognizing the, 91; one-sided, 121; unlimited, assumption about, 94. *See also* Sacrifice; Sacrificial love
Sendak, M., 167
Sentimentalization: of children, 62; of family life, 83
Separation, attachment and, anxiety over, 167, 194. *See also* Letting go
Series of Unfortunate Events, A (Snicket), 169
Seuss, Dr., 9, 159, 160, 161, 162, 163, 165
Sexism: addressing, in daily life, 120; facing, 105
Shabbat worship, 154–155
Shadowlands, 1
Shared responsibility: advocating, xv; hope for, 91; increase in, 11, 87
Shema, 113, 117, 155
Shoes, taking off, 39–40
Sibling rivalry, stories of, 162
Siblings: practicing on, 114; respect for, 119
Silence: and charity, 80; conversation alongside, 9; danger of, 9; focus on, xii; as a means to love God, 8, 9; place for, 9–10; tension between words and, holding the, 12, 13; words supplementing and enriching, 153
Silverstein, S., 80, 81
Simplification, strategies of, issue with, 45
Sin, 64, 70, 182, 184, 187, 191
Singing, 32
Sinlessness, sources of, 8
Sirach 30:9–10, 143
Slack line, living on a, 12–14
Sleep, issue of, 30–31, 44
Small Catechism (Luther), 25
Snicket, L., 169
Social action, addressing, in daily life, 120

Other Books in the Practices of Faith Series

Practicing Our Faith
A Way of Life for a Searching People
DOROTHY C. BASS
Paper
ISBN: 0–7879–3883–1

"As wise as grandparents, a good guide to living within our families and communities with integrity and generosity."

— Kathleen Norris author of *Dakota* and *The Cloister Walk*

Many Christians are looking for ways to deepen their relationship with God by practicing their faith in everyday life. Some go on retreats but are often disappointed to find that the integrated life they experienced in a place apart is difficult to recreate in their day-to-day world. Many thoughtful, educated Christians search for spiritual guidance in Eastern religious traditions, unaware of the great riches within their own heritage.

To all these seekers, *Practicing Our Faith* offers help that is rooted in Christian faith and tradition. The contributors examine twelve central Christian practices—such as keeping Sabbath, honoring the body, and forgiving one another—by placing each in historical and biblical context, reexamining relevance to our times, and showing how each gives depth and meaning to daily life. Shaped by the Christian community over the centuries yet richly grounded in the experiences of living communities today, these practices show us how Christian spiritual disciplines can become an integral part of how we live each day.

DOROTHY C. BASS is a noted church historian and director of the Valparaiso Project on the Education and Formation of People in Faith. She lives with her husband and children in Valparaiso, Indiana.

Other Books in the Practices of Faith Series

Receiving the Day
Christian Practices for Opening the Gift of Time
DOROTHY C. BASS
Paper
ISBN: 0–7879–5647–3

"With wisdom, clarity, and sacred practicality, Dorothy Bass changes our relationship with Time. It needn't control us. Rather, the day, the week, and the year are each an opportunity for us to shape our lives in the peace and kindness of God. God's story becomes our story. This is a book of genuine insight and gentle leadership. Let it turn your calendar from a taskmaster into a gift from the Creator for creation and for you."

> — Walter Wangerin Jr., author, *The Book of God*

"Those who struggle with pressures and limits of time—that is, all of us! will find this book a rich resource to be tasted and tried. This deeply spiritual book dramatically reorients the heart of the reader . . . challenging our time-obsessed society and teaching the wisdom of religious practices."

> — Bonnie J. Miller-McLemore, author, *And Also a Mother:*
> *Work and Family as Theological Dilemma*

"A profoundly useful book . . . It reminds us forcibly that we are embodied creatures gifted by God with time too precious to fritter or work away. In its recommendations for healing our relationship to time it is often unsettlingly revolutionary, frequently subversive of our secular culture, and always full of Dorothy Bass's honest and generous reflections on her own life. It is a pleasure to recommend it."

> — Roberta Bondi, author, *A Place to Pray: Reflections on the*
> *Lord's Prayer and Memories of God*

A spiritual reconsideration of our frantic approach to time, *Receiving the Day* invites readers to embrace the temporal landmarks of our lives as opportunities for deeper relationship with God and one another.

A Song to Sing, A Life to Live
Reflections on Music as Spiritual Practice
DON SALIERS, EMILY SALIERS
Paper
ISBN: 0–7879–8377–2

"The Indigo Girl and her father focus on the many dimensions of music in one's spiritual life."

— *Publishers Weekly,* February 9, 2004

Indigo Girl Emily Saliers and her father Don Saliers explore the many dimensions of music as it relates to our spiritual lives. Music is a central practice in most expressions of spirituality and faith–whether it's the Christian music of seeker services, traditional hymnody, liturgical chant and singing, or popular music ballads about the meaning of life. In this rich exploration of music across all these settings and styles, authors Don and Emily Saliers interweave their own stories as well as those of others to reveal the importance of music as spiritual practice and a force for good in our lives, looking at such topics as music and justice, music and grief, music and delight, and music and hope.

Don Saliers (Atlanta, GA) is professor of theology at Candler School of Theology at Emory University. **Emily Saliers** (Atlanta, GA) is a member of the Indigo Girls, an award-winning folk-rock duo known for their social activism.

Other Books in the Practices of Faith Series

Testimony
Talking Ourselves into Being Christian
Thomas G. Long
Cloth
ISBN: 0–7879–6832–3

"Thomas G. Long has long been one of our most effective Christian talkers, and now in this trenchant testimony, the harvest of a rich and provoking ministry, he helps us all the better to talk about our Christian faith. Never have we had a greater need for authentic discourse, nor have we ever been better served."

> — The Reverend Professor Peter J. Gomes, Plummer Professor of Christian Morals and Pusey Minister in the Memorial Church, Harvard University

"In the rich vocabulary and cadence of his own speech, Thomas G. Long teaches us how to bring faith to speech in the everyday occurrences of life. One comes away from this book with an emboldened sense of how to speak of God in public places and spaces. Ever the innovative teacher, Long demonstrates for us once again why he belongs in the upper echelons of contemporary writers on matters of Christian faith and practice."

> — Cleophus J. LaRue, Princeton Theological Seminary

In this groundbreaking book, Thomas G. Long–a theologian and respected authority on preaching–explores how Christians talk when they are not in church. Testimony breaks the stained-glass image of religious language to show how ordinary talking in our everyday lives–talk across the backyard fence, talk with our kids, talk about politics and the events of the day–can be sacred speech. In a world of spin, slick marketing, mindless chatter, and easy deceptions, *Testimony* shows that the hunger for truthful, meaningful, and compassionate speech is ultimately grounded in truth about God.

Thomas G. Long is Bandy Professor of Preaching, Candler School of Theology, Emory University. He is a former pastor and associate editor of the *Journal for Preachers*. Long is the author of fourteen books.

Honoring the Body
Meditations on a Christian Practice
STEPHANIE PAULSELL
Paper
ISBN: 0–7879–6757–2

"This latest installment in Jossey-Bass's Practices of Faith series is at once a highly organized survey of human embodiment and free-flowing meditation on the same."
— *Publishers Weekly,* January 14, 2002

"Here is a book we have needed for a long time, a book that will help Christians—who affirm that 'the Word became flesh'—overcome their baffling historic aversion to the body and learn to honor it. Stephanie Paulsell is a wise and compassionate guide, and she has given us the most compelling treatment of this topic I've ever read. May her insights be received, and embodied, by many."
— Parker Palmer, author, *Let Your Life Speak* and *The Courage to Teach*

"*Honoring the Body* is an elegantly written book. It is filled with wisdom, insight from the Christian tradition, and incisive analysis of a crucial yet vexing practice of Christian life. It also is eminently practical, a call to transformed thinking and living. I heartily commend it."
— L. Gregory Jones, author, *Embodying Forgiveness* and dean of Duke Divinity School

In this exquisite and sensitive book, author Stephanie Paulsell draws on resources from the Christian tradition to show how we can learn to celebrate the body's pleasures, protect the body's vulnerabilities, and develop the practices that will ultimately transform our troubled relationship with our bodies to one of honor and joy. A practical resource, *Honoring the Body* weaves together scripture, history, and lively stories that can help us recover and sustain an appreciation for ourselves as physical beings.

Stephanie Paulsell teaches at Harvard Divinity School. She is the former director of ministry studies and senior lecturer in religion and literature at the University of Chicago Divinity School, and is a minister in the Christian Church (Disciples of Christ).

Let the Children Come
Reimagining Childhood from a Christian Perspective
BONNIE J. MILLER-MCLEMORE
Hardcover
ISBN: 0–7879–5665–1

"*Let the Children Come* is not only engagingly written and filled with common sense, it is also theologically illuminating and pastorally astute."

— From the Foreword by Lisa Sowle Cahill, J. Donald Monan, S.J. Professor of Theology, Boston College

"This book will help us to live with and care for children with greater understanding, compassion, and respect."

— Dorothy C. Bass, editor, Practicing Our Faith

"In this appealing book, Bonnie J. Miller-McLemore rescues the traditional themes of Christian theology for a positive, practical theology of children and child raising."

— Rosemary Radford Ruether, Carpenter Professor of Feminist Theology, Graduate Theological Union, Berkeley, California

In this important and much-needed book, theologian, author, and teacher Bonnie J. Miller-McLemore writes about the struggle to raise children with integrity and faithfulness as Christians in a complex postmodern society. *Let the Children Come* shows that the care of children is in itself a religious discipline and a communal practice that places demands on both congregations and society as a whole. The author calls for clearer and more defined ways in which Christians can respond to the call to nurture all children (not just their own) as manifestations of God's presence in the world. Miller-McLemore raises and investigates questions that up until now have largely been left unasked, such as: What are the dominant cultural perceptions of children including religious perceptions with which parents must grapple? How have Christians defined children and parenting, and how should they today?